Creative Management and Development

Third Edition

Edited by Jane Henry

⑤ SAGE Publications

London ● Thousand Oaks ● New Delhi

First edition published 1991
Second edition published 2001
This third edition published 2006

 SAGE Publications Ltd
1 Oliver's Yard
55 City Road
London EC1Y 1SP

SAGE Publications Inc.
2455 Teller Road
Thousand Oaks, California 91320

SAGE Publications India Pvt Ltd
B-42, Panchsheel Enclave
Post Box 4109
New Delhi 110 017

British Library Cataloguing in Publication data

A catalogue record for this book is available
from the British Library

ISBN-10 1-4129-2247-X   ISBN-13 978-1-4129-2247-0
ISBN-10 1-4129-2248-8   ISBN-13 978-1-4129-2248-7 (pbk)

Library of Congress Control Number: 2006927104

Typeset by C&M Digitals (P) Ltd, Chennai, India
Printed in Great Britain by The Cromwell Press Ltd, Trowbridge, Wiltshire
Printed on paper from sustainable resources

Contents

Contents

About the authors

Professor Teresa M Amabile, Harvard Business School, Boston, US

Professor Chris Argyris, Organizational Behaviour, Harvard University, Cambridge, Massachusetts, US

Professor Guy Claxton, Graduate School of Education, University of Bristol, Bristol, UK

Professor Mihaly Csikszentmihalyi, Drucker School of Management, Claremont Graduate University, Claremont, California, US

Professor Goran Ekvall, FA Institute, Stockholm, Sweden

Daniel Goleman, Co-chairman of the Consortium for Research on Emotional Intelligence in Organizations, Graduate School of Applied and Professional Psychology, Rutgers University, Piscataway, New Jersey, US

Professor Sarah Hampson, Psychology Department, University of Surrey, UK

Professor Charles Handy, London Business School, UK

Jeffrey R Hanson, President, J R Hanson Company, New York, US

Paul Hawken, Smith and Hawken and Datafusion, US

Dr Jane Henry, Head of Centre for Human Resources and Change Management, Open University Business School, Milton Keynes, UK

Professor Michael Kirton, Occupational Research Centre, Hertfordshire, UK

Professor David Krackhardt, Carnegie Mellon University, US

Amory Lovins, Research Director, Rocky Mountain Institute, Colorado, US

L Hunter Lovins, CEO, Rocky Mountain Institute, Colorado, US

Professor Ikujiro Nonaka, Hitotsubashi University, Japan

Professor Richard Pascale, Templeton College, Oxford University, UK

Claudia Sacramento, Work and Organisational Psychology, Aston University, UK

Ricardo Semler, CEO Semco, Brazil

Dr Vandana Shiva, Director, Research Foundation for Science, Technology and Ecology, Delhi, India

Professor John Sparrow, Business School, University of Central England, UK

Professor Hirotaka Takeuchi, Hitotsubashi University, Japan

Professor Michael West, Work and Organisational Psychology, Aston University, UK

Acknowledgements

Grateful acknowledgement is made to the following sources for permission to reproduce material in this book.

A CREATIVITY
1 *A Systems Perspective on Creativity*
Edited excerpt from M Csikszentmihalyi, 'A systems perspective on creativity' pp. 313–335 in M. Sternberg (Ed.) *Handbook of Creativity*, 1999. © Cambridge University Press 1999.
Updated Figure 1.1 © Mihaly Csikszentmihalyi

2 *How to Kill Creativity*
Reprinted by permission of *Harvard Business Review*. Excerpt from "How to kill creativity" by T Amabile, September 1998. © 1998 by the Harvard Business School Publishing Corporation; all rights reserved.

B COGNITION
3 *Flourishing in Teams: Developing Creativity and Innovation*
M. West and C. Sacramento, Commissioned Chapter. Business School, Aston University © The Open University.

4 *Beyond Cleverness: How to be Smart Without Thinking*
G. Claxton, Commissioned Chapter. Graduate School Education, University of Bristol, Bristol. © The Open University.

5 *Organizational Knowledge Creation*
I. Nonaka and H. Takeuchi, pp. 56–94 from Chapter 3 in *The Knowledge Creating Company*. © 1995 by Oxford University Press, Inc. By permission of Oxford University Press Inc.

6 *Beyond Sense-making: Emotion, Imagery and Creativity*
J. Sparrow, Commissioned Chapter. Business School, University of Central England, Birmingham. © The Open University.

C STYLE

7 Personality: State of the Art

S Hampson, 'Personality: State of the art'. This article originally appeared in The Psychologist 12(6), June 1999. The Psychologist is published by the British Psychological Society: see www.thepsychologist.org.uk

8 Adaptors and Innovators

Reprinted from Long Range Planning 1984, 17(2), M Kirton, 'Adaptors and innovators'. pp. 137–43. © 1984, with permission of Elsevier.

9 What Makes a Leader

Reprinted by permission of *Harvard Business Review*. Excerpt from 'What makes a leader' by D Goleman, November 1998. © 1998 by the Harvard Business School Publishing Corporation; all rights reserved.

D CULTURE

10 Organizational Conditions and Levels of Creativity

Edited excerpt from G Ekvall, 'Conditions and levels of creativity' from *Creativity and Innovation Management* 6(4) 1997, pp. 195–205. Reproduced by permission of Blackwell Publishing.

11 The Citizen Company

C Handy, 'The Citizen Company' from *The Hungry Spirit* by Charles Handy, published by Hutchinson. Reprinted by permission of The Random House Group Ltd.
© 1998 by Charles Handy. Used by permission of Broadway Books, a division of Random House, Inc.

12 Why My Former Employees Still Work For Me

Reprinted by permission of *Harvard Business Review*. Excerpt from 'Why my former employees still work for me' by R Semler, January 1994. © 1994 by the Harvard Business School Publishing Corporation; all rights reserved.

13 Creativity, Development and Well-being

J. Henry, Commissioned Chapter. Open University Business School, Milton Keynes. © The Open University.

E DEVELOPMENT

14 Empowerment: The Emperor's New Clothes

Reprinted by permission of *Harvard Business Review*. Excerpt from 'Empowerment: The emperor's new clothers' by C Argyris, May 1998. © 1998 by the Harvard Business School Publishing Corporation; all rights reserved.

15 *Informal Networks: The Company Behind the Chart*
Reprinted by permission of *Harvard Business Review*. Excerpt from 'Informal networks: The company behind the chart' by D Krackhardt and JR Hanson, 1993.
© 1993 by the Harvard Business School Publishing Corporation; all rights reserved.

F PERCEPTION

16 *Monocultures of the Mind*
V Shiva, 'Monocultures of the Mind' edited excerpt from Chapter 1 of *Monocultures of the Mind*, London: Zed Books, 1993. Reproduced with permission of the publisher.

17 *A Road Map for Natural Capitalism*
Reprinted by permission of *Harvard Business Review*. Excerpt from 'Natural capitalism' by A Lovins, H Lovins, P Hawken, May 1999. © 1999 by the Harvard Business School Publishing Corporation; all rights reserved.

18 *Surfing the Edge of Chaos*
Richard T Pascale, 'Surfing the Edge of Chaos', *MIT Sloan Management Review*, Spring 1999, 40(3). © 1999 by Massachusetts Institute of Technology. All rights reserved. Distributed by Tribune Media Services.

Preface

The rapid rate of technological development has led to an increase in the pace of change, and globalization and deregulation have led to increased competition. To survive, organizations need to be continuously creative and innovative, especially in high wage economies. This has led to talk of the entrepreneurial society and increased interest in ways of developing and sustaining creativity and innovation at work. We now have a better idea of how creativity emerges in organizations and a more developed idea of the principles that lay behind creative management than when the first edition of this book was published fifteen years ago.

This edition is divided into six parts – creativity, cognition, style, culture, development and perception. The contributors include many of the most prominent researchers in the fields of creative management and development.

The first part of the book, on creativity and cognition, charts the shift to a more systemic view of creativity and the greater attention now paid to the role of tacit knowledge. The middle sections, on style and culture, elaborate on the way in which cognitive style and personality type affect how we set about problem-solving, decision-making and change, and the different kinds of culture organizations need to encourage creativity. The last part discusses ways of developing in a sustainable manner, that take account of our own and the planet's well-being.

In terms of creativity (Section A) two key changes in our understanding are the increased emphasis now placed on the role of intrinsic motivation and the importance of the social field or community of practice in which the endeavour arises. Csikszentmihalyi has addressed how creativity emerges from a social field. Amabile has drawn attention to the key role of intrinsic motivation in creative endeavour. West and Sacramento draw together research on the impact of team tasks, group composition, organizational context and team processes on team innovation.

Our understanding of human cognition (Section B) has been revolutionized in the last twenty years, in particular our understanding about the importance of unconscious information processing and the limitations of rational thought. Claxton summarizes recent findings on the key role of implicit learning, intuition and tacit knowledge in creativity, thinking and know-how. Nonaka and Takeuchi illustrate the important role of tacit knowledge in innovation and knowledge creation and point out the greater extent to which this is recognized in Eastern organizations compared to their Western counterparts. Sparrow discusses the neglected role of emotion and imagery in cognition and their relationship to creativity.

Another factor that affects both what we attend to and the way we set about tasks is our cognitive preferences and personality type (Section C). Hampson provides a brief overview of some key dimensions on which individuals differ. Kirton expounds upon the implications of a natural preference for adaption as opposed to innovation and the consequence for problem-solving, creativity, decision-making and change management style. Goleman argues that emotional intelligence is a key factor in differentiating the good from the bad leader.

Culture (Section D) can have a major impact on creativity in organizations. Generally an open climate is associated with creative organizations but Ekvall argues that different types of people and tasks need different sorts of climate to bring out the creativity appropriate for the task. Handy argues that the changed business environment necessitates a new relationship between management and workers, one he likens to the idea of citizenship. He advocates more workplace democracy as a means of building trust. Semler describes his experience of transforming a conservative traditional organization into an entrepreneurial self-organizing network of loosely related businesses.

Development (Section E) is increasingly important as knowledge changes with increasing rapidity and staff become more empowered. Henry discusses the relationship between development, creativity and well-being. Argyris explains the importance of walking the talk in change programmes and illustrates how defensive behaviour can get in the way. Krackhardt and Hanson illustrate the importance of informal networks and the benefits of mapping.

Finally Perception (Section F) addresses the question of how our assumptions affect the way we choose to develop. Shiva asserts that the reductionist bias in Western thought leads to a neglect of local knowledge in international development and argues that much modern agriculture and forestry is inherently unsustainable. Lovins, Lovins and Hawken argue that a shift in values, towards a more natural form of capitalism that mimics nature, would allow business to operate profitably in more sustainable ways. Pascale shows how the science of complexity offers a new understanding that focuses attention away from trying to control proceedings and towards the facilitation of emergent ideas and relationships.

Readers of the previous editions will notice some continuity of theme in the sections on creativity, cognition, style and perception. The second edition expanded material on culture, learning and emotion. This edition expands the material on development, complexity and team innovation.

Jane Henry
j.a.henry@open.ac.uk
2006

A

Creativity

The section contains chapters by some giants of recent creativity and innovation research: Mihaly Csikszentmihalyi, Teresa Amabile and Michael West. All emphasize how the community in which a person operates affects creative and innovative outcomes.

Mihaly Csikszentmihalyi has drawn attention to the social context out of which creativity and innovation emerge. For example, he has demonstrated the beneficial role of working at a place and time in which other individuals are engaged in related creative activities: painting and sculpture in Florence in the 14th century, the development of computers in Northern California in the 1960s and 70s, industrialization in SE Asia in the last quarter of the 20th century. Here Csikszentmihalyi outlines his systems theory of creativity, relating creative effort by individuals to the state of the domain they are working in and the characteristics of those who assess the worth of the creative endeavour in the field concerned. This offers a penetrating analysis of how creative endeavour emerges within a social field. Drawing on years of research in the field, Csikszentmihalyi discusses the interplay between knowledge about the domain, gatekeepers in the field and creative individuals. Many of the points made here in relation to other domains apply equally well to creativity and innovation in organizational settings.

Teresa Amabile has drawn attention to the importance of intrinsic motivation in creative endeavour. Business has traditionally rewarded people extrinsically with pay and promotion but creative actions often arise out of a long-standing commitment to and interest in a particular area. She appreciates this is only one part of the equation, and that expertise in the domain concerned and sufficient mental flexibility to question assumptions and play with ideas, are also important. Here she summarizes some of the implications of her studies among scientists, researchers and managers in organizations for creativity and innovation. She points out the critical importance of challenge, for example, matching people to tasks they are interested in and have expertise in, allowing people freedom as to how they achieve innovation, setting a sufficiently diverse team the task of innovation, along with sufficient resources, encouragement and support.

Michael West and Claudia Sacramento draw together research on team task, team composition, organizational context and team processes that affect the level of team innovation in organizations. They consider the effect of intrinsic motivation and differing levels of extrinsic demands on team tasks, noting that though high levels of external demand may limit the development of new creative ideas early on in the innovation process, a moderate level of external demand often facilitates the implementation of innovation in groups. They go on to consider the role of diversity and selection procedures on the group composition, the part played by the organizational climate and rewards, and the role of group norms that encourage attempts at innovation and reflection, the effect of handling conflict constructively, actively seeking cross-team links, and the benefits of clear leadership that is sensitive to others needs.

A Systems Perspective on Creativity

Mihaly Csikszentmihalyi

Psychologists tend to see creativity exclusively as a mental process [but] creativity is as much a cultural and social as it is a psychological event. Therefore what we call creativity is not the product of single individuals, but of social systems making judgements about individual's products. Any definition of creativity that aspires to objectivity, and therefore requires an intersubjective dimension, will have to recognize the fact that the audience is as important to its constitution as the individual to whom it is credited.

An Outline of the Systems Model

This environment has two salient aspects: a cultural, or symbolic, aspect which here is called the domain; and a social aspect called the field. Creativity is a process that can be observed only at the intersection where individuals, domains, and fields interact (Figure 1.1).

For creativity to occur, a set of rules and practices must be transmitted from the domain to the individual. The individual must then produce a novel variation in the content of the domain. The variation then must be selected by the field for inclusion in the domain.

Creativity occurs when a person makes a change in a domain, a change that will be transmitted through time. Some individuals are more likely to make such changes, either because of personal qualities or because they have the good fortune to be well positioned with respect to the domain – they have better access to it, or their social circumstances allow them free time to experiment. For example until quite recently the majority of scientific advances were made by men who had the means and the leisure: clergymen like Copernicus, tax collectors like Lavoisier, or physicians like Galvani could afford to build their own laboratories and to concentrate on their thoughts. And, of course, all of these individuals lived in cultures with a tradition of systematic observation of nature and a tradition of record keeping and mathematical

Source: M. Csikszentmihalyi (1999) Edited extract from R. Sternberg (Ed.) *Handbook of Creativity*. Cambridge: Cambridge University Press, 313–35.

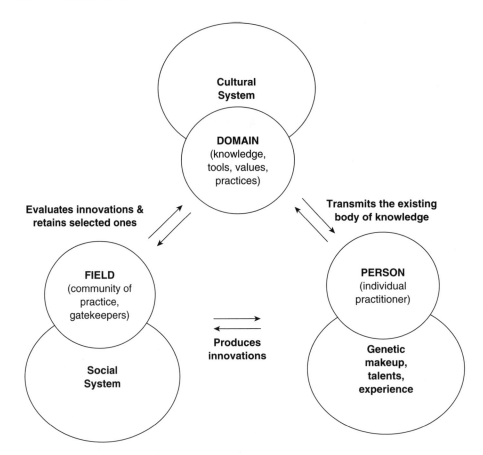

Figure 1.1   *A systems model of creativity*

symbolization that made it possible for their insights to be shared and evaluated by others who had equivalent training.

But most novel ideas will be quickly forgotten. Changes are not adopted unless they are sanctioned by some group entitled to make decisions as to what should or should not be included in the domain. These gatekeepers are what we call here the field. Here field refers only to the social organization of the domain – to the teachers, critics, journal editors, museum curators, agency directors, and foundation officers who decide what belongs to a domain and what does not. In physics, the opinion of a very small number of leading university professors was enough to certify that Einstein's ideas were creative. Hundreds of millions of people accepted the judgement of this tiny field and marvelled at Einstein's creativity without understanding what it was all about. It has been said that in the United States 10,000 people in Manhattan constitute the field in modern art. They decide which new paintings or sculptures deserve to be seen, bought, included in collections, and therefore added to the domain.

The Cultural Context

Creativity presupposes a community of people who share ways of thinking and acting, who learn from each other and imitate each other's actions. It is useful to think about creativity as involving a change in memes – the units of imitation that Dawkins (1976) suggested were the building blocks of culture. Memes are similar to genes in that they carry instructions for action. The notes of a song tell us what to sing, the recipe for a cake tells us what ingredients to mix and how long to bake it. But whereas genetic instructions are transmitted in the chemical codes that we inherit on our chromosomes, the instructions contained in memes are transmitted through learning. By and large we can learn memes and reproduce them without change; when a new song or a new recipe is invented, then we have creativity.

Cultures as a Set of Domains

It is useful to think about cultures as systems of interrelated domains. Cultures differ in the way that memes (i.e. technical procedures, kinds of knowledge, styles of art, belief systems) are stored. As long as they are recorded orally and can be transmitted only from the mind of one person to another, traditions must be strictly observed so as not to lose information. Therefore, creativity is not likely to be prized, and it would be difficult to determine in any case. Development of new media of storage and transmission (e.g. books, computers) will have an impact on rates of novelty production and its acceptance.

Another dimension of cultural difference is the accessibility of information. With time, people who benefit from the ability to control memes develop protective boundaries around their knowledge, so that only a few initiates at any given time will have access to it. Priestly castes around the world have evolved to keep their knowledge esoteric and out of reach of the masses. Even in the times of Egyptian civilization, craft guilds kept much of their technical knowledge secret. Until recently in the West, knowledge of Latin and Greek was used as a barrier to prevent the admittance of the masses to professional training. The more such barriers, the less likely it becomes that potentially creative individuals will be able to contribute to a domain.

Similarly, how available memes are also bears on the rate of creativity. When knowledge is concentrated in a few centres, libraries, or laboratories, or when books and schools are rare, most potentially creative individuals will be effectively prevented from learning enough to make a contribution to existing knowledge.

Cultures differ in the number of domains they recognize and in the hierarchical relationship among them. New memes most often arise in cultures that, either because of geographical location or economic practices, are exposed to different ideas and beliefs. The Greek traders collected information from Egypt, the Middle East, the north coast of Africa, the Black Sea, Persia and even Scandinavia, and this disparate information was amalgamated in the crucible of the Ionian and Attic city-states. In the Middle Ages, the Sicilian court welcomed techniques and knowledge from China and Arabia, as well as from Normandy, Florence in the Renaissance was a centre of trade and manufacture, and so was Venice; later the maritime trade of the Iberian Peninsula, the Netherlands, and Great Britain moved the centre of information exchange to those regions. Even now, when the diffusion of information is almost instantaneous, useful new ideas are likely to arise from centres where people from different cultural backgrounds are able to interact and exchange ideas.

The Role of the Domain in the Creative Process

Cultures are made up of a variety of domains: music, mathematics, religion, various technologies, and so on. Innovations that result in creative contributions do not take place directly in the culture, but in one of such domains.

There are times when the symbolic system of a domain is so diffuse and loosely integrated that it is almost impossible to determine whether a novelty is or is not an improvement on the status quo. Chemistry was in such a state before the adoption of the periodic table, which integrated and rationalized knowledge about the elements. Earlier centuries may have had many potentially creative chemical scientists, but their work was too idiosyncratic to be evaluated against a common standard. Or, conversely, the symbolic systems may be so tightly organized that no new development seems possible: this resembles the situation in physics at the end of the preceding century, before the revolution in thinking brought about by quantum theory. Both of these examples suggest that creativity is likely to be more difficult before a paradigmatic revolution. On the other hand, the need for a new paradigm makes it more likely that if a new viable contribution does occur despite the difficulty, it will be hailed as a major creative accomplishment.

At any historical period, certain domains will attract more gifted young people than at other times, thus increasing the likelihood of creativity. The attraction of a domain depends on several variables: its centrality in the culture, the promise of new discoveries and opportunities that it presents, the intrinsic rewards accruing from working in the domain. For instance, the Renaissance in early-fifteenth-century Florence would have not happened without the discovery of Roman ruins, which yielded a great amount of new knowledge about construction techniques and sculptural models and motivated many young people who otherwise would have gone into the professions, to become architects and artists instead. The quantum revolution in physics at the beginning of this century was so intellectually exciting that, for several generations, some of the best minds flocked to physics or applied its principles to neighbouring disciplines such as chemistry, biology, medicine, and astronomy. Nowadays similar excitement surrounds the domains of molecular biology and computer science.

As Thomas Kuhn (1962) remarked, potentially creative young people will not be drawn to domains where all the basic questions have been solved and which, therefore, appear to be boring – that is, offer few opportunities to obtain the intrinsic and extrinsic rewards that follow from solving important problems.

Domains also vary in terms of their accessibility. Sometimes rules and knowledge become the monopoly of a protective class or caste, and others are not admitted to it. Creative thought in Christianity was renewed by the Reformation, which placed the Bible and its commentaries in reach of a much larger population, which earlier had been excluded by an entrenched priestly caste from perusing it directly. The enormously increased accessibility of information on the Internet might also bring about a new peak in creativity across many different domains, just as the printing press did over four centuries ago.

Finally, some domains are easier to change than others. This depends in part on how autonomous a domain is from the rest of the culture or social system that supports it. Until the seventeenth century in Europe it was difficult to be creative in the many branches of science that the Church had a vested interest in protecting – as the case of Galileo illustrates. In Soviet Russia, the Marxist-Leninist dogma took precedence over scientific domains, and many new ideas that conflicted with it were not accepted. Even in our time, some topics in the social (and even in the physical and biological) sciences are considered less politically correct than others and are given scant research support as a consequence.

Creativity is the engine that drives cultural evolution. The notion of evolution does not imply that cultural changes necessarily follow some single direction or that cultures are getting any better as a result of the changes brought about by creativity. Evolution in this context means increasing complexity over time. Complexity means that cultures tend to become differentiated over time, that is, they develop increasingly independent and autonomous domains [and that] the domains within a culture become increasingly integrated, that is, related to each other and mutually supportive of each others' goals. Creativity contributes to differentiation, but it can easily work against integration, [as] new ideas, technologies, or forms of expression often break down the existing harmony between different domains.

The Social Context

In order to be called creative, a new meme must be socially valued. Without some form of social valuation it would be impossible to distinguish ideas that are simply bizarre from those that are genuinely creative. But this social validation is usually seen as something that follows the individual's creative act and can be – at least conceptually – separated from it. The stronger claim made here is that there is no way, even in principle, to separate the reaction of society from the person's contribution. The two are inseparable. As long as the idea or product has not been validated, we might have originality, but not creativity.

Nowadays everyone agrees that Van Gogh's paintings show that he was a very creative artist. It is also fashionable to sneer at the ignorant bourgeoisie of his period for failing to recognize Van Gogh's genius and letting him die alone and penniless. But we should remember that a hundred years ago those canvases were just the hallucinatory original works of a sociopathic recluse. They became creative only after a number of other artists, critics, and collectors interpreted them in terms of new aesthetic criteria and transformed them from substandard efforts into masterpieces.

Without this change in the climate of evaluation, Van Gogh would not be considered creative even now. In the sciences as well as in the arts, creativity is as much the result of changing standards and new criteria of assessment, as it is of novel individual achievements.

Societal Conditions Relevant to Creativity

The second main element of the systems model is society, or the sum of all fields. Fields are made up of individuals who practice a given domain and have the power to change it. For example, all the accountants who practice by the same rules comprise the field of accountancy, and it is they who have to endorse a new way of keeping accounts if it is to be accepted as a creative improvement.

Other things being equal, a society that enjoys a material surplus is in a better position to help the creative process. A wealthier society is able to make information more readily available, allows for a greater rate of specialization and experimentation, and is better equipped to reward and implement new ideas. Subsistence societies have fewer opportunities to encourage and reward novelty, especially if it is expensive to produce. Only societies with ample material reserves can afford to build great cathedrals, universities, scientific laboratories. But it seems that there is often a lag between social affluence and creativity: the impact of wealth may take several generations to manifest itself. So the material surplus of the nineteenth-century United States was first needed to build a material infrastructure for society (canals, railroads, factories), before it was invested in supporting novel ideas such as the telephone or the mass production of cars and planes.

Whether a society is open to novelty or not depends in part on its social organization. A farming society with a stable feudal structure, for instance, would be one where tradition counts more than novelty. Societies based on commerce, with a strong bourgeois class trying to be accepted by the aristocracy, have on the other hand been usually favourable to novelty. Whenever the central authority tends toward absolutism, it is less likely that experimentation will be encouraged (Therivel, 1995). Ancient Chinese society is a good example of a central authority supported by a powerful bureaucracy that was able to resist for centuries the spread of new ideas.

Rentier societies, where the ruling classes lived off the profits of land rent, pensions, or stable investments, have been historically reluctant to change because any novelty was seen to potentially threaten the status quo that provided the livelihood of the oligarchy. This condition might become relevant again as the United States moved more toward an economy where pensions and retirement plans are a major source of income for an increasing number of people.

A different and more controversial suggestion is that egalitarian societies are less likely to support the creative process than those where relatively few people control a disproportionate amount of the resources. Aristocracies or oligarchies may be better able to support creativity than democracies or social regimes, simply because when wealth and power are concentrated in a few hands, it is easier to use part of it for risky or 'unnecessary' experiments. Also, the development of a leisure class often results in a refinement of connoisseurship that in turn provides more demanding criteria by which a field evaluates new contributions.

Societies located at the confluence of diverse cultural streams can benefit more easily from that synergy of different ideas that is so important for the creative process. It is for this reason that some of the greatest art, and the earliest science, developed in cities that were centres of trade. The Italian Renaissance was in part due to the Arab and Middle Eastern influences that businessmen and their retinues brought into Florence and the seaports of Venice, Genoa, and Naples. The fact that periods of social unrest often coincide with creativity (Simonton, 1991) is probably due to the synergy resulting when the interests and perspectives of usually segregated classes are brought to bear on each other. The Tuscan cities supported creativity best during a period in which noblemen, merchants, and craftsmen fought each other bitterly and when every few years, as a different political party came to power, a good portion of the citizenry was banished into exile.

External threats also often mobilize society to recognize creative ideas that otherwise might not have attracted much attention. Florence in the fifteenth century spent so many resources on the arts in part because the leaders of the city were competing against their enemies in Sienna, Lucca, and Pisa and tried to outdo them in the beauty of their churches and public squares (Heydenreich, 1974). The reason that high-energy physics became such an important field after World War II is that practically every nation wished to have the technology to build its own nuclear arsenal.

Finally, the complexity of a society also bears on the rates of innovation it can tolerate. Too much divisiveness, as well as its opposite, too much uniformity, are unlikely to generate novelty that will be accepted and preserved. Ideal conditions for creativity would be a social system that is highly differentiated into specialized fields and roles, yet is held together by what Durkheim (1912/1967) called the bonds of 'organic solidarity'.

The Role of the Field

What does it take for a new meme to be accepted into the domain? Who has the right to decide whether a new meme is actually an improvement, or simply a mistake to be discarded? In the systems model, the gatekeepers who have the right to add memes to a domain are collectively designated the field. Some domains may have a very small field consisting of a dozen or so scholars across the world. Others, such as electronic engineering, may include many thousands of specialists whose opinion would count in recognizing a viable novelty. For mass-market products such as soft drinks or motion pictures, the field might include not only the small coterie of product developers and critics, but the public at large. For instance, if New Coke is not a part of the culture, it is because although it passed the evaluation of the small field of beverage specialists, it failed to pass the test of public taste.

Some of the ways in which fields influence creativity follow. The first issue to be considered is the field's access to economic resources. In some domains it is almost impossible to do novel work without access to capital. To build a cathedral or to make a movie required the collaboration of people and materials, and these must be made available to the would-be creative artists. The masterpieces of Florence were built with the profits that the city's bankers made throughout Europe: the masterpieces of Venice were the fruit of that city's seagoing trade. Dutch painters and scientists blossomed after Dutch merchants began to dominate the sea-lanes: then it was the turn of France,

England, Germany, and, finally, the United States. As resources accumulate in one place, they lay down the conditions that make innovation possible.

A field is likely to attract original minds to the extent that it can offer scope for a person's experimentations and promises rewards in case of success. Even though individuals who try to change domains are in general intrinsically motivated – that is, they enjoy working in the domain for its own sake – the attraction of extrinsic awards such as money and fame are not to be discounted.

Leonardo da Vinci, one of the most creative persons on record in terms of his contributions to the arts and the sciences, constantly moved during his lifetime from one city to another, in response to changing market conditions. The leaders of Florence, the dukes of Milan, the popes of Rome, and the king of France waxed and waned in terms of how much money they had to devote to new paintings, sculptures, or cutting-edge scholarship: and as their fortunes changed, Leonardo moved to wherever he could pursue his work with the least hindrance.

The centrality of a field in terms of societal values will also determine how likely it is to attract new persons with an innovative bent. In this particular historical period, bright young men and women are attracted to the field on computer sciences because it provides the most exciting new intellectual challenges; others to oceanography because it might help to save the planetary ecosystem; some to currency trading because it provides access to financial power; and some to family medicine because it is the medical specialty most responsive to societal needs. Any field that is able to attract a disproportionate number of bright young persons is more likely to witness creative breakthroughs.

In the domains of movies or popular music, which are much more accessible to the general public, the specialized field is notoriously unable to enforce a decision as to which works will be creative. It is instructive to compare the list of Nobel Prize winners in literature with those in the sciences: few of the writers from years past are now recognized as creative compared with the scientists.

In order to establish and preserve criteria, a field must have a minimum of organization. However, it is often the case that instead of serving the domain, members of the field devote most of their energies to serving themselves, making it difficult for new ideas to be evaluated on their merits. It is not only the Church that has hindered the spread of new ideas for fear of losing its privileges. Every industry faces the problem that better ideas that require changing the status quo will be ignored, because so much effort and capital has been invested in existing production methods.

Another important dimension along which fields vary is the extent to which they are ideologically open or closed to new memes. The openness of a field depends in part on its internal organization, in part on its relation to the wider society. Highly hierarchical institutions, where knowledge of the past is greatly valued, generally see novelty as a threat. For this reason, churches, academies, and certain businesses based on tradition seek to promote older individuals to leadership positions as a way of warding off excessive change. Also, creativity is not welcome in fields whose self-interest requires keeping a small cadre of initiates performing the same routines, regardless of efficiency: some of the trade unions come to mind in this context.

It requires an adroit balancing act for those responsible for evaluating novelty to decide which new ideas are worth preserving. If a historical period is stagnant, it is probably not because there were no potentially creative individuals around, but because of the ineptitude of the relevant fields.

It might be objected that some of the most influential new ideas or processes seem to occur even though there is no existing domain or field to receive them. For instance, Freud's ideas had a wide impact even before there was a domain of psycho-analysis or a field of analysts to evaluate them. Personal computers were widely adopted before there was a tradition and a group of experts to judge which were good, which were not. But the lack of a social context in such cases is more apparent than real. Freud, who was immersed in the already-existing domain of psychiatry, simply expanded its limits until his conceptual contributions could stand on their own as a separate domain. Without peers and without disciples, Freud's ideas might have been original, but they would not have had an impact on the culture, and thus would have failed to be creative. Similarly, personal computers would not have been accepted had there not been a domain – computer languages that allowed the writing of software and therefore, various applications – and an embryonic field – people who had experience with mainframe computers, with video games, and so on who could become 'experts' in this emerging technology.

In any case, the point is that how much creativity there is at any given time is not determined just by how many original individuals are trying to change domains, but also by how receptive the fields are to innovation. It follows that if one wishes to increase the frequency of creativity, it may be more advantageous to work at the levels of fields than at the level of individuals. For example, some large organizations such as Motorola, where new technological interventions are essential, spend a large quantity of resources in trying to make engineers think more creatively. This is a good strategy as far as it goes, but it will not result in any increase in creativity unless the field – in this case, management – is able to recognize which of the new ideas are good and has ways for implementing them, that is, including them in the domain. Whereas engineers and managers are the field who judge the creativity of new ideas within an organization such as Motorola, the entire market for electronics becomes the field that evaluates the organization's products once these have been implemented within the organization. Thus, at one level of analysis the system comprises the organization, with innovators, managers, and production engineers as its parts but at a higher level of analysis the organization becomes just one element of a broader system that includes the entire industry.

The Individual in the Creative Process

The great majority of psychological research assumes that creativity is an individual trait, to be understood by studying individuals. The systems model makes it possible to see that before a person can introduce a creative variation, he or she must have access to a domain and must want to learn to perform according to its rules. This implies that motivation is important. But it also suggests a number of additional factors that are usually ignored, for instance, that cognitive and motivational factors interact with the state of the domain and the field.

Second, persons who are likely to innovate tend to have personality traits that favor breaking rules and early experiences that make them want to do so. Divergent thinking, problem finding, and all the other factors that psychologists have studied are relevant in this context.

Finally, the ability to convince the field about the virtue of the novelty one has produced is an important aspect of personal creativity. The opportunities that one has to get access to the field, the network of contacts, the personality traits that make it possible for one to be taken seriously, the ability to express oneself in such a way as to be understood, are all part of the individual traits that make it easier for someone to make a creative contribution.

But none of these personal characteristics are sufficient, and probably they are not even necessary. Conservative and unimaginative scientists have made important contributions to science by stumbling on important new phenomena. At the same time, it is probably true that persons who master a domain, and then want to change it, will have a higher proportion of their efforts recognized as creative.

The Background of Creative Individuals

One of the first issues to consider is whether an individual is born in an environment that has enough surplus energy to encourage the development of curiosity and interest for its own sake. The following personal background factors can affect the incidence of creativity:

- A child is likely to be discouraged from expressing curiosity and interest if the material conditions of existence are too precarious
- Ethnic and family traditions can have a very important role in directing the child's interest toward specific domains
- Cultural capital (i.e. home learning, schooling) is essential for a child to develop expertise in a domain
- Tutors, mentors, and connections are often indispensable for advancing far enough to have one's ideas recognized
- Marginality (social, ethnic, economic, religious) seems to be more conducive to wanting to break out of the norm than a conventional, middle-class background

Even though it is said that necessity is the mother of invention, too much deprivation does not seem to lead to innovative thinking. When survival is precarious – as it has been and still is in most of the world – there is little energy left for learning and experimenting. It is not impossible for a talented person to emerge from a ghetto or a third-world country, but much potential is lost for lack of access to the basic tools of a domain.

Ethnic groups, and families within them, differ in the amount of importance they place on different domains. Jewish tradition has emphasized the importance of learning, and Asian-American families have instilled strong academic and artistic motivation in their children (Kao, 1995). Some cultural groups emphasize musical abilities, others focus on engineering or technology. Such traditions help to focus a child's interest on a particular domain, thus providing the preconditions for further innovation.

It has been observed that many creative individuals grew up in atypical conditions, on the margins of the community. Many of them were orphaned early, had to struggle against relative poverty and prejudice, or were otherwise singled out as different from their peers (Csikszentmihalyi and Csikszentmihalyi, 1993). For example, all seven of the creative geniuses of this century described by Gardner (1993) were outsiders to the societies in which they worked. Einstein moved from Germany to Switzerland, Italy, and the United States; Gandhi grew up in South Africa; Stravinsky left Russia; Eliot settled in England; Martha Graham as a child moved from the South to California, where she became exposed to and influenced by Asian art; Freud was Jewish in Catholic Vienna; and Picasso left Spain for France. It seems that a person who is comfortably settled in the bosom of society has fewer incentives to change the status quo.

Personal Qualities

Having the right background conditions is indispensable but certainly not sufficient for a person to make a creative contribution. He or she must also have the ability and inclination to introduce novelty into the domain.

The following individual qualities seem to affect the incidence of creativity:

- In certain domains (e.g. music, mathematics) genetic inheritance may play an important role in directing interest to the domain and in helping to master it
- A great deal of intrinsic motivation is needed to energize the person to absorb the relevant memes and to persevere in the risky process of innovation
- Cognitive ability such as fluency, flexibility, and discovery orientation seem necessary to engage successfully in the process of generating novelty
- To be able to innovate successfully, a person needs to have apppropriate traits – which may vary depending on the field and the historical period. In general, one must persevere and be open to experience, as well as adopt apparently contradictory behaviors

Talent, or innate ability, refers to the fact that it is easier to be creative if one is born with a physical endowment that helps to master the skills required by the domain. Great musicians seem to be unusually sensitive to sounds even in their earliest years. It would not be surprising, however, to find that interest or skill in certain domains can be inherited. Howard Gardner's (1983, 1993) postulate of seven or more separate forms of intelligence also seems to support the notion that each of us might be born with a propensity to respond to a different slice of reality, and hence to operate more effectively in one domain rather than another. Many creative individuals display unusual early abilities that are almost at the level of child prodigies described by Feldman (1986). On the other hand, a roughly equal number who have achieved comparable creative contributions appear to have had rather undistinguished childhoods and were not recognized as exceptional until early adulthood.

Cerebral lateralization research has led many people to claim that left-handers or ambidextrous individuals, who are presumed to be using the right side of their brains more than right-handers, are more likely to be creative. Left-handers are apparently over-represented in such fields as art, architecture, and music: many exceptional individuals from Alexander the Great to Leonardo, Michelangelo, Raphael, Picasso, Einstein, and the three presidential candidates of the 1992 election – Clinton, Bush, Perot – were all left-handers (Coren, 1992; Paul, 1993).

Perhaps the most salient characteristic of creative individuals is a constant curiosity, an ever-renewed interest in whatever happens around them. This enthusiasm for experience is often seen as part of the 'childishness' attributed to creative individuals (Csikszentmihalyi, 1996; Gardner, 1993). Without this interest, a person would be unlikely to become immersed deeply enough in a domain to be able to change it. Another way of describing this trait is that creative people are intrinsically motivated. They find their reward in the activity itself, without having to wait for external rewards or recognition. A recurring refrain among them goes something like this: 'You could say that I worked every day of my life, or with equal justice you could say that I never did any work in my life.' Such an attitude greatly helps a person to persevere during the long stretches of the creative process when no external recognition is forthcoming.

The importance of motivation for creativity has long been recognised, Cox (1926) advised that if one had to bet on who is more likely to achieve a creative break-through, a highly intelligent but not very motivated person, or one less intelligent but more motivated, one should always bet on the second. Because introducing novelty in a system is always a risky and usually an unrewarded affair, it takes a great deal of motivation to persevere in the effort. One recent formulation of the creative person's willingness to take risks is the 'economic' model of Sternberg and Lubart (1995).

Probably the most extensively studied attributes of the creative cognitive style are divergent thinking (Guilford, 1967) and discovery orientation (Getzels and Csikszentmihalyi, 1976). Divergent thinking is usually indexed by fluency, flexibility, and originality of mental operations. Whether divergent thinking tests also relate to creativity in 'real' adult settings is not clear, although some claims to that effect have been made (Milgram, 1990; Torrance, 1988). Discovery orientation, or the tendency to find and formulate problems where others have not see any, has also been measured in selected situations, with some encouraging results (Baer, 1993; Runco, 1995). As Einstein and many others have observed the solution of problems is a much simpler affair than their formulation. Anyone who is technically proficient can solve a problem that is already formulated: but it takes true originality to formulate a problem in the first place (Einstein and Infeld, 1938).

Some scholars dispute the notion that problem finding and problem solving involve different thought processes: for example, the Nobel Prize – winning economist and psychologist Herbert Simon (1985, 1989) has claimed that all creative achievements are the result of normal problem solving.

The personality of creative persons has also been exhaustively investigated (Barron, 1969, 1988). Psychoanalysis theory has stressed the ability to regress into the unconscious while still maintaining conscious ego controls as one of the hallmarks of creativity (Kris, 1952). The widespread use of multifactor personality inventories suggest that creative individuals tend to be strong on certain traits, such as introversion and self-reliance, and low on others, such as conformity and moral certainty (Csikszentmihalyi and Getzels, 1973; Getzels and Csikszentmihalyi, 1976; Russ, 1993).

One view I have developed on the basis of my studies is that creative persons are characterized not so much by single traits, as by their ability to operate through the entire spectrum of personality dimensions. So they are not just introverted, but can be both extroverted and introverted, depending on the phase of the process they happen to be involved in at the moment. When gathering ideas, a creative scientist is gregarious and sociable: when starting to work, he or she might become a secluded hermit for weeks on end. Creative individuals are sensitive and aloof, dominant and humble, masculine and feminine, as the occasion demands (Csikszentmihalyi, 1996). What dictates their behavior is not a rigid inner structure, but the demands of the interaction between them and the domain in which they are working.

In order to want to introduce novelty into a domain, a person should first of all be dissatisfied with the status quo. It has been said that Einstein explained why he spent so much time developing a new physics by saying that he could not understand the old physics. Greater sensitivity, naivety, arrogance, impatience, and higher intellectual standards have all been adduced as reasons why some people are unable to accept the conventional wisdom in a domain and feel the need to break out of it.

Values also play a role in developing a creative career. There are indications that if a person holds financial and social goals in high esteem, it is less likely that he or she will continue for long to brave the insecurities involved in the production of novelty, and will tend to settle instead for a more conventional career (Csikszentmihalyi et al., 1984; Getzels and Csikszentmihalyi, 1976). A person who is attracted to the solution of abstract problems (theoretical value) and to order and beauty (aesthetic value) is more likely to persevere.

In order to function well within the creative system, one must internalize the rules of the domain and the opinions of the field, so that one can choose the most promising ideas to work on, and do so in a way that will be acceptable to one's peers. Practically all creative individuals say that one advantage they have is that they are confident that they can tell which of their own ideas are bad, and thus they can forget the bad ones without investing too much energy in them. For example Linus Pauling, who won the Nobel Prize twice, was asked at his 60th birthday party how he had been able to come up with so many epochal discoveries. 'It's easy,' he is said to have answered. 'You can think of a lot of ideas, and throw away the bad ones'. To be able to do so, however, implies that one has a very strong internal representation of which ideas are good and which are bad, a representation that matches closely the one accepted by the field.

Conclusion

Creativity cannot be recognized except as it operates within a system of cultural rules, and it cannot bring forth anything new unless it can enlist the support of peers. It follows that the occurrence of creativity is not simply a function of how many gifted individuals there are, but also of how accessible the various symbolic systems are and how responsive the social system is to novel ideas. Instead of focusing exclusively on individuals, it will make more sense to focus on communities that may or may not nurture genius. In the last analysis, it is the community and not the individual who makes creativity manifest.

References

Baer, J. (1993) *Creativity and Divergent Thinking*. Hillsdale, NJ: Erlbaum.

Barron, F. (1969) *Creative Person and Creative Process*. New York: Holt, Rinehardt, and Winston.

Barron, F. (1988) Putting creativity to work. In R.J. Sternberg (Ed.) *The Nature of Creativity*. Cambridge: Cambridge University Press. (pp. 76–98).

Coren, S. (1992) *The Left-handed Syndrome: The Causes and Consequences of Left-handedness*. New York: Free Press.

Cox, C. (1926) *Genetic Studies of Genius: The Early Mental Traits of Three Hundred Geniuses* (Vol. 2). Stanford, CA: Stanford University Press.

Cox, C. (1926) *The Early Mental Traits of Three Hundred Geniuses*. Stanford, CA: Stanford University Press.

Csikszentmihalyi, M. (1988a) Motivation and creativity: Toward a synthesis of structural and energistic approaches to cognition. *New Ideas in Psychology, 6*(2), 159–76.

Csikszentmihalyi, M. (1988b) Society, culture, person: A systems view of creativity. In R.J. Sternberg (Ed.) *The Nature of Creativity*. Cambridge: Cambridge University Press. (pp. 325–339).

Csikszentmihalyi, M. (1988c) Solving a problem is not finding a new one: A reply to Simon. *New Ideas in Psychology, 6*(2), 183–6.

Csikszentmihalyi, M. (1990) The domain of creativity. In M.A. Runco and R.S. Albert (Eds) *Theories of Creativity*. Newbury Park, CA: Sage. (pp. 190–212).

Csikszentmihalyi, M. (1993) *The Evolving Self: A Psychology for the Third Millennium*. New York: HarperCollins.

Csikszentmihalyi, M. (1996) *Creativity: Flow and the Psychology of Discovery and Invention*. New York: HarperCollins.

Csikszentmihalyi, M. and Csikszentmihalyi I.S. (1993) Family influences on the development of giftedness. In *The Origins and Development of High Ability*. Chichester: Wiley (Ciba Foundation Symposium 178). (pp. 18–206).

Csikszentmihalyi, M, and Getzels, J.W. (1973) The personality of young artists: an empirical and theoretical exploration. *British Journal of Psychology, 64*(1), 91–104.

Csikszentmihalyi, M. and Getzels, J.W. (1988) Creativity and problem finding. In F.G. Farley and R.W. Heperud (Eds) *The Foundations of Aesthetics, Art, and Art Education*. New York: Praeger. (pp. 91–106).

Csikszentmihalyi, M., Getzels, J.W. and Kahn, S.P. (1984) *Talent and achievement: A longtitudinal study of artists*. (A report to the Spencer Foundation.). Chicago: University of Chicago.

Csikszentmihalyi, M., Rathunde, K. and Whalen, S. (1993) *Talented Teenagers: The Roots of Success and Failure*. Cambridge: Cambridge University Press.

Csikszentmihalyi, M, and Sawyer, K. (1995) Shifting the focus from the organizational creativity. In G.M. Ford and D.A. Gioia (Eds) *Creative Action in Organizations*. Thousand Oaks, CA: Sage. (pp. 167–72).

Dawkins, R. (1976) *The Selfish Gene*. Oxford: Oxford University Press.

Durkheim, E. (1912/1967) *The Elementary Forms of Religious Life*. New York: Free Press.

Einstein, A., and Infeld, L. (1938) *The Evolution of Physics*. New York: Simon & Schuster.

Feldman, D. (1986) *Nature's Gambit: Child Prodigies and the Development of Human Potential*. New York: Basic Books.

Feldman, D., Csikszentmihalyi, M. and Gardner, H. (1994) *Changing the World: A Framework for the Study of Creativity*. Westport, CT: Praeger.

Gardner, H. (1983) *Art Education, 36(2)*, Art and the Mind, March, 47–49.

Gardner, H. (1993) *Creating Minds*. New York: Basic Books.

Getzels, J.W. and Csikszentmihalyi, M. (1976) *The Creative Vision: A Longitudinal Study of Problem Finding in Art*. New York: Wiley.

Gruber, H. (1988) The evolving systems approach to creative work. *Creativity Research Journal*, 1(1), 27–51.

Guilford, J.P. (1967) *The Nature of Human Intelligence*. New York: McGraw-Hill.

Heydenreich, L.H. (1974) *Il primo rinascimento*. Milan: Rizzoli.

Kao, G. (1995) Asian Americans as model minorities? A look at their academic performance. *American Journal of Education, 103*, 121–59.

Kasof, J. (1995) Explaining creativity: The attributional perspective. *Creativity Research Journal*, 8(4), 311–66

Kris, E. (1952) *Psychoanalytic Explorations in Art*. New York: International Universities Press.

Kuhn, T.S. (1962) *The Structure of Scientific Revolutions*. Chicago: University of Chicago Press.

Maslow, A.H. (1963) The creative attitude. *Structuralist, 3*, 4–10.

Milgram, R.N. (1990) Creativity: an idea whose time has come and gone? In M.A. Runco and R.S. Albert (Eds) *Theories of Creativity*. Newbury Park, CA: Sage. (pp. 215–33).

Paul, D. (1993) *Left-handed Helpline*. Manchester: Dextral.

Runco, M.A. (1991) *Divergent Thinking*. Norwood, NJ: Ablex.

Runco, M.A. (Eds) (1995) *Problem finding*. Norwood, NJ: Ablex.

Russ, S.W. (1993) *Affect and Creativity*. Hillsdale, NJ: Erlbaum.

Simon, H.A. (1985) *Psychology of scientific discovery*. Keynote presentation at the 93rd Annual meeting of the American Psychological Association. Los Angeles, CA.

Simon, H.A. (1989) Creativity and motivation: A response to Csikszentmihalyi. *New Ideas in Psychology, 6(2)*, 177–81.

Simonton, D.K. (1988) *Scientific Genius*. Cambridge: Cambridge University Press.

Simonton, D.K. (1990) Political pathology and societal creativity. *Creativity Research Journal*, 3(2), 85–99.

Simonton, D.K. (1991) Personality correlates of exceptional personal influence. *Creative Research Journal, 4*, 67–8.

Simonton, D.K. (1994) *Greatness: Who Makes History and Why*. New York: Guilford.

Sternberg, R.J. and Lubart, T.I. (1995) *Defying the Crowd: Cultivating Creativity in a Culture of Conformity*. New York: Free Press.

Therivel, W.A. (1995) Long-term effect of power on creativity. *Creativity Research Journal*, 8, 73–92.

Torrance, E.P. (1988) The nature of creativity as manifest in its testing. In R.J. Sternberg (Ed.) *The Nature of Creativity*. Cambridge: Cambridge University Press. (pp. 43–75).

2

How to Kill Creativity

Teresa Amabile

When I consider all the organizations I have studied and worked with over the past 22 years, there can be no doubt: creativity gets killed much more often than it gets supported. For the most part, this isn't because managers have a vendetta against creativity. On the contrary, most believe in the value of new and useful ideas. However, creativity is undermined unintentionally every day in work environments that were established – for entirely good reasons – to maximize business imperatives such as co-ordination, productivity, and control.

Managers cannot be expected to ignore business imperatives, of course. But in working toward these imperatives, they may be inadvertently designing organizations that systematically crush creativity. My research shows that it is possible to develop the best of both worlds: organizations in which business imperatives are attended to and creativity flourishes. Building such organizations, however, requires us to understand precisely what kinds of managerial practices foster creativity – and which kill it.

The Three Components of Creativity

Within every individual, creativity is a function of three components: expertise, creative-thinking skills, and motivation. Can managers influence these components? The answer is an emphatic yes – for better and for worse – through workplace practices and conditions.

Expertise is, in a word, knowledge – technical, procedural and intellectual. *Creative-thinking skills* determine how flexibly and imaginatively people approach problems. Do their solutions up-end the status quo? Do they persevere through dry spells?

Not all *motivation* is created equal. An inner passion to solve the problem at hand leads to solutions far more creative than external rewards, such as money. This component – called intrinsic motivation – is the one that can most immediately be influenced by the work environment.

Source: T. Amabile (1998) *Harvard Business Review*, September, 77–87.

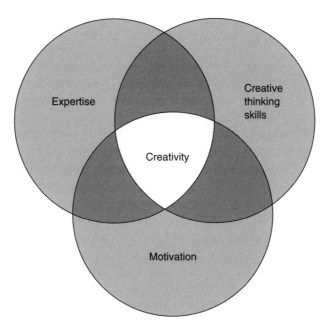

Figure 2.1   *The three components of creativity*

Managing Creativity

[Amabile's research has identified six general categories of managerial practice that affect creativity. These are challenge, freedom, resources, work-group features, supervisory encouragement, and organizational support.] Taking the six categories that have emerged from our research in turn, let's explore what managers can do to enhance creativity – and what often happens instead. It is important to note that creativity-killing practices are seldom the work of lone managers. Such practices usually are systemic – so widespread that they are rarely questioned.

Challenge

Of all the things managers can do to stimulate creativity, perhaps the most efficacious is the deceptively simple task of matching people with the right assignments. Managers can match people with jobs that play to their expertise and their skills in creative thinking, *and* ignite intrinsic motivation. Perfect matches stretch employees' abilities. The amount of stretch, however, is crucial: not so little that they feel bored but not so much that they feel overwhelmed and threatened by a loss of control.

Making a good match requires that managers possess rich and detailed information about their employees and the available assignments. Such information is often difficult and time consuming to gather. Perhaps that's why good matches are so rarely made. In fact, one of the most common ways managers kill creativity is by not trying to obtain the information necessary to make good connections between people and jobs. Instead, something of a shotgun wedding occurs. The most eligible employee is wed to the most eligible – that is, the most urgent and open – assignment. Often, the results are predictably unsatisfactory for all involved.

Freedom

When it comes to granting freedom, the key to creativity is giving people autonomy concerning the means – that is, concerning the process – but not necessarily the ends. People will be more creative, in other words, if you give them freedom to decide how to climb a particular mountain. You needn't let them choose which mountain to climb. In fact, clearly specified strategic goals often enhance people's creativity.

I'm not making the case that managers should leave their subordinates entirely out of goal- or agenda-setting discussions. But they should understand that inclusion in those discussions will not necessarily enhance creative output and certainly will not be sufficient to do so. It is far more important that whoever sets the goals also makes them clear to the organization and that these goals remain stable for a meaningful period of time. It is difficult, if not impossible, to work creatively toward a target if it keeps moving.

Autonomy around process fosters creativity because giving people freedom in how they approach their work heightens their intrinsic motivation and sense of ownership. Freedom about process also allows people to approach problems in ways that make the most of their expertise and their creative-thinking skills. The task may end up being a stretch for them, but they can use their strengths to meet the challenge.

How do executives mismanage freedom? There are two common ways. First, managers tend to change goals frequently or fail to define them clearly. Employees may have freedom around process, but if they don't know where they are headed, such freedom is pointless. And second, some managers fall short on this dimension by granting autonomy in name only. They claim that employees are 'empowered' to explore the maze as they search for solutions but, in fact, the process is proscribed. Employees diverge at their own risk.

Resources

The two main resources that affect creativity are time and money. Managers need to allot these resources carefully. Like matching people with the right assignments, deciding how much time and money to give to a team or project is a sophisticated judgement call that can either support or kill creativity.

Consider time. Under some circumstances, time pressure can heighten creativity. Say, for instance, that a competitor is about to launch a great product at a lower price than your offering or that society faces a serious problem and desperately needs a solution – such as an AIDS vaccine. In such situations, both the time crunch and the importance of the work legitimately make people feel that they must rush. Indeed, cases like these would be apt to increase intrinsic motivation by increasing the sense of challenge.

Organizations routinely kill creativity with fake deadlines or impossibly tight ones. The former create distrust and the latter cause burnout. In either case, people feel over-controlled and unfulfilled – which invariably damages motivation. Moreover, creativity often takes time. It can be slow going to explore new concepts, put together unique solutions, and wander through the maze. Managers who do not allow time for exploration or do not schedule in incubation periods are unwittingly standing in the way of the creative process.

When it comes to project resources, again managers must make a fit. They must determine the funding, people, and other resources that a team legitimately needs to complete an assignment – and they must know how much the organization can legitimately afford to allocate to the assignment. Then they must strike a compromise. Interestingly, adding more resources above a 'threshold of sufficiency' does not boost creativity. Below the threshold, however, a restriction of resources can dampen creativity. Unfortunately, many managers don't realize this and therefore often make another mistake. They keep resources tight, which pushes people to channel their creativity into finding additional resources, not in actually developing new products or services.

Another resource that is misunderstood when it comes to creativity is physical space. It is almost conventional wisdom that creative teams need open, comfortable offices. Such an atmosphere won't hurt creativity, and it may even help, but it is not nearly as important as other managerial initiatives that influence creativity. Indeed, a problem we have seen time and time again is managers paying attention to creating the 'right' physical space at the expense of more high-impact actions, such as matching people to the right assignments and granting freedom around work processes.

Work-group Features

If you want to build teams that come up with creative ideas, you must pay careful attention to the design of such teams. That is, you must create mutually supportive groups with a diversity of perspectives and backgrounds. Why? Because when teams comprise people with various intellectual foundations and approaches to work – that is, different expertise and creative thinking styles – ideas often combine and combust in exciting and useful ways.

Diversity, however, is only a starting point. Managers must also make sure that the teams they put together have three other features. First, the members must share excitement over the team's goal. Second, members must display a willingness to help their teammates through difficult periods and setbacks. And third, every member must recognize the unique knowledge and perspective that other members bring to the table. These factors enhance not only intrinsic motivation but also expertise and creative-thinking skills.

Again, creating such teams requires managers to have a deep understanding of their people. They must be able to assess them not just for their knowledge but for their attitudes about potential fellow team members and the collaborative process, for their problem-solving styles, and for their motivational hot buttons. Putting together a team with just the right chemistry – just the right level of diversity and supportiveness – can be difficult, but our research shows how powerful it can be.

It follows, then, that one common way managers kill creativity is by assembling homogeneous teams. The lure to do so is great. Homogeneous teams often reach 'solutions' more quickly and with less friction along the way. These teams often report high morale, too. But homogeneous teams do little to enhance expertise and creative thinking. Everyone comes to the table with a similar mind-set. They leave with the same.

Supervisory Encouragement

Most managers are extremely busy. They are under pressure for results. It is therefore easy for them to let praise for creative efforts – not just creative successes but unsuccessful efforts, too – fall by the wayside. One very simple step managers can take to foster creativity is to not let that happen.

The connection to intrinsic motivation here is clear. Certainly, people can find their work interesting or exciting without a cheering section – for some period of time. But to *sustain* such passion, most people need to feel as if their work matters to the organization or to some important group of people. Otherwise, they might as well do their work at home and for their own personal gain.

Managers in successful, creative organizations rarely offer specific extrinsic rewards for particular outcomes. However, they freely and generously recognize creative work by individuals and teams – often before the ultimate commercial impact of those efforts is known. By contrast, managers who kill creativity do so either by failing to acknowledge innovative efforts or by greeting them with skepticism. In many companies, for instance, new ideas are met not with open minds but with time-consuming layers of evaluation – or even with harsh criticism. When someone suggests a new product or process, senior managers take weeks to respond. Or they put that person through an excruciating critique.

Not every new idea is worthy of consideration, of course, but in many organizations, managers habitually demonstrate a reaction that damages creativity. They look for reasons to not use a new idea instead of searching for reasons to explore it further. An interesting psychological dynamic underlies this phenomenon. Our research shows that people believe that they will appear smarter to their bosses if they are more critical – and it often works. In many organizations, it is professionally rewarding to react critically to new ideas.

Unfortunately, this sort of negativity bias can have severe consequences for the creativity of those being evaluated. How? First, a culture of evaluation leads people to focus on the external rewards and punishments associated with their output, thus increasing the presence of extrinsic motivation and its potentially negative effects on intrinsic motivation. Second, such a culture creates a climate of fear, which again undermines intrinsic motivation.

Finally, negativity also shows up in how managers treat people whose ideas don't pan out: often, they are terminated or otherwise warehoused within the organization.

Of course, ultimately, ideas do need to work; remember that creative ideas in business must be new *and* useful. The dilemma is that you can't possibly know beforehand which ideas will pan out. Furthermore, dead ends can sometimes be very enlightening. In many business situations, knowing what doesn't work can be as useful as knowing what does. But if people do not perceive any 'failure value' for projects that ultimately do not achieve commercial success, they'll become less and less likely to experiment, explore, and connect with their work on a personal level. Their intrinsic motivation will evaporate.

Supervisory encouragement comes in other forms besides rewards and punishment. Another way managers can support creativity is to serve as role models, persevering through tough problems as well as encouraging collaboration and communication within the team. Such behavior enhances all three components of the creative process, and it has the added virtue of being a high-impact practice that a single manager can take on his or her own. It is better still when all managers in an organization serve as role models for the attitudes and behaviors that encourage and nurture creativity.

Organizational Support

Encouragement from supervisors certainly fosters creativity, but creativity is truly enhanced when the entire organization supports it. Such support is the job of an organization's leaders, who must put in place appropriate systems or procedures and emphasize values that make it clear that creative efforts are a top priority. For example, creativity-supporting organizations consistently reward creativity, but they avoid using money to 'bribe' people to come up with innovative ideas. Because monetary rewards make people feel as if they are being controlled, such a tactic probably won't work. At the same time, not providing sufficient recognition and rewards for creativity can spawn negative feelings within an organization. People can feel used, or at least under-appreciated, for their creative efforts. And it is rare to find the energy and passion of intrinsic motivation coupled with resentment.

Most important, an organization's leaders can support creativity by mandating information sharing and collaboration and by ensuring that political problems do not fester. Information sharing and collaboration support all three components of creativity. Take expertise. The more often people exchange ideas and data by working together, the more knowledge they will have. The same dynamic can be said for creative thinking. In fact, one way to enhance the creative thinking of employees is to expose them to various approaches to problem solving. With the exception of hardened misanthropes, information sharing and collaboration heighten peoples' enjoyment of work and thus their intrinsic motivation.

Whether or not you are seeking to enhance creativity, it is probably never a good idea to let political problems fester in an organizational setting. Infighting, politicking, and gossip are particularly damaging to creativity because they take peoples' attention away from work. That sense of mutual purpose and excitement so central to intrinsic motivation invariably lessens when people are cliquish or at war with one another. Indeed, our research suggests that intrinsic motivation increases when people are aware that those around them are excited by their jobs. When political problems abound, people feel that their work is threatened by others' agendas.

Finally, politicking also undermines expertise. The reason? Politics get in the way of open communication, obstructing the flow of information from point A to point B. Knowledge stays put and expertise suffers.

3

Flourishing in Teams: Developing Creativity and Innovation

Michael A. West and Claudia A. Sacramento

Introduction

Team working offers a powerful and ubiquitous strategy for managing organizational change, and team innovation is often the manifestation of teams' efforts to cope success-fully with the changes in their work environments. Developing team innovation will enhance an organization's ability to redirect and focus resources effectively, appropriately and more quickly than its competitors, because it enables all members of the organization to respond to the demands for change, and to make appropriate changes at a local level.

In order to manage and implement change we therefore need to understand how to develop innovative teams. In this chapter, we review relevant research and present twelve principles that theorists and practitioners can use as guides for understanding and promoting innovation in teams.

Innovation can be defined as '… the intentional introduction and application within a job, work team or organization of ideas, processes, products or procedures which are new to that job, work team or organization and which are designed to ben-efit the job, the work team or the organization.' (West and Farr, 1990, p. 9). Innovation is a two-component non-linear process, encompassing both creativity and innovation implementation. At the outset of the process, creativity dominates, to be superseded later by innovation implementation processes.

Innovation represents a particular category of change – it is intentional, designed to benefit, and new to the unit of adoption. If a change incorporates these three elements, according to this definition, it is innovation.

A Framework for Research on Team Innovation

In this chapter we describe research which examines the relationships between aspects of the *team task* (intrinsically and extrinsically motivating task characteristics); *team composition* (personality of team members, skill and diversity); *organizational context* (rewards, learning and development practices, climate); *team processes* (including norms for innovation, leadership, reflexivity, inter-group relations, conflict and dissent) and the likely effectiveness of team innovation.

The task
1   Intrinsically motivating
2   High level of extrinsic demands

Group composition
3   Selection of innovative people
4   Diversity in skills and demography

The organizational context
5   Rewards for innovation
6   A learning and development climate
7   A climate for innovation

Process
8   Norms for innovation
9   Reflexivity
10 Leadership supportive for innovation
11 Conflict and dissent
12 Bridging across teams

1 Ensure the Team Task is Intrinsically Motivating

The task a group performs is a fundamental influence on the team, defining its composition, structure, processes and functioning. A lifeboat rescue team will be very different on all these dimensions from a pharmaceuticals research and development (R & D) team. The content of tasks also motivates team members to innovate. For example, Oldham and Cummings (1996) found that the five core job characteristics – skill variety and challenge, task identity, task significance, task feedback, and autonomy (Hackman and Oldham, 1980), predicted individual innovation at work. Skill variety refers to the degree to which a job requires different activities in order for the work to be carried out and the degree to which the range of skills and talents of the person working within the role is used. Task identity is the degree to which the job represents a whole piece of work. It is not simply adding a rubber band to the packaging of a product, but being involved in the manufacture of the product throughout the process, or at least in a meaningful part of the process. Task significance is the impact of task completion upon other people within the organization or in the world at large. Monitoring the effectiveness of an organization's debt collection is less significant than addressing the well-being of elderly people in rural settings, and may therefore evoke less innovation. When people receive feedback on their performance they are more likely to become aware of 'performance gaps'. Consequently they are more attuned to the need to initiate new ways of working in order to fill the gaps. Of course, this also implies that they have clear job objectives. Finally, autonomy refers to the freedom, independence and discretion of employees in how they perform the task – determining how to do their work and when to do it.

Gulowsen (1972) suggests the degree of autonomy of the work group can be assessed in relation to group influence over:

- the formulation of goals – what and how much it is expected to produce
- where to work and number of hours (when to work overtime and when to leave)
- choice about further activities beyond the given task
- selection of production methods
- internal distribution of task responsibilities within the group
- membership of the group (who and how many people will work in the group)
- leadership – whether there will be a leader and who will be the leader and how to carry out individual tasks.

To encourage innovation in teams we could therefore ensure they have a whole task which: requires a broad range of appropriate high level skills; requires members to work interdependently to perform the task; is perceived by team members as significant; and allows team members to have autonomy in deciding the means to achieve their task goals and accurate and timely feedback on team performance.

2 Ensure a High Level of Extrinsic Demands

The external context of the group's work, be it organizational climate, support systems, market environment, or environmental uncertainty, is likely to have a highly significant influence both on its creativity and innovation implementation. People, groups and organizations will innovate partly in response to external demands. But such demands can inhibit creativity. Several studies suggest that, in general, creative cognition occurs when individuals feel free from pressure, safe, and experience relatively positive affect (Claxton, 1997, 1998). For example, using the Luchins Water jars problems, Rokeach (1950) demonstrated how time pressures inhibit creative problem-solving. Moreover, psychological threats to face or identity are associated with rigid thinking (Cowen, 1952). Time pressure can also increase rigidity of thinking on work-related tasks such as selection decisions (Kruglansky and Freund, 1983). Wright (1954) asked people to respond to Rorschach inkblots tests; half were hospital patients awaiting an operation and half were 'controls'. The former gave more stereotyped responses, and were less fluent and creative in completing similes (e.g. 'as interesting as …'), indicating the effects of stress or threat upon their capacity to generate creative responses.

In contrast, among individual health workers we have found in a number of studies that high work demands are significant predictors of individual innovation (Bunce and West, 1995, 1996; West, 1989). Indeed, studies of work role transitions show that changing role objectives, strategies or relationships is a common response to the demands of new work environments (West, 1987). Of course, excessive work demands can have detrimental effects also on stress levels, absenteeism and turnover. But the point here is that individuals innovate at least partly in response to high levels of demand. Borrill et al. (2000a) explored innovation in 100 UK primary health care teams. The external demands of the health care environment were assessed using a UK government index of health and illness for each local area (the Jarman Index). Perceived levels of participation by team members were measured using the Team Climate Inventory (Anderson and West, 1998). Where levels of participation in the team were high, team innovation was also high, but only in environments characterized by high levels of ill health, with associated strong external demands on the health care professionals. Our research in manufacturing organizations and in hospitals suggests that external demands have a significant impact also upon organizational innovation (and therefore will likely have an impact upon group innovation). A longitudinal study of 81 manufacturing organizations showed that the lower the market share of the companies in relation to their primary products, the higher the level of companies' product and technological innovation. It seems that the threat of being a small player in a competitive situation spurs innovation. Moreover, the extent of environmental uncertainty reported by senior managers in these organizations (in relation to suppliers, customers, market demands and government legislation), was a significant predictor of the degree of innovation in organizational systems, i.e., in work organization and people management practices (West et al., 1998). Taken together, these findings suggest that if the environment of teams and organizations is demanding and uncertain, it is likely that they will innovate in order to reduce the uncertainty and level of demand.

It is suggested therefore that external demands will *inhibit* creativity which occurs in the earlier stages of the innovation process, but that they will *facilitate* innovation (via innovation implementation) at later stages. Creativity requires an undemanding environment, while implementation requires precisely the opposite. Innovation implementation involves changing the status quo, which implies resistance, conflict and a requirement for sustained effort. A team that attempts to implement innovation is likely to encounter resistance and conflict among others in the organization, and therefore sustained effort is required to overcome these disincentives to innovate. But effort itself is aversive – like most species, we strive to achieve our goals while expending the minimum effort necessary. The effort required to innovate can be motivated, at least partly, by external demands. External demands often take the form of *uncertainty* (which can be experienced as potentially threatening). There is a strong relationship between environmental uncertainty and more organic structures in organizations, which themselves facilitate innovation. The price of crude oil is a constant uncertainty in petroleum refining and retailing organizations, and this prompts continuous innovation in retail operations to win customer loyalty. Another form of external demand is *time constraints* imposed by the organization or environment. Where customers demand ever-shorter lead times (the time from placing an order to its delivery), manufacturers or suppliers of services must innovate in their work processes in order to satisfy their customers' demands. *Competition* is clearly a form of demand which economists have long identified as a force for innovation. The *severity or challenge* of the environment is also an important influence. For example, two health care teams may perform exactly the same diagnostic, treatment and preventive health care functions, but the team operating in a deprived inner city environment faces far greater demands than that in a well-to-do suburban area.

What is intuitively apparent is that the relationship between external demands and innovation implementation cannot be linear. Extreme demands or sustained high levels are likely to produce paralysis or learned helplessness. When individuals are confronted by sustained demands that they cannot meet, they are likely to respond with apathy or learned helplessness (Maier and Seligman, 1976). So either very low or very high levels of demands will be associated with relatively low levels of innovation implementation – an inverted U relationship.

Create conditions within which teams are exposed to high but not excessive levels of external demands.

3 Select a Team of Innovative People

To build an innovative team, we must ensure that members are inclined towards innovation. Researchers examining the relationships between team members' 'Big Five' personality characteristics and innovation have found teams made up of individuals with high levels of 'openness' display high levels of innovation (whilst the other four characteristics: conscientiousness, extraversion, agreeableness and neuroticism do not predict innovation) (Barrick et al., 1998).

More specifically there is some evidence that innovative team members are both creative and good at implementing innovation. They are people who have a preference for thinking in novel ways; who think globally instead of locally (distinguishing the wood from the trees). They have appropriate intellectual abilities, including synthetic abilities (to see problems in new ways and escape the bounds of conventional thinking); analytic abilities to recognize which ideas are worth pursuing; and the practical contextual abilities to persuade others of the value of their ideas (Sternberg and Lubart, 1996). To be innovative we also require sufficient knowledge of the field to be able to move it forward, while not being so conceptually trapped in it that we are unable to conceive of alternative courses (Mumford and Gustafson, 1988). People who are confident of their abilities are more likely to innovate in the workplace. In a study of role innovation among more than 2000 UK managers, Nicholson and West (1988) found that confidence and motivation to develop knowledge and skills predicted innovation following job change.

Innovative people also tend to be self-disciplined, with a high degree of drive and motivation, and a concern with achieving excellence (Mumford and Gustafson, 1988). This perseverance against social pressures presumably reduces the dangers of premature abandonment. Innovative people have a high need for freedom, control and discretion in the workplace and appear to find bureaucratic limitations or the exercise of control by managers frustrating (Barron and Harrington, 1981; West, 1987; West and Rushton, 1989).

Include team members who have the personality trait of openness, who think in novel and non-conventional ways, who are persuasive, knowledgeable about their field, confident, with high tolerance for ambiguity, and who are self-disciplined and persistent.

4 Select People with Diverse Skills and Backgrounds

One can differentiate diversity in attributes that are relevant to the person's role or task in the organization (e.g. organizational position and specialized knowledge), and differences that are inherent in the person (e.g. age, gender, ethnicity, social status and personality) (Maznevski, 1994). Jackson (1992) believes that the effects of diversity on team performance are complex: task-related and relations-oriented diversity have different effects that depend also on the team task. For tasks requiring creativity and a high quality of decision-making, the available evidence supports the conclusion that task diversity is associated with better quality team decision-making (Jackson, 1996).

The relationship between group diversity and group innovation has interested many scholars (O'Reilly and Williams, 1998). One significant study of innovation in teams is a UNESCO sponsored international effort to determine the factors influencing the scientific performance of 1222 research teams (Andrews, 1979; see also Payne, 1990). Diversity was assessed in six areas: projects; interdisciplinary orientations; specialities; funding resources; R & D activities; and professional functions. Overall, diversity accounted for 10% of the variance in scientific recognition, R & D effectiveness, and number of publications, suggesting that diversity does influence team innovation.

One explanation for these findings is that creativity and innovation require diversity of knowledge, professional orientation or disciplinary background because the integration of diverse perspectives creates the potential for combinations of ideas from different domains. For example, having doctors, nurses, counsellors, social workers, and physiotherapists in primary health care teams is associated with high levels of innovation in patient care (Borrill et al., 2000b). If people who work together in teams have different professional training, skills, experiences, and orientations, they will bring usefully differing perspectives to the group. Such a divergence of views will create multiple perspectives, disagreement and conflict. If informational conflict is processed in the interests of effective decision-making and task performance rather than on the basis of motivation to win or prevail, this generates improved performance and more innovative actions will be the result (De Dreu, 1997; Hoffman and Maier, 1961; Pearce and Ravlin, 1987; Porac and Howard, 1990; Tjosvold, 1985, 1991, 1998). But diversity also demands extra efforts at integration since diversity creates the potential for conflict as much as for creativity (De Dreu, 1997; Pelled et al., 1999).

Are teams which are composed of very different people (gender, culture, age, organizational tenure) more innovative than those whose members are similar? There is some evidence that heterogeneity in both relations-oriented and task-oriented domains is associated with group innovation, including heterogeneity in personality (Hoffman and Maier, 1961), leadership abilities (Ghiselli and Lodahl, 1958), attitudes (Willems and Clark, 1971), gender, (Wood, 1987), and education (Smith et al., 1994). Empirical research on the effects of demographic diversity on work team outcomes has provided mixed results (Milliken and Martins, 1996; Webber and Donahue, 2001; Jehn et al., 1999). 'Sometimes the effect of diversity seems positive, at other times negative, and in other situations, there seems to be no effect at all' (Shaw and Barret-Power, 1998: 1307). The relationship between demographic diversity and innovation may therefore be curvilinear (see also West, 2002). One study to test this possibility showed a curvilinear relationship between age, gender and tenure diversity and team innovation, and this was usually mediated by the task focus of the team. If teams were tightly focused on the task then moderate levels of demographic diversity seemed to promote innovation. Very high or low levels of demographic diversity were associated with low levels of innovation (Gonzalez-Roma et al., 2002).

Select team members who have task relevant skills, a diverse a range of skills and professional backgrounds and ensure the team is tightly focused on getting the work done.

5 Provide Organizational Rewards for Innovation

The organizational context of team work has a significant effect on the team's innovation (Guzzo, 1996; Hackman, 1990). Organizational cultures that resist innovation will of course reduce the likelihood that teams will innovate. One of the most tangible marks of organizational support for innovation is whether employees' attempts to introduce new and improved ways of doing things are rewarded. While some theories of creativity and flow suggest that creative work is primarily sustained by intrinsic motivation (Amabile, 1983; 1988), emerging research evidence suggests that rewards can complement intrinsic motivation. Rewards appear to be counter-productive only if they serve to displace attention from the task towards the reward (Eisenberger and Cameron, 1996). There is evidence that extrinsic rewards encourage both creativity and innovation implementation (Abbey and Dickson, 1983; Eisenberger and Cameron, 1996). There is also a body of work examining 'gainsharing' as a device for stimulating productivity and innovation that suggests the value of reward for innovation (Cotton, 1996; Heller et al., 1998). Gainsharing is the term used to describe systems used in commercial organizations to involve staff in developing new and more effective means of production. If employees develop ways of increasing production or improving quality, they are rewarded with a share of the financial gains of the innovation. Evaluations of 'gainsharing' programmes suggest they are effective in increasing innovation, productivity and employee involvement in decision-making (Cotton, 1996).

It makes sense to argue that what should be rewarded is not the success of innovation but genuine attempts at innovation. Otherwise it is likely that employees will simply play safe with innovations that are neither radical nor novel (staying within existing paradigms).

Find ways of rewarding teams that innovate, even if the innovations don't work out.

6 Create a Learning and Development Climate in the Organization

For teams to innovate in organizations they must learn, be it from customers, suppliers, training experiences or any other domain. Learning means changing our understanding, and changing understanding is fundamental to innovation. Those who study organizational learning emphasize the importance of practices that encourage 'outward focus' in order to bring new knowledge into the company (Burgoyne et al., 1999). Recruitment and selection can help determine whether or not people are employed with the necessary attributes to make a contribution to the knowledge creation process. Induction and training activities can help shape the psychological contract, potentially enhancing motivation and developing skills as well as the required questioning, sharing and challenging behaviours. Appraisal and remuneration strategies play a role in clarifying expectations and rewarding effective performance, defined in terms of willingness to learn, take risks and communicate well. Human Resource Management (HRM) activity therefore can help shape the learning agenda, providing the impetus and incentive for individuals to explore learning and develop their communication and team-working skills with others.

Various organizational learning mechanisms can assist in generating a variety of perspectives in teams. Presenting team members with the opportunity to visit customers or suppliers, regardless of their job role, potentially provides liaison with the external environment and provokes questioning of the appropriateness of organizational practices and goals (McGrath, 1984). Similarly, intra-organizational secondments are likely to be beneficial in challenging thinking and generating the flow of new ideas. Opportunities for team members to learn outside the constraints of their immediate jobs will facilitate the transfer of knowledge internally and enrich individuals' perceptions of the challenges faced by other organizational members (Tsai, 2001). The extent to which knowledge is then captured and disseminated can play an important role in determining whether or not the opportunities presented for variety can be made available across the organization as a whole (Kogut and Zander, 1992). Companies can develop these learning mechanisms in several ways. Firstly, they can enable visits to external suppliers or customers for teams that would not normally have such contact as part of their job responsibilities. Furthermore, teams working on the factory floor in one department can be seconded to another department so that they can learn more about the processes and procedures in that area. Companies can also provide support for team member learning/training that is not directly work related. Finally, companies can implement systems that keep record of teams' solutions to problems and facilitate knowledge transfer (problem solutions or best practice) across teams.

Encourage team innovation by developing supportive HRM practices (recruitment, selection, induction, training and appraisal), and encourage organizational learning via secondments, visits to external organizations, a broad approach to training support, and knowledge management which involves recording and communicating teams' solutions and best practices.

7 Develop a Climate for Innovation in the Organization

In a study comparing the work environments of highly creative projects against less creative projects, Amabile and colleagues found that five aspects of the work environment consistently differed between the two groups (Amabile et al., 1996). These were challenge, organizational encouragement, work group support, supervisory encouragement, and organizational impediments.

Challenge is regarded as a moderate degree of workload pressure that arises from an urgent, intellectually challenging problem (Amabile, 1988; Amabile et al., 1996; Hennessey, 2003). The authors distinguish challenge from excessive workload pressure, which they argue is negatively related to innovation, and suggest that time pressure may add to the perception of challenge in the work if it is perceived as a concomitant of an important, urgent project. This challenge, in turn, may be positively related to intrinsic motivation and creativity.

Organizational encouragement includes three aspects of the work environment. The first is encouragement of risk taking and idea generation, a valuing of innovation from the highest to the lowest levels of management. The second refers to a fair and supportive evaluation of new ideas; the authors underline this by referring to studies that showed that whereas threatening and highly critical evaluation of new ideas was shown to undermine creativity in laboratory studies, in field research, supportive, informative evaluation can enhance the intrinsically motivated state that is most conducive to creativity. The final aspect refers to the important role of collaborative idea flow across the organization, participative management, and decision-making, in the stimulation of innovation.

Work group support indicates the encouragement of activity through the particular work group. The four aspects thought to be relevant for this are team member diversity, mutual openness to ideas, constructive challenging of ideas, and shared commitment to the project; whereas the former two may influence creativity through exposing individuals to a greater variety of unusual ideas, the latter two are thought to increase intrinsic motivation.

The supervisory encouragement measure includes goal clarity, open supervisory interactions, and perceived supervisory or leader support. Goal clarity is likely to enable more focused problem-solving laying the groundwork for insightful and creative work. Amabile and colleagues (1996) argue that open supervisory interactions as well as perceived supervisory support may influence creativity through preventing people from experiencing fear of negative criticism that can undermine the intrinsic motivation necessary for creativity.

In reporting the last of the five factors, organizational impediments, Amabile et al. (1996) refer to a few studies indicating that internal strife, conservatism, and rigid, formal management structures represent obstacles to creativity. The authors suggest that because these factors may be perceived as controlling, their likely negative influence on creativity may evolve from an increase in individual extrinsic motivation (a motivation through external factors but not the task itself) and a corresponding decrease in the intrinsic motivation necessary for creativity. However, research on impediments to creativity is still comparatively limited.

Senior managers should focus on managing the climate or culture of the organization in order to increase employees' experience of positive challenge; organizational encouragement for innovation; teamworking; supervisory goal clarity, support and openness; and to decrease their perceptions of chronic organizational hostility, conservatism and rigid formal structures. Determining and increasing the factors that promote employee satisfaction may also lead to higher levels of team innovation.

8 Establish Team Norms for Innovation

Support for innovation involves the expectation, approval and practical support of attempts to introduce new and improved ways of doing things in the work environment

(West, 1990). Within teams, new ideas may be routinely rejected or ignored, or attract verbal and practical support. Such group processes powerfully shape individual and group behaviour and those which support innovation will encourage team members to introduce innovations. In a longitudinal study of 27 hospital top management teams, support for innovation was the most powerful predictor of team innovation of any of the group processes or group composition factors examined (Anderson and West, 1998; West and Anderson, 1996).

A manufacturing organization on the Isle of Wight that we visited provides a good example of how innovative team norms may develop from relatively seemingly trivial events. The main production team on the shop floor had complained about the storage of dirty materials, and was given time off from production, and a budget to design and build a suitable storage extension for the factory. They completed the task under time and budget, and thereafter began to suggest many more innovations in work processes and structures. The team, as a result of their good experience, developed clear norms for valuing and discovering innovation. In effect, the team was provided with the conditions to be innovative and, once empowered, proactively fostered innovative team norms.

Encourage teams to be innovative and verbally and practically support team members' ideas for new and improved products, services, or ways of working.

9 Encourage Reflexivity in Teams

Our research suggests that a key indicator of innovation in work teams is reflexivity. Team reflexivity is the extent to which team members collectively reflect upon the team's objectives, strategies and processes as well as their wider organizations, and adapt them accordingly (West, 1996; 2000).

Reflexivity can lead to radical change in the status quo and sometimes the creative destruction of existing processes. For example, one plastics packaging production team which we studied succeeded in removing management controls on intervention so they were able to discuss product specifications, pricing and delivery dates directly with customers. Productivity and quality improved, and the time from customers placing their orders to delivery dropped by a factor of three.

Reflexivity requires a degree of safety however, since reflection is likely to reveal gaps between how the team is performing and how it would like to perform. Edmondson's (1996; 1999) work helps us to understand the conditions within a team which encourage reflexivity or learning. She found major differences between newly formed intensive care nursing teams in their management of medication errors. In some teams, members openly acknowledged and discussed their medication errors (giving too much or too little of a drug, or administering the wrong drug) and discussed ways to avoid their occurrence. In others, members kept information about errors to themselves. Learning about the causes of these errors, as a team, and devising innovations to prevent future errors were only possible in teams of the former type. Edmondson gives an example of how, in one learning-oriented team, discussion of a recent error led to innovation in equipment. An intravenous medication pump was identified as a source of consistent errors and so was replaced by a different type of pump. She also illustrates how failure to discuss errors and generate innovations led to the costly failure of the Hubble telescope development project. In particular, Edmondson (1996; 1999) argues that learning and innovation will only take place where group members trust other members' intentions. This manifests in a group level belief that well-intentioned action will not lead to punishment or rejection by the team, which Edmondson calls 'team safety': 'The term is meant to suggest a realistic, learning oriented attitude about effort, error and change – not to imply a careless sense of permissiveness, or an unrelentingly positive affect. Safety is not the same as comfort; in contrast, it is predicted to facilitate risk.' (Edmondson, 1999: 14). European research on error management broadly supports Edmondson's interpretations (e.g. Van Dyck, 2000).

Teams benefit from taking time out from working to reflect on their work habits, objectives, team processes and outcomes, make plans for change, implement them and reflect again. A sense of safety helps teams self-reflectively explore in this way.

10 Ensure there is Clarity of Leadership in the Team and that the Leadership Style is Appropriate for Encouraging Innovation

The team leader normally has a potent and pervasive influence on team innovation and in particular team processes (Tannenbaum et al., 1996). The leader brings task expertise, abilities and attitudes to the team that can influence the group design and group norms (Hackman, 1990; 1992; 2002), and, through monitoring, feedback and coaching, can help develop these processes, to assist the team to achieve its tasks (McIntyre and Salas, 1995) and to innovate. The extent to which the leader defines team objectives and helps organize the team to ensure progress towards achieving these objectives can affect the level of team innovation.

Clarity of team leadership (team members are clear about where the leadership of the team resides) is critical to the role of leadership in fostering team innovation (regardless of whether leadership is shared). In a test of this proposition, West et al. (2003a) sampled 3447 respondents from 98 primary health care teams, 113 community mental health teams, and 72 breast cancer care teams. The results revealed that leadership clarity was associated with clear team objectives, high levels of participation, commitment to excellence and support for innovation. Team processes consistently predicted team innovation across all three samples. Clarity of team leadership predicted innovation in the latter two samples and team processes partially mediated this relationship.

Several leadership scholars (c.f. Barry, 1991; Kim et al., 1999; McCall, 1988) identified roles which are central to effective project work and innovation. They concluded that leaders must engage in boundary spanning behaviour, facilitate teamwork, drive innovation and direct project work.

Leadership boundary spanning involves the management of external relationships including co-ordinating tasks, negotiating resources and goals with stakeholders as well as scanning for information and ideas. Waldman and Atwater (1994) studied 40 R & D projects teams and found that, out of a range of leadership behaviours examined (including transformation leadership and goal setting behaviour), boundary spanning was the strongest predictor of research managers' ratings of project performance and innovation.

Facilitative leadership refers to encouraging safe team interactions, participation, sharing of ideas and open discussion of different perspectives. Kim et al. (1999) surveyed 87 R & D teams in six Korean organizations and found that the leader's performance of the team builder role was a significant predictor of team ratings of innovation. A leader who acts as an innovator envisions project opportunities and new approaches by questioning team assumptions and challenging the status quo. Leaders who question approaches and suggest innovative ways of performing tasks tend to lead innovative teams (Keller, 1992). Likewise Kim and colleagues (1999) found that the leader's technical problem-solving ability, in particular appraisal of problems and identification of new ideas, was significantly correlated with R & D project performance. Yukl et al. (1990) found that leaders who clarified tasks by communicating instructions and setting priorities, deadlines and standards, were most effective in leading innovative teams.

It generally helps to ensure that leadership in the team is clear to all team members and that there is no conflict over leadership. Ensure that leaders fulfil the roles that are critical to innovation such as boundary spanning, facilitating, and directing; but also train leaders to be aware of group processes; listen in order to understand rather than to appraise or refute; assume responsibility for accurate team communication; be sensitive to unexpressed feelings; protect minority views; keep the discussion moving; and develop skills in summarising.

11 Manage Conflict Constructively and Encourage Minorities to Dissent within Teams

Many scholars argue that the management of competing perspectives is fundamental to the generation of creativity and innovation (Mumford and Gustafson, 1988; Nemeth and Owens, 1996; Tjosvold, 1998). Such processes are characteristic of task-related conflict (as opposed to conflicts of relationship and process conflict, see De Dreu, 1997; Jehn, 1997). They can arise from a common concern with the quality of task performance in relation to shared objectives. Task conflict is an awareness of differences in viewpoints and opinions about a task. In essence, team members are more committed to performing their work effectively and excellently than they are either to bland consensus or to personal victory in conflict with other team members over task performance strategies or decision options.

Dean Tjosvold and colleagues (Tjosvold, 1982; Tjosvold and Field, 1983; Tjosvold and Johnson, 1977; Tjosvold et al., 1986; Tjosvold, 1998) have presented cogent arguments and strong supportive evidence that constructive (task-related) controversy in a co-operative group context, improves the quality of decision-making and creativity (Tjosvold, 1991). Constructive controversy is characterised by full exploration of opposing opinions and frank analyses of task-related issues. It occurs when decision-makers believe they are in a co-operative group context, where mutually beneficial goals are emphasized, rather than in a competitive context, where decision-makers feel their personal competence is confirmed rather than questioned, and where they perceive processes of mutual influence rather than attempted dominance.

For example, the most effective self-managing teams in a manufacturing plant that Alper and Tjosvold (1993) studied were those which had compatible goals and promoted constructive controversy. Members of teams which promoted inter-dependent conflict management (people co-operated to work through their differences), compared to teams with win/lose conflict (where team members tended to engage in a power struggle when they had different views and interests), felt confident that they could deal with differences. Such teams were rated as more productive and innovative by their managers. Apparently, because of this success, members of these teams were committed to working as a team.

Another perspective on conflict and innovation comes from minority influence theory. A number of researchers have shown that minority consistency of arguments over time is likely to lead to change in majority views in groups (Maass and Clark, 1984; Nemeth, 1986; Nemeth and Chiles, 1988; Nemeth and Kwan, 1987; Nemeth and Owens, 1996; Nemeth and Wachtler, 1983).

De Dreu and De Vries (1993; 1997) suggest that a homogenous workforce, in which minority dissent is suppressed, will reduce creativity, innovation, individuality and independence (see also Nemeth and Staw, 1989). Disagreement about ideas within a group can be beneficial and some researchers even argue that team task or information-related conflict is valuable, whether or not it occurs in a collaborative context, since it can improve decision-making and strategic planning (Cosier and Rose, 1977; Mitroff et al., 1977; Schweiger et al., 1989). This is because task-related conflict may lead team members to re-evaluate the status quo and adapt their objectives, strategies or processes more appropriately to their situation (Coser, 1970; Nemeth and Staw, 1989; Roloff, 1987; Thomas, 1979). However, De Dreu and Weingart (2003) suggest that high levels of conflict in teams, regardless of whether the conflict is focused on relationships or task, will inhibit team effectiveness and innovation.

In two studies involving postal work teams, De Dreu and West found that minority dissent did indeed predict team innovation (as rated by the teams' supervisors), but only in teams with high levels of participation (De Dreu and West, 2001). It seems that the social processes in the team necessary for minority dissent to influence the innovation process are characterized by high levels of team member interaction, influence over decision-making, and information sharing.

Encourage moderate task-related (as distinct from emotional or interpersonal) conflict and minority dissent, along with high levels of participation since this will lead to debate and to consideration of alternative interpretations of information available. This in turn will prompt integrated and creative solutions to work-related problems – to innovation.

12 Don't Just Bond ... Bridge

The strengths of team-working in organizations are the involvement of all in contributing their skills and knowledge, in good collective decision-making and innovation – team bonding enables innovation. The fundamental weakness is the tendency of team based organizations to be driven by intergroup competition, hostility and rivalry with likely consequent negative impacts on organizational performance overall; in short, inter-group bias. Consequently, teams need to be persuaded to bridge these divides.

Mohrman et al. (1995) have pointed out that there are likely to be innovation benefits of good linkages between groups and teams and across departments within organizations. The cross-disciplinarity, cross-functionality and cross-team perspectives that such interactions can produce are likely to generate the kinds of dividends related to innovation that heterogeneity within teams could offer.

In a study of 45 new product teams in five high technology companies, Ancona and Caldwell (1992) found that when a work group recruited a new member from a functional area in an organization, communication between the team and that area went up dramatically. This would favour innovation through the incorporation of diverse ideas and models gleaned from these different functional areas. Consistent with this, the researchers discovered that the greater the group's functional diversity, the more team members communicated outside the work group's boundaries and the higher ratings of innovation they received from supervisors. The UNESCO research described above (Andrews, 1979) also showed that the extent of communication between research teams had strong relationships with scientific recognition of the teams, R & D effectiveness, number of publications, and the applied value of their work (all surrogate measures of innovation).

How can teams encourage good inter-group working? A fruitful avenue may be to look at the two main causes of dysfunctional inter-group relations: conflicting interests or goals, and the disruptive dynamics of salient social categorisation (Turner, 1985). One way for *the team* to improve relationships with other teams would be to make such improvement one of its four or five core work objectives. Teams can also use secondments and set up cross team work projects. Another strategy is to improve and encourage contact and open communication between teams. Such contacts usually lead to a weakening of perceptions of conflicting goals (Tjosvold, 1998). Open and collaborative communication are a means by which trusting cross team relationships can be created; such trusting relationships enable conflicts of interest to be managed constructively.

There are many ways *for the organization* to encourage inter-group working (see West et al., 2003a), including encouraging teams to downplay the salience of group boundaries by developing a common super-ordinate identity within the organization; rewarding the maintenance and development of cross team relationships; making team boundaries more permeable, e.g. through rotating team members in different teams (see also Katz and Allen, 1988).

Encourage different teams to work together, share best practice, develop joint projects and strive to find a common super-ordinate identity within the organization in order to encourage the innovation that springs from bridging boundaries. Reward inter-team working.

Conclusions

Based on research findings, we outlined a number of practical recommendations that can be applied in organizational settings where the intent is to encourage teams to be innovative. These recommendations can be summarized in four main points.

First the team's task must be a whole task: one that is perceived by the team as significant to the organization or the wider society; one that makes varied demands on team members and requires them to use their knowledge and skills interdependently; one that provides opportunities for social contact between them; and one that provides opportunities for learning, skill development and task development. The group should be relatively autonomous in the conduct of its work.

Second, the group should be given time during the early stages of the innovation process, in an unpressured environment, to generate creative ideas for new and improved products or ways of working. This may mean taking time away from the usual workplace and working in (ideally) a pleasant and relaxing environment. The services of a skilled facilitator, knowledgeable about research evidence on group creative processes (as opposed to popular belief and consultancy mythology), can help groups to maximize their creative output. An intra-group psychosocial environment experienced by group members as unthreatening will best facilitate such processes.

Third, at later stages of the innovation process, if group members feel pressured, or uncertain, they are more likely to implement innovations, as long as the demands and uncertainties are created by extra- not intra-group agents (this is sometimes called the 'burning platform' effect) and the level of demand is not crippling. Today, competition, threat, pressure and uncertainty are characteristic of most public and commercial sector environments, particularly as globalization increases apace – there is rarely reason to increase the level of demand. But there is much more reason to improve the level of safety and the integration skills of team members.

Fourth and above all, group members must individually and collectively develop the skills to work well as a team, encouraging integrating group processes to ensure that they innovate effectively. This means continually clarifying and ensuring group member commitment to shared objectives; encouraging information sharing, regular group member interaction, and shared influence over decision-making; and encouraging high levels of emphasis on quality, and practical support (time, money, and co-operation) for innovation. It means encouraging group members to regularly reflect upon and adapt their objectives, strategies and processes – consciously and continually improving their functioning as a group.

In sum, for creativity and innovation implementation to emerge from group functioning – for groups to be sparkling fountains of ideas and changes – the context must be demanding but there must be strong group integration processes and a high level of intra-group safety. This requires that members have the integration abilities to work effectively in teams; and that they develop a safe psychosocial climate and appropriate group processes (clarifying objectives, encouraging participation, constructive controversy, reflexivity and support for innovation). Such conditions are likely to produce high levels of group innovation, but crucially too, the well-being which is a consequence of effective human interaction in challenging and supportive environments.

References

Abbey, A. and Dickson, J.W. (1983) R & D work climate and innovation in semiconductors. *Academy of Management Journal, 26*(2), 362–8.

Alper, S. and Tjosvold, D. (1993) Cooperation theory and self-managing teams on the manufacturing floor. Paper presented at the International Association for Conflict Management, Eugene, OR.

Amabile, T.M. (1983) The social psychology of creativity: A componential conceptualization. *Journal of Personality and Social Psychology, 45,* 357–76.

Amabile, T.M. (1988) A model of creativity and innovation in organizations. In B.M. Staw and L.L. Cummings (Eds) *Research in Organizational Behavior, 10.* Greenwich, CT: JAI Press. (pp. 123–67).

Amabile, T.M. Conti, R., Coon, H., Lazenby, J., and Herron, M. (1996) Assessing the work environment for creativity. *Academy of Management Journal, 39,* 1154–84.

Ancona, D.G. and Caldwell, D.F. (1992) Bridging the boundary: external process and performance in organizational teams. *Administrative Science Quarterly, 37,* 634–65.

Anderson, N. and West, M.A. (1998) Measuring climate for work group innovation: Development and validation of the Team Climate Inventory. *Journal of Organizational Behavior, 19,* 235–58.

Andrews, F. M. (Ed.) (1979) *Scientific Productivity.* Cambridge, England: Cambridge University Press.

Barrick, M.R., Stewart, G.L., Neubert, M.J., Mount, M.K. (1998) Relating member ability and personality to work-team processes and team effectiveness. *Journal of Applied Psychology, 83,* 377–91.

Barron, F.B. and Harrington, D.M. (1981) Creativity, intelligence and personality. In M.R. Rosenzweig and L.W. Porter (Eds) *Annual Review of Psychology, 32,* 439–76. Palo Alto, CA: Annual Reviews.

Barry, D. (1991) Managing the bossless team: Lessons in distributed leadership. *Organizational Dynamics, 20,* 31–47.

Borrill, C.S., Carletta, J., Carter, A.J., Dawson, J., Garrod, S., Rees, A., Richards, A., Shapiro, D. and West, M.A. (2000a) *The Effectiveness of Health Care Teams in the National Health Service,* Birmingham: Aston Centre for Health Service Organization Research.

Borrill, C.S., West, M.A., Shapiro, D. and Rees, A. (2000b) Team Working and Effectiveness in Health Care. *British Journal of Health Care Management, 6,* 364–71.

Bunce, D. and West, M.A. (1995) Changing work environments: Innovative coping responses to occupational stress. *Work and Stress, 8,* 319–31.

Bunce, D. and West, M.A. (1996) Stress management and innovation interventions at work. *Human Relations, 49,* 209–32.

Burgoyne, J., Pedler, M. and Boydell, T. (1999) *The Learning Company, a Strategy for Sustainable Development.* New York: Maidenhead.

Claxton, G.L. (1997) *Have Brain, Tortoise Mind: Why intelligence increases when you think less.* London: Fourth Estate.

Claxton, G.L. (1998) Knowing without Knowing why: Investigating human intuition. *The Psychologist, 11,* 217–20.

Cotton, J.L. (1996) Employee involvement. In C.L. Cooper and I.T. Robertson (Eds) *International Review of Industrial and Organizational Psychology, 11.* John Wiley & Sons Ltd. (pp. 219–42).

Coser, L.A. (1970) *Continuities in the Study of Social Conflict.* New York: Free Press.

Cosier, R., and Rose, G. (1977) Cognitive conflict and goal conflict effects on task performance. *Organizational Behavior and Human Performance, 19,* 378–91.

Cowen, E.L. (1952) The influence of varying degrees of psychological stress on problem-solving rigidity. *Journal of Abnormal and Social Psychology, 47,* 420–4.

De Dreu, C.K.W. (1997) Productive Conflict: The importance of conflict management and conflict issue. In C.K.W. De Dreu and E. Van De Vliert (Eds) *Using Conflict in Organizations*. London: Sage. (pp. 9–22).

De Dreu, C.K.W. and De Vries, N.K. (1993) Numerical support, information processing and attitude change. *European Journal of Social Psychology*, *23*, 647–62.

De Dreu, C.K.W. and De Vries, N.K. (1997) Minority dissent in organizations. In C. K. W. De Dreu and E. Van De Vliert (Eds) *Using Conflict in Organizations*. London: Sage. (pp. 72–86).

De Dreu, C.K.W. and Weingart, L.R. (2003) A Contingency Theory of Task Conflict and Performance in Groups and Organizational Teams. In M. West, D. Tjosvold and K. Smith (Eds) *International Handbook of Organizational Teamwork and Cooperative Working*. Chichester, England: Wiley. (pp. 151–65).

De Dreu, C.K.W. and West, M.A. (2001) Minority dissent and team innovation: The importance of participation in decision-making. *Journal of Applied Psychology, 68,* 1191–201.

Economist (2003) Innovating by numbers. *Economist: Economist Technology Quarterly*, June 21st, 2003, 3.

Edmondson, A.C. (1996) Learning from mistakes is easier said than done: Group and organizational influences on the detection and correction of human error. *Journal of Applied Behavioral Science, 32,* 5–28.

Edmondson, A.C. (1999) Psychological safety and learning behavior in work teams. *Administrative Science Quarterly, 44,* 350–83.

Eisenberger, R. and Cameron, J. (1996) Detrimental effects of reward: Reality of myth? *American Psychologist, 51*(11), 1153–66.

Ghiselli, E.E. and Lodahl, T.M. (1958) Patterns of managerial traits and group effectiveness. *Journal of Abnormal and Social Psychology. 57,* 61–66.

Gonzalez-Roma, V., Peiro, J.M. and Tordera, N. (2002) An examination of the antecedents and moderator influences of climate strengths. *Journal of Applied Psychology, 87(3),* 465–73.

Gulowsen, J.A. (1972) A measure of work group autonomy. In L.E. Davis and J.C. Taylor (Eds) *Design of Jobs*. Harmondsworth, England: Penguin. (pp. 374–90).

Guzzo, R.A. (1996) Fundamental considerations about work groups. In M.A. West (Ed.) *Handbook of Work Group Psychology*. Chichester, England: Wiley.

Hackman, J.R. (1990) *Groups that Work (and Those that don't)*. San Francisco: Jossey Bass.

Hackman, J.R. (1992) Group influences on individuals in organizations. In M.D. Dunnette and L.M. Hough (Eds) *Handbook of Industrial and Organizational Psychology (Vol. 3)*. Palo Alto, CA: Consulting Psychologists Press. (pp. 199–267).

Hackman, J.R. (2002) *Leading Teams: Setting the Stage for Great Performances*. Harvard, CN: Harvard Business School.

Hackman, J.R. and Oldham, G.R. (1980) *Work Redesign*. Reading, MA: Addison-Wesley.

Heller, F., Pusic, E., Strauss, G. and Wilpert, B. (1998) *Organizational Participation: Myth and Reality*. Oxford: Oxford University Press.

Hennessey, B.A. (2003). Is the Social Psychology of Creativity Really Social?: Moving Beyond a Focus on the Individual. In P. Paulus and B. Nijstad (Eds) *Group Creativity: Innovation through Collaboration*. New York: Oxford University Press. (pp. 181–201).

Hoffman, L.R. and Maier, N.R.F. (1961) Sex differences, sex composition, and group problem-solving. *Journal of Abnormal and Social Psychology*, *63*, 453–6.

Jackson, S.E. (1992) Consequences of group composition for the interpersonal dynamics of strategic issue processing. *Advances in Strategic Management, 8,* 45–82.

Jackson, S.E. (1996) The consequences of diversity in multidisciplinary work teams. In M.A. West (Ed.) *Handbook of Work Group Psychology*. Chichester, England: Wiley. (pp. 53–75).

Jehn, K.A. (1997) A qualitative analysis of conflict types and dimensions in organizational groups. *Administrative Science Quarterly, 42,* 530–57.

Jehn, K.A., Northcraft, G.B. and Neale, M.A. (1999) Why differences make a difference: A field study of diversity, conflict, and performance in workgroups. *Administrative Science Quarterly, 44,* 741–63.

Katz, R. and Allen, T.J. (1988) Investigating the Not Invented Here (NIH) syndrome: A look at the performance, tenure, and communication patterns of 50 R & D project groups. In Michael L. Tushman and William L. Moore (Eds) *Readings in the Management of Innovation* (2nd ed.). (pp. 293–309).

Keller, R.T. (1992) Transformational leadership and the performance of research and development research groups. *Journal of Management, 18*, 489–501.

Kim, Y., Min, B. and Cha, J. (1999) The roles of R & D team leaders in Korea: A contingent approach. *R & D Management, 29*, 53–165.

Kogut, B. and Zander, U. (1992) Knowledge of the firm, combinative capabiltiies, and the replication of technology. *Organization Science, 3*, 383–97.

Kruglansky, A.W. and Freund, T. (1983) The freezing and unfreezing of lay influences: effects on impressional primacy, ethnic stereotyping and numerical anchoring. *Journal of Experimental Social Psychology, 19*, 448–68.

Maass, A., and Clark, R.D. (1984) Hidden impacts of minorities: fifty years of minority influence research. *Psychological Bulletin, 95*, 428–50.

Maier, S.F. and Seligman, M. (1976) Learned helplessness: Theory and evidence. *Journal of Experimental Psychology: General, 105*, 3–46.

Maznevski, M.L. (1994) Understanding our differences: Performance in decision-making groups with diverse members. *Human Relations, 47*, 531–52.

McCall, M.W. Jr. (1988) Leadership and the professional. In Katz, R. (Ed.) *Managing Professionals in Innovative Organizations*. Cambridge, MA: Ballinger.

McGrath, J.E. (1984) *Groups, Interaction and Performance*. Englewood Cliffs, NJ: Prentice-Hall.

Mclntyre, R.M. and Salas, E. (1995) Measuring and managing for team performance: lessons from complex environments. In R.Guzzo and E. Salas (Eds) *Team Effectiveness and Decision-making in Organizations*. San Francisco, CA: Jossey-Bass.

Milliken, F.J. and Martins, L.L. (1996) Searching for common threads: Understanding the multiple effects of diversity in organizational groups. *Academy of Management Review, 21*(2), 402–33.

Mitroff, J., Barabba, N., and Kilmann, R. (1977) The application of behavior and philosophical technologies to strategic planning: a case study of a large federal agency. *Management Studies, 24*, 44–58.

Mohrman, S.A., Cohen, S.G. and Mohrman, A.M. (1995) *Designing Team-based Organizations: New Forms for Knowledge Work*. San Francisco, CA: Jossey Bass.

Mumford, M.D. and Gustafson, S.B. (1988) Creativity syndrome: Integration, application and innovation. *Psychological Bulletin, 103*, 27–43.

Nemeth, C. (1986) Differential contributions of majority and minority influence. *Psychological Review, 93*, 23–32.

Nemeth, C., and Chiles, C. (1988) Modelling courage: the role of dissent in fostering independence. *European Journal of Social Psychology, 18*, 275–80.

Nemeth, C., and Kwan, J. (1987) Minority influence, divergent thinking and the detection of correct solutions. *Journal of Applied Social Psychology, 9*, 788–99.

Nemeth, C. and Owens, P. (1996) Making work groups more effective: The value of minority dissent. In M.A. West (Ed.) *Handbook of Work Group Psychology*. Chichester, England: John Wiley. (pp. 125–42).

Nemeth, C. and Staw, B.M. (1989) The trade offs of social control and innovation within groups and organizations. In L. Berkowitz (Ed.) *Advances in Experimental Social Psychology*. New York: Academic Press. (pp. 175–210).

Nemeth, C.J. and Wachtler, J. (1983). Creative problem solving as a result of majority vs minority influence. *European Journal of Social Psychology, 13*, 45–55.

Nicholson, N. and West, M.A. (1988) *Managerial Job Change: Men and Women in Transition*. Cambridge: Cambridge University Press.

Oldham, G.R. and Cummings, A. (1996) Employee creativity: Personal and contextual factors at work. *Academy of Management Journal, 39*(3), 607–34.

O'Reilly, C. and Williams, K.Y. (1998) Group demography and innovation: Does diversity help? In Deborah H Gruenfeld, (Ed.) *Research on Managing Groups and Teams, Vol. 1.* (pp. 183–207).

Payne, R.L. (1990) The effectiveness of research teams: A review. In M.A. West and J.L. Farr (Eds) *Innovation and Creativity at Work: Psychological and Organizational Strategies.* Chichester, England: Wiley. (pp. 101–22).

Pearce, J.A. and Ravlin, E.C. (1987) The design and activation of self-regulating work groups. *Human Relations, 40,* 751–82.

Pelled, H.L., Eisenhardt, K.M. and Xin, K.R. (1999) Exploring the black box: An analysis of work group diversity, conflict, and performance. *Administrative Science Quarterly, 44,* 1–28.

Porac, J.F. and Howard, H. (1990) Taxonomic mental models in competitor definition. *Academy of Management Review, 2,* 224–40.

Rokeach, M. (1950) The effect of perception of time upon the rigidity and concreteness of thinking. *Journal of Experimental Psychology, 40,* 206–16.

Roloff, M.E. (1987) Communication and conflict. In C.R. Berger and S.H. Chaffee (Eds) *Handbook of Communication Science.* Newbury Park, CA: Sage. (pp. 484–534).

Schweiger, D., Sandberg, W. and Rechner, P. (1989) Experimental effects of dialectical inquiry, devil's advocacy, and other consensus approaches to strategic decision making. *Academy of Management Journal, 32,* 745–72.

Shaw, J. B. and Barrett-Power, E. (1998) The effects of diversity on small work group processes and performance. *Human Relations, 51*(10), 1307–25.

Smith, K.G. Smith, K.A., Bannon, D.P., Olian, J.D., Sims, H.P. and Scully, J. (1994) Top Management Team demography and process: The role of social integration and communication. *Administrative Science Quarterly, 39,* 412.

Sternberg, R.J. and Lubart, T.I. (1996) Investing in creativity. *American Psychologist, 51,* 677–88.

Tannenbaum, S.I., Salas, E. and Cannon-Bowers, J.A. (1996). Promoting team effectiveness. In M.A. West (Ed.) *Handbook of Work Group Psychology.* Chichester, UK: Wiley. (pp. 503–29).

Thomas, K.W. (1979) Organizational conflict. In S. Kerr (Ed.) *Organizational Behavior.* Columbus, OH: Grid Publishing. (pp. 151–84).

Tjosvold, D. (1982) Effects of approach to controversy on superiors' incorporation of subordinates' information in decision making. *Journal of Applied Psychology, 67,* 189–93.

Tjosvold, D. (1985) Implications of controversy research for management. *Journal of Management, 11,* 21–37.

Tjosvold, D. (1991) *Team Organization: An Enduring Competitive Advantage.* Chichester, England: Wiley.

Tjosvold, D. (1998) Co-operative and competitive goal approaches to conflict: accomplishments and challenges. *Applied Psychology: An International Review, 47,* 285–342.

Tjosvold, D. and Field, R.H.G. (1983) Effects of social context on consensus and majority vote decision making. *Academy of Management Journal, 26,* 500–6.

Tjosvold, D., and Johnson, D.W. (1977) The effects of controversy on cognitive perspective-taking. *Journal of Education Psychology, 69,* 679–85.

Tjosvold, D., Wedley, W.C. and Field, R.H.G. (1986) Constructive controversy, the Vroom-Yetton Model, and managerial decision-making. *Journal of Occupational Behavior, 7,* 125–38.

Tsai, W. (2001) Knowledge transfer in intraorganizational networks: Effects of network position and absorptive capacity on business unit innovation and performance. *Academy of Management Journal, 44*(5), 996–1004.

Turner, J.C. (1985) Social categorization and the self-concept: A social cognitive theory of group behavior. In E.J. Lawler (Ed.) *Advances in Group Processes: Theory and research,* vol. 2. Greenwich, CT: JAI Press. (pp. 77–121).

Van Dyck, C. (2000) *Putting Errors to Good Use: Error Management Culture in Organizations.* Amsterdam: Kurt Lewin Institute.

Waldman, D.A. and Atwater, L.E. (1994) The nature of effective leadership and championing processes at different levels in a R & D hierarchy. *The Journal of High Technology Management Research, 5,* 233–45.

Webber, S.S. and Donahue, L.M. (2001) Impact of highly and less job-related diversity on work group cohesion and performance: A meta-analysis. *Journal of Management, 27*(2), 141–62.

West, M.A. (1987) Role innovation in the world of work. *British Journal of Social Psychology, 26,* 305–15.

West, M.A. (1989) Innovation among health care professionals. *Social Behavior, 4, 173–84.*

West, M.A. (1990) The social psychology of innovation in groups. In M.A. West and J.L. Farr (Eds) *Innovation and Creativity at Work: Psychological and Organizational Strategies.* Chichester, England: John Wiley. (pp. 309–33).

West, M.A. (1996) Reflexivity and work group effectiveness: A conceptual integration. In M.A. West (Ed.) *Handbook of Work Group Psychology.* Chichester, England: Wiley. (pp. 555–79).

West, M.A. (2000) Reflexivity, revolution, and innovation in work teams. In M.M. Beyerlein, D.A. Johnson and S.T. Beyerlein (Eds) *Advances in Interdisciplinary Studies of Work Teams: Product Development Teams.* Stamford, CT: JAI Press. (pp. 1–29).

West, M.A. (2002) Sparkling fountains or stagnant ponds: An integrative model of creativity and innovation implementation in work groups. *Applied Psychology: An International Review. 51,* 355–87.

West, M.A. and Anderson, N. (1996) Innovation in top management teams. *Journal of Applied Psychology, 81,* 680–93.

West, M.A., Borrill, C.S., Dawson, J.F., Brodbeck, F., Shapiro, D.A. and Haward, B. (2003a) Leadership clarity and team innovation in health care. *The Leadership Quarterly, 14*(4–5), 393–410.

West, M.A., and Farr, J.L. (1990) Innovation at work. In M.A. West and J.L. Farr (Eds), *Innovation and Creativity at Work: Psychological and Organizational Strategies.* Chichester, England: Wiley. (pp. 3–13).

West, M.A., Hirst, G., Richter, A. and Shipton, H. (2004) Twelve steps to heaven: Successfully managing change through developing innovative teams. *European Journal of Work and Organizational Psychology, 13*(2), 269–99.

West, M.A., Patterson, M., Pillinger, T. and Nickell, S. (1998) *Innovation and Change in Manufacturing.* Institute of Work Psychology, University of Sheffield, Sheffield, S10 2TN.

West, M.A. and Rushton, R. (1989) Mismatches in work role transitions. *Journal of Occupational Psychology, 62,* 271–86.

West, M.A., Tjosvold, D. and Smith, K.G. (2003b) (Eds), *International Handbook of Organisational Teamwork and Co-operative Working.* Chichester, England: Wiley.

Willems, E.P. and Clark, R.D. III (1971) Shift toward risk and heterogeneity of groups. *Journal of Experimental and Social Psychology, 7,* 302–12.

Wood, W. (1987) Meta-analytic review of sex differences in group performance. *Psychological Bulletin, 102,* 53–71.

Wright, M. (1954). A study of anxiety in a general hospital setting. *Canadian Journal of Psychology, 8,* 195–203.

Yukl, G., Wall, S. and Lepsinger, R. (1990) Preliminary report on validation of the Managerial Practices Survey. In K.E. Clark and M.B. Clark (Eds), *Measures of Leadership.* NJ: Leadership Library of America.

Note: This chapter is an abridged version of West, M.A., Hirst, G. et al. (2004). Twelve steps to heaven: Successfully managing change through developing innovative teams. *European Journal of Work and Organizational Psychology, 13*(2), 269–299.

B

Cognition

The authors in this section show that if organizations wish to capitalize on creativity, innovation and knowledge they are well advised to allow space for implicit, analogical and other non-formal ways of thinking. Claxton outlines the importance of intuitive expertise and implicit learning. Nonaka and Takeuchi illustrate how Japanese firms make use of metaphor and hands on experience to assist knowledge creation. Sparrow outlines the role of emotion and imagery in creative cognition.

Guy Claxton, a cognitive psychologist and educator, outlines the reasons why creativity and innovation may benefit from a receptive form of thinking that allows intuitive knowledge to be heard. Studies of what managers actually do by Mintzberg and others have shown that managers, like the rest of the population, rely heavily on hunches and intuitive thinking to understand situations, make decisions and guide action, but they normally feel obliged to justify their thinking explicitly. Cognitive psychologists have found that intuitive thinking can be especially critical in complex and uncertain situations and that the ability to explain one's actions follows long behind intuitive wisdom. This chapter seeks to illustrate why we need to find a place for intuitive expertise and non-reflective judgement, and how creative thinking draws on tacit thought processes.

Ijuro Nonaka and Hirotaka Takeuchi are Japanese Professors who have studied knowledge creation in innovative Japanese companies. This chapter presents a cogent account of the deficiency of Western conceptualizations of innovation and knowledge, locating the information processing bias found in the West firmly within its longstanding tradition of rational and dualistic thinking. The emphasis on explicit doing in the West contrasts with the East, where tacit knowledge has long been recognized as an important counterpart to rational ways of knowing. Perhaps partly because of their pictographic language, the Japanese have a less atomistic and dualistic way of thinking than in the West, so the split between subject and object is less cavernous, and the concept of knowledge is less separated from its development. Nonaka charges that Westerners tend to ignore the process of knowledge creation, emphasizing explicit thought processes at the expense of implicit ways of knowing, which are especially important in the early phase of problem formulation. Nonaka goes on to show how organizations in Japan make space for implicit ways of knowing during organizational innovation processes.

Sparrow's chapter focuses on emotion. In a number of settings positive mood has been found to be associated with greater openness and a greater capacity for divergent thinking, whereas fear is known to restrict the range of options explored. Sparrow highlights the interdependence of emotion, imagery and cognition and illustrates their relationship to creative work. He points out that emotion tends to be marginalised in many work environments and argues for greater acknowledgement of both emotion and imaginistic thinking at work.

Beyond Cleverness: How to be Smart Without Thinking

Guy Claxton

> It is a profoundly erroneous truism, repeated by all eminent people when they are making speeches, that we should cultivate the habit of thinking of what we are doing. The precise opposite is the case … Operations of thought are like cavalry charges in battle – they are strictly limited in number, they require fresh horses, and they must only be made at decisive moments.
>
> A.N. Whitehead

There is a stupid rumour going round that intelligence is essentially rational, and that hard problems are invariably best tackled as explicitly, clearly, logically and articulately as possible. It's not true. As Whitehead says, logical clarity is *one* form of intelligence, but to assume that it is always the best, and the more of it the better, is as daft as to say that running is always the best way of getting around, or a screwdriver is always the best tool. The rumour is stupid because it makes you less intelligent, mistaking one useful faculty of mind for the whole repertoire of useful mind states and modes. People who are good at being articulate and analytical, but who confuse this with being all-round intelligent are, we might say, 'clever' – but clever is not the same as smart.

This error is widely perpetrated in education, in law, increasingly in medicine, and, unfortunately, in business. Clever people are good on paper. They can mount plausible arguments, fast. They can spot the flaws in other people's ideas, and score points by being quick to do so. They have good memories and can spout facts and statistics to support their case. They often have impressive qualifications, because first class degrees from Oxford and Harvard MBAs are designed to select and train those who are fast and clear and fluent. But such qualities, when overused or misapplied, can lead to quite unintelligent behaviour. (The stupid cleverness of lawyers is legendary.) As Robert Bernstein said, when he was CEO of publishing giant Random House, 'That's what frightens me about business schools. They train their students to sound wonderful. But it's necessary to find out if there's any *judgment* behind their language' (Rowan, 1986).

Over the last two decades, cognitive scientists have revealed a variety of ways in which 'clever' turns out not to be so smart; and conversely, some of the kinds of smart that do not involve mere cleverness. This science-based, more balanced view of intelligence is beginning to seep into the professions, and into areas such as management education. Managers, for example, are waking up to the fact that some ways of being smart are not clear, not articulate, not quick, not analytical – sometimes not even conscious.

But the stranglehold of the old lop-sided model of cleverness is proving hard to break. The distrust of non-clever forms of intelligence reflects 300 years of European cultural history. The Cartesian slogan 'Cogito ergo sum' encapsulated the successful attempt to reduce the human mind only to its most conscious and rational regions, and to persuade people that their very identity resided in the exercise of this explicit, articulate, analytical form of intelligence. The Enlightenment of the eighteenth century picked out just this single way of knowing and, in raising it to a high art, implicitly ignored or disabled any others: those that were not so clinical and cognitive, and were instead more bodily, sensory, affective, mythic or aesthetic.

In some ways, this distrust is justified. On one hand, rather grandiose claims have been made for 'intuition' that are simply not defensible. Descartes thought intuition gave direct access to the Mind of God, but it doesn't for most of us. And some people have claimed infallible status for their 'gut feelings', where the rest of us can remember only too well the times our intuition let us down – about stock market movements, horse races or people to be trusted or loved. On the other hand, recent forms of lip-service to the non-rational – 'right-brain thinking', 'brainstorming', 'emotional intelligence' and so on – have often been founded more in consultant's hype than in scientific research. Too often they have presented simplistic nostrums as if they were, indeed, God's Truth – leaving a justifiable residue of scepticism, rather than an expanded sense of possibility.

But cynicism can be as self-defeating as credulity, if it leads people to treat all 'knowledge' or 'opinion' that comes without a rational pedigree as if it had no claim on our time or our respect. It is not smart to treat action that is not planned or premeditated, answers that come without reasons, understandings that cannot instantly be clearly and quickly put into words, as inevitably second-rate. It is stupid to treat all forms of learning that do not involve articulation, and all ways of judging that have no explicit criteria, as lazy and inadequate. Where professional cultures become obsessed with planning, deliberation, calculation, measurement, justification and accountability, they are being less smart than they could be.

In this chapter, I want to review some of the research that is helping to rehabilitate a smarter view of what it means to be truly smart. Cognitive science is reminding us of aspects of intelligence that do not involve clear thinking; and of the occasions on which the attempt to maintain or impose such thinking is counter-productive. For example, I shall illustrate the importance of *intuitive expertise*; of *learning without thinking*; of *non-reflective judgement*; of perceptual *sensitivity to clues* and patterns; and of *receptive creativity* and problem-solving. From a consideration of these will emerge some basic principles about what makes for smart, as opposed to stupid, mind-sets, and also about the kinds of organizational cultures that encourage either genuinely smart or stupid-clever forms of thinking.

Intuitive Expertise

The first of the unclever ways of being smart involves allowing the unfolding of smooth mastery of complex but familiar domains, such as a family, a sports team or a company. Such performance is usually at its best when it is unpremeditated and unself-conscious. As Mihaly Csikszentmihalyi has captured with his research on 'flow', we are often at our smartest and most fluid when we are so immersed in a situation that we are doing completely without thinking (Csikszentmihalyi, 1990). The expert manager may go through a whole meeting, adjusting intentions and moderating time as he/she goes, without being conscious of much reasoning, and without being able to say why or how he/she made the 'decisions' they did, or to what clues he/she was responding. Indeed it is well-known that becoming too aware of and reflective about one's action, in the heat of the moment, may result in a loss of fluency and even, in extremes of self-consciousness, in paralysis. Thinking about what you are doing, or consciously monitoring what you are doing, as you are doing it, can be deleterious, as the eminent philosopher A.N. Whitehead notes in the quotation at the beginning of this chapter. Intuitive virtuosity unrolls, for the most part, without the help (or the hindrance) of deliberation. Occasionally the expert in mid-performance may 'stop to think', but the moments at which these 'cavalry charges' are made must be well-timed, and not prolonged (Dreyfus and Dreyfus, 1986).

In the context of unfolding expertise, the role of conscious thinking is best conceived as the voice of an 'internalized coach'. A good coach lodges in learners' minds bits of advice about what to do, or what to attend to, at critical moments. Such bits of advice are designed to interrupt an unfolding habit and remind us of an alternative way of proceeding, or an alternative source of feedback to attend to, that is not yet automated in our system. When the coach is present, they can spot the 'psychological moment' at which to do this bit of astute reminding. Being sparing and appropriate with advice is a crucial part of the coaches' skill. Talking to ourselves and 'thinking about what we are doing' ought to have the same function. It should remind us, in the midst of action, of alternatives that we might benefit from. From this point of view, talking to ourselves too much, or doing so at inappropriate or unnecessary moments, or doing so in a critical and undermining way, rather than supportively and instructively, can all be as counterproductive as they would be if there were a bad coach in front of us. Thinking about what you are doing is not a 'good thing' in its own right; and it is certainly not the case that 'the more of it the better'.

Learning Without Thinking

The substantial gap between what a skilled manager can do, and what they can tell you about what they are doing, means, therefore, that learning, as well as fluent performance itself, may need to proceed intuitively. As Michael Polanyi (1958) perceptively commented nearly 40 years ago:

> Maxims are rules, the correct application of which is part of the art which they govern … Maxims cannot be understood, still less applied, by anyone not already possessing a good practical knowledge of the art. They derive their interest from our appreciation of the art and cannot themselves either replace or establish that appreciation … [And therefore] an art which [necessarily] cannot be specified in detail, cannot be transmitted by prescription, since no prescription for it exists.

It is not just that the expert has not yet got round to articulating his/her expertise, but could do so, given the time and the inclination. Polanyi's point is that virtuosity cannot, *in principle,* be fully explicated, for it embodies observations, distinctions and nuances that are too fine-grain to be caught accurately in a web of words. And this means that, while some bits of judicious thinking may *guide* the process of learning, they cannot, by themselves, establish the nuanced expertise of the virtuoso professional or performer. For that, experience is needed – and much of this experiential learning happens best without the intervention of conscious thought or regulation.

Many psychological studies of so-called 'implicit learning', in which a person tries to gain mastery of a complex domain via an extended process of trial and error, have revealed four important findings. First, what such learning needs is an attitude of open-minded attention rather than of earnest 'problem-solving'. If you are trying to guess what is going to happen next, test out a pre-determined idea, or apply what you can remember of what you learned in a seminar, all that cognitive activity – those forms of cleverness – may well blind you to what is actually going on. You are so busy trying to impose a theory on the situation that you fail to pick up the subtle – and probably unexpected – contingencies that are actually there. You learn faster and better if you can turn off your thinking. For example, Coulson (1996), in some preliminary studies, has shown that the ability to soak up the details of a complex situation through implicit learning is facilitated by a state of confusion. If people have given up the attempt to try to figure out what is going on, and simply interact with the situation in a 'mindless' but observant manner, they come to master it, at an intuitive level – they do the right thing without knowing why – faster than those who keep struggling for conscious comprehension.

Second, this kind of 'learning by osmosis' can detect and make use of subtleties that are too fine for conscious thinking to detect at all. Lewicki et al. (1992) have found that such implicit learning can pick out and make use of patterns of information in a complex situation (such as a work team) that are too subtle to be captured in a conscious, articulate account. They showed that people can make non-conscious use of information that they are totally unable to describe, despite being well-motivated to articulate the very patterns they had been using.

Third, when people are learning to manage a complex environment, their intuitive grasp – their 'know how' – develops much faster than their ability to describe what they are doing. Expertise precedes explanation. However, during the pre-articulate phase, people often dramatically under-estimate their own level of performance. They make perfectly good decisions and actions on the basis of hunches, yet may believe that they are merely guessing (Berry and Dienes, 1993). Their 'feelings' are reliable, yet their confidence in those feelings is weak. Clearly, the rationalist idea that 'if you can't explain it, you can't have learned it ("properly")' is at work here. Having been led, by their education as much as anything, to equate 'learning with understanding', they distrust their own demonstrably effective but unarticulated competence. That is not smart.

Fourth, when people's learning does not incorporate the intuitive stage, their conscious knowledge seems unable to guide their actions. Patients with damage to certain parts of the frontal lobes of the brain are as good as normal people at eventually being able to explain what is going on in such complex environments. They have lost none of their ability to construct accurate accounts on the basis of their experience. However, this knowledge turns out to be of no real use, for their practical expertise never improves. And their 'learning' is not accompanied by any intuitive promptings, as it is for normal people. It is as if our hunches and feelings, far from being primitive or irrational, are a vital part of our learning and understanding. Antonio Damasio (1994), who conducted these studies of brain damaged patients, concludes that 'intuition' is actually the glue that holds intelligent action and conscious understanding together. Without it they become disconnected, and the level of 'articulate incompetence' becomes dangerous (Bechara et al., 1997).

The manager's job is to do or say the right thing: the thing that moves things forward and helps to get the job done well. Continually anticipating the need to justify their interventions often, as we well know, makes people 'play safe' and 'cover their backs', and such priorities can interfere with getting the job done. Management education's job is to help people get to the point where they do and say the right things most of the time, in ever more uncertain and complex situations. Being articulate about what they are doing is only of relevance to the extent that it leads to this end, and is a hindrance when it distracts from it, or *assumes* that 'comprehension leads to competence' without checking. It often doesn't.

Non-Reflective Judgement

> When making a decision of minor importance, I have always found it
> advantageous to consider all the pros and cons. In vital matters however …
> the decision should come from the unconscious, from somewhere within
> ourselves.
>
> Sigmund Freud

I have already alluded to the fact that expert judgement in many professions is often wholly or largely intuitive. The art connoisseur has a 'feeling' that the putative Giotto is 'school of', and not by the master himself. The doctor has a hunch that this combination of symptoms is not as straightforward as it looks – though could not say why. The experienced manager 'just knows' that the morale in the sales division is poor, though everyone is putting on a brave face. In a whole variety of spheres, what the medical profession refers to as 'clinical judgement' is ubiquitous and indispensable, and seems to accrue gradually as a result of extensive experience, and not through erudition. Although the current emphasis on measurable accountability is rightly intended to safeguard against the bias and injustice that is the shadow of unbridled subjectivity, the issue is again not black and white. There are costs in swinging too far in the direction of 'objectivity', not least the undermining of people's confidence in their own judgement, and a reluctance to use intuitive judgement when it is necessary and appropriate.

The value of intuitive judgement has again been demonstrated recently in the laboratory. Timothy Wilson and Jonathan Schooler (1991) asked students to taste and rate a number of different makes of strawberry jam. The jams had recently been the subject of a 'Which?'-type consumer report, and those given to the students had been ranked 1st, 11th, 32nd and 44th by the 'experts'. Some of the students were told that they would be asked to explain the reasons for their preferences, and to think hard about their judgements. The others were free to choose more intuitively. The results showed that those students who had been left to their own devices, and who evaluated the jams intuitively, showed a much higher agreement with the experts' choices, while those who had tried to produce explicit justifications made judgements that were more idiosyncratic. What this did *not* reflect, it turned out, was the students tuning in more carefully to their own personal tastes. In a follow-up study, Schooler tested to see whether, despite their divergence from 'received wisdom' the students remained happy with their decisions over a period of time. Far from becoming more content with their choices, those students who had thought most carefully declared themselves **less** satisfied. It turns out that, in cases where much of the 'data' on which a decision is based is sensory, subtle or holistic, the effort to force the judging process into a form that demands explicit, articulate reasoning is counter-productive.

Ap Dijksterhuis of the University of Amsterdam has shown that explicit, methodical thinking breaks down as the number of variables to be considered increases beyond a certain point (Dijksterhuis, 2003). In an elegant series of studies, he faced people with choices that depended on up to a dozen different variables – as, for example, is involved in the task of choosing between applicants for a job. People who were encouraged to think most carefully made worse choices, and they did so because of the limitations of conscious thinking. We can only bear in mind – i.e. think consciously about – a handful of factors at once. As the variables proliferate, so pre-rational decisions have to be made about which factors are to be included in the conscious set, and which are to be dropped. (Imagine someone who can only juggle three balls being thrown a fourth and a fifth – they either have to ignore the incoming balls, or drop some of the original ones.) Intuition, on the other hand, seems able to provide a running résumé of the decision-making process that remains more sensitive to the whole range of factors. Forcing people to be articulate requires them to focus on only a sub-set of all the available information, and to pick out the factors that are most 'sayable' rather than the most salient.

Sensitivity to Clues

The fourth kind of intuitive intelligence reflects a heightened sensitivity to clues. To say of someone that they are 'very intuitive' can imply that they extract the maximum amount of significance from the available information: they see the meaning in the detail that others may have overlooked. Such clues may not themselves be registered consciously by the 'intuiter', yet they can still contribute to an accurate 'feeling of knowing'. This ability to be attentive to detail, whether consciously or subliminally, may underlie the kind of 'clinical judgement' which we have just discussed, and it certainly provides a non-mystical account of the famous 'sixth sense' that some people seem to display. Scott Fitzgerald (1934), who was himself fascinated by the phenomenon of subliminal perception, illustrates in *Tender is the Night* how the so-called sixth sense may actually reduce to an acute employment of the other five.

> In an inhabited room there are refracting objects only half noticed: varnished wood, more or less polished brass, silver and ivory, and beyond these a thousand conveyors of light and shadow so mild that one scarcely thinks of them as that: the tops of picture frames, the edges of pencils or ashtrays, or crystal or china ornaments; the totality of this refraction appealing to equally subtle reflexes of the vision as well as to those associational fragments in the subconscious that we seem to hang on to, as the glass-fitter keeps the irregular shaped pieces that may do, sometime. This fact might account for what Rosemary afterwards mystically describes as realising there was some one in the room, before she could determine it.

There is now a wealth of experimental evidence that attests to the existence and the value of such subtle clues, and the abilities to make use of them (see Claxton, 1997). As long ago as 1884, philosopher C.S. Pierce and his graduate student Joseph Jastrow conducted a long series of studies on unconscious perception, at the end of which they concluded that their research had:

> … highly important bearings, since it gives new reason for believing that we gather what is passing in one another's minds in large measure from sensations so faint that we are not aware of having them, and can give no account of how we reach our conclusions about such matters. The insight of females as well as certain 'telepathic' phenomena may be explained in this way. Such faint sensations ought to be fully studied by the psychologist and assiduously cultivated by everyman.

Westcott (1968) gave people problems to solve, and offered them a series of clues which they could take up one by one. They could opt to take only one or two clues before venturing a solution, or they could be more cautious and wait until they had more information. Westcott found that his subjects divided into four groups, according to whether they were willing to answer on the basis of a little information, or needed more; and, within each of these two groups, whether their solutions tended to be correct or not. One group – those whom Westcott identified as the 'successful intuitives' – did consistently well with only a little information, while another, the 'conservative failures', did poorly no matter how much information they had asked for. Clearly the 'intuitives' were able to extract the significance of each of the clues more successfully than their more cautious or more insensitive colleagues.

Of particular interest were the ways in which the different groups scored differently on tests of personality. Intuitive people, Westcott found, tend to be introverted: they like to keep out of the social limelight, but feel self-sufficient and trust their own judgement. They like to make up their own minds about things, and tend to resist being controlled by others. They tend to be unconventional, and comfortable in their unconventionality. In Westcott's words, 'they explore uncertainties and entertain doubts far more than the other groups do, and they live with these doubts and uncertainties without fear. They enjoy taking risks, and are willing to expose themselves to criticism and challenge. They can accept or reject criticism as necessary, and they are willing to change in ways they deem to be appropriate' (p. 55). So when risk and uncertainty exist, it is the 'intuitives' you want on your team; not those who insist on gathering every last shred of data before they dare make a move.

Too much hard thinking undermines intelligence by closing people off to their own existing resources of knowledge and experience. It renders their perception of current events coarser and more conventional. When people are searching earnestly, anxiously or impatiently for a solution, they tend to see what they expect or want to see, and the incongruous detail or the small but vital clue gets overlooked. The good tracker, or the insightful detective, possess a large body of knowledge, skill and experience – much of which is not systematically formulated in consciousness. The way they make use of this rich memory is more through 'resonance' than rationality. They take time to absorb the fine details of the situation, and to allow this subtle image to resonate gently with their accumulated wisdom in a way that could not be described as intellectual or explicit. Sherlock Holmes, you may recall, when faced with a particularly difficult case, would not spend hours, as it were, checking the Interpol database on his computer, but having inspected the scene of the crime would retire to his room with a full tobacco pouch, saying 'Do not disturb me, Watson. This is, I think, a three pipe problem'. Holmes embodies a mature form of intelligence that relies as much on quiet reflection as on busy reasoning.

It is as if there is a variable threshold between the conscious and the unconscious minds, and an analytical, critical attitude, or too much pressure for results, causes this threshold to be raised, so that information that is subtle or equivocal becomes unavailable. This happens even at the level of bare perception. People who are looking at a screen in order to detect faint flashes of light are better at doing so when they are not trying too hard. Perception is more sensitive when you are relaxed, just allowing what is faintly there to 'pop up' by itself. Interestingly, however, this effect is reduced when people do not feel comfortable adopting such a receptive attitude. For people who find it difficult to allow themselves to respond spontaneously, or who rate themselves as more highly motivated to do well, the advantage of the 'pop up' condition is removed (Snodgrass et al., 1993). Learning to ease up, and let the mind 'do its own thing' clearly has its advantages.

Creativity and Problem-solving

Creativity is perhaps the area *par excellence* where hard thinking and data analysis have periodically to give way to more ruminative or even hazy forms of cognition. In the autobiographical writings of creative scientists and artists there has been, for a long time, a recognition of the creative power of unconscious mental processes. A satisfying product may appear not as the result of conscious cognitive labour, but as a gift from 'out of the blue', and this process may be encouraged and stimulated, but it cannot be forced or controlled. Quite the reverse: the gifts appear only in a mood of relaxed reverie and rumination, when they are not being earnestly sought or worked on at all.

Now there is experimental evidence for these anecdotal conclusions, too. Janet Davidson (1995) asked people to solve simple 'insight' problems such as:

> George wants to cook three steaks as quickly as possible, but unfortunately his grill can only cook two steaks at a time. The steaks take three minutes a side to cook. What is the shortest time in which George can cook all three steaks?

See Note at the end of the chapter for the solution.

In general an insight problem is one in which people's 'first take' on the problem is likely to embody a plausible assumption which turns out to be illicit; and/or one in which the solution depends on an holistic perception of the elements of the problem in relationship, rather than on analytical, sequential reasoning. Davidson found that people who were most successful at solving such puzzles thought more slowly than those who became stuck and failed. Even though 'intelligence' is generally associated with faster processing, in the case of problems that require insight, rather than brute reasoning, it is 'slow and steady' that wins the race. What happens is that people who tend to rush at the problem are more likely to make some false assumptions, and get locked in to an erroneous way of thinking about it from which they cannot then escape.

Jonathan Schooler has shown that people who are good at solving these kinds of 'insight problems' are able to let their minds go blank and admit to themselves that they are temporarily stuck. People who persist with conscious thinking are less likely to make the breakthrough. As Schooler says: 'Verbalization may cause such a ruckus in the front of one's mind that one is unable to attend to the new approaches that may be emerging in the back of the mind' (Schooler et al., 1993). The more keenly one seeks a solution or an explanation, the more likely one is to come up with thoughts that are conventional and uncreative. Thus a young executive, baffled by the poor reception of a well-planned presentation, may be more likely to generate a creative alternative for themselves as their mind wanders drowsily in the evening than they are in a serious, anxious debriefing session with their team leader or mentor straight after the event.

The clever mind tends to be relentless in its search for solutions. It sees no value in less focused mental activity or in 'time off task'. Yet this is another of the ways in which it stifles creativity. For there is plenty of evidence that the innovative mind needs to move between open-minded playfulness and concentrated purposefulness, and to do so with a range of different rhythms and tempi. We have already seen the value of allowing pauses and gaps in the train of thought. A few seconds of 'down time' can allow a fuller and more integrated mental picture of a situation to emerge, enabling a response to be less impulsive and more 'thoughtful'.

Taking a few minutes away from a problem that is proving recalcitrant can also be very productive. Studies have shown that problems on which people have got stuck are more likely to be solved after a break of a few minutes than if problem-solving is persistent (Smith, 1995). Dijksterhuis (2003) found that the people in his complex judgement situations made better choices if the decisions were preceded by a few minutes' delay in which they were prevented from thinking about the problem. In clever mode, it is easy to get locked in, as we have seen, to a view of the problem that may contain some unnecessary or misleading assumptions. By taking a break and thinking about something else, you increase the likelihood that these assumptions will lose their strength and dissolve away, so that when you return to the problem, you may be able to take a fresh approach. Collectively, it can be very helpful to suggest such a 'hunch break' in a meeting that has become blocked, or where positions have become entrenched. Even a ten minute recess can allow minds to soften and emotions to cool, so that greater creativity can emerge.

On a slightly longer time-scale, it has been shown that creative individuals tend to structure their daily routines so that they contain significant periods of playtime or rest. A recent survey of outstandingly creative people in the US found that: 'Many of the individuals we interviewed structured their day to include a period of solitary time that follows a period of hard work ... Without this solitary quiet time, they would never have their most important ideas. Several respondents kept their minds idle by engaging in repetitive physical activity'. For example, one said: 'Generally the really high ideas come to me when I'm gardening, or when I'm doing something steadying with my hands' (Csikszentmihalyi and Sawyer, 1996). Longer-term still, there are too many accounts to ignore of people who discovered solutions to complex problems whilst they were on holiday. The 30 page document that outlined the structure of the first consumer banking enterprise in the US has become widely known in financial circles as the 'memo from the beach'.

Balancing the Different Modes of Mind

Taken together, these observations and research studies make a powerful case for the importance of kinds of intelligent cognition that do not involve elegant, clear-cut, systematic reasoning, but which are more intuitive, sensory and embodied. And they also show that these forms of intelligence can be overridden and undermined by too strong a determination to maintain conscious comprehension, clarity and control. However, we must be aware of jumping out of the rationalistic frying-pan into the intuitive fire. Just as logic can lead you astray, so can intuition. Both are perfectly capable of being applied badly, or at the wrong time. The extra ingredient of real intelligence is knowing when and how to draw on each of these different kinds of smart, and how to integrate and slide between them.

For example, intuitions often come with a kind of built-in confidence rating, a subjective feeling of 'rightness', that may vary in its strength from 'complete guess' to 'absolute certainty'. Mangan (1993) has suggested that this feeling acts as a summary in consciousness of a set of unconscious processes and judgements that cannot – at least at that moment, and perhaps in principle – surface as such. He uses the metaphor of the 'menu bar' on a computer word processing screen: a set of symbols and icons indicating the status of different variables, and the availability of various options, which act as pointers and reminders, but which do not take up very much of the limited space on the screen itself. Intuition in general, in Mangan's view, comprises such short-hand references which inhabit the 'fringe' of consciousness, and he reminds us of William James' perceptive concern with 'the reinstatement of the vague to its proper place in our mental life'.

Intuition can be shown to have significantly greater validity than its author gives it credit for. Bowers et al. (1990), for example, have demonstrated that we frequently undervalue faint hunches, inklings or even what feel like total guesses. Their subjects were given clues to the solution of a puzzle one at a time, and after each one were required to come up with an attempt at the answer, even if they thought it was a complete shot in the dark. Bowers was able to show that these 'complete guesses' began to converge on an acceptable solution well before the solution itself actually appeared, even though subjects' confidence in them was non-existent.

However, arguing for greater respect for the feeling of rightness in our mental life does not entail always taking it at face value, or treating it as infallible. The feeling may be *indicative* of an idea that is worth taking seriously, but it is rarely *definitive*. Despite famous examples of unshakable intuitive confidence, such as Gauss's 'I have my result, but I do not yet know how to get it', the feelings of rightness – or wrongness – can both be misleading. For instance, when people are solving analytical problems, their sense of how 'warm' they are is an accurate predictor of an imminent successful solution. But with insight problems, the feeling of warmth is actually predictive of failure. People think they are getting closer to a solution when they are actually barking up the wrong tree (Metcalfe and Wiebe, 1987).

As I said earlier, one of the reasons that intuition got a bad name was the apparent contradiction between some of the grandiose claims of incorrigibility – of direct revelation of unquestionable 'truth' – on the one hand, and the transparent fact that it is blatantly and frequently wrong, on the other. Sometimes people's inklings and premonitions, their gut feelings and gut reactions, turn out to be perceptive and appropriate; other times, they don't. People can end up falling in love with each other despite unfavourable first impressions. Promising hunches regularly turn out to be blind alleys. A manager's first guesses about how to deal with a problematic situation can be distressingly misguided. Intuition can be mistaken and misleading; but does that mean, if we shed the inflated expectations, that it is of no value, or that it cannot be educated to become *more* reliable and perceptive?

Take a famous example – one often used by Wittgenstein in his seminars – of a stubbornly false intuition. Imagine that the Earth is smoothed into a perfect sphere, and that a ribbon is tied snugly round the equator. Now untie the ribbon, and add just six feet to its total length. Space it out, so that the gap thus created is equal all the way round. How big is the gap? A micron? A hair's breadth? A paperback book? A foot? Most people's strong intuition is that the gap would be tiny. In fact it is easy to prove mathematically that it is nearly a foot. You could crawl under it. The intuition is false; but the interesting question is *why* is it false? It turns out that its basis is the assumption that 'if you add a little to a lot, it won't make much difference.' Now there are many situations, superficially similar to Wittgenstein's puzzle, where this assumption is both valid and useful. If you were to turn the oceans into a giant cylinder, and add six gallons to it, the height would indeed rise by only a negligible amount.

The fault comes in an over-reliance on an *holistic unconscious analogy*; the unanalysed assimilation of this problem to a class of situations to which, despite appearances, it does not actually belong. This unconscious analogizing is a vital and ubiquitous mental process. It is a way of getting cognition going by giving it a *prima facie* sensible guess to work on. Often these guesses are productive, and sometimes they turn out to be misleading (Bruner and Clinchy, 1972). The new boss tacitly assumes a model of management and leadership, both consciously and unconsciously imbibed from previous experiences of being managed and led, which may be appropriate and adequate for his/her particular personality and this particular organizational culture, or it may not. It may be a good first guess that can be trimmed and tuned, or it may be quite the wrong place to start, that is only going to cause grief and strife. It depends. The intuition serves us well if we take it as an hypothesis, rather than as the God-given truth. If we take it as gospel, and try to force situations or ourselves to fit what is in fact an inaccurate template, then we may end up stymied and frustrated. A balanced view of intuition is one which sees it as a valuable source of hypotheses, which are nonetheless capable of being interrogated.

This simultaneous respect for the fallibility and the value of intuition is reflected time and again in the literature of creativity – both artistic, scientific and pragmatic. An on-going survey of Nobel science laureates by Marton and colleagues in Sweden (e.g. Fensham and Marton, 1992) – to take just one of these spheres – reveals the absolutely central place which they give to intuitive forms of intelligence. Michael Brown (Nobel Prize for Chemistry, 1985), for example, says:

> And so, as we did our work, we almost felt at time that there was a hand guiding us. Because we would go from one step to the next, and somehow we would know which was the right way to go. And I can't really tell you how we knew that.

Intuition seems also to offer a vital way of evaluating leading-edge results, where no explicit criteria yet exist. Stanley Cohen (Nobel Prize for Medicine, 1986) says:

> To me it is a feeling of 'Well, I don't really believe this result', or 'This is a trivial result', or 'This is an important result' ... I am not always right, but I do have feelings about what is an important observation, and what is probably trivial.

In a classic description of incubation, Rita Levi-Montalcini (Nobel Prize for Medicine, 1986) says:

> You've been thinking about something without willing to for a long time ... Then, all of a sudden, the problem is opened to you in a flash, and you suddenly see the answer.

While Konrad Lorenz (Nobel Prize for Medicine, 1973) emphasizes both the reliance of intelligence on a large database of experience, and the need for a relaxed and gentle attitude towards problem-solving:

> This apparatus which intuits has to have an enormous basis of known facts at its disposal with which to play. And it plays in a very mysterious manner, because ... it sort of keeps all known facts afloat, waiting for them to fall into place, like a jigsaw puzzle. And if you press ... if you try to permutate your knowledge, nothing comes of it. You must give a sort of mysterious pressure, and then rest, and suddenly BING!, the solution comes.

So rehabilitating the less 'clever' ways of knowing seems to be largely a matter of regaining balance: the balance between effort and playfulness, which Lorenz has just described, and the balance between intuition itself and reason. Mathematician Henri Poincaré summed it up by saying 'It is through logic we prove; it is through intuition we discover.' It is as though the well-tempered mind has available to it a number of modes that needed to work in concert, each taking the lead in turn; or as if creativity demanded a cycle of cognitive 'seasons', some of them involving busily planting, harvesting or threshing, and others, the fallow 'winter months', requiring patience, and a tolerance for seeming inactivity, which is, despite appearances, necessary and productive. The classic model of creativity (Wallas, 1926) in fact divides it into four stages: *preparation,* in which data is gathered, reason is applied, and eventually an impasse reached; *incubation,* in which the problem is not consciously worked at or attended to; *illumination,* in which an intuitive solution emerges into consciousness; and *verification,* in which purposeful analysis is applied to check the intuition out, and find ways to communicate it.

Interestingly, this balance is also acknowledged by artists. Henry Moore wrote:

> It is a mistake for a sculptor or a painter to speak or write very often about his job. It releases tension needed for his work. By trying to express his aims with rounded-off logical exactness, he can easily become a theorist whose actual work is only a caged-in exposition of concepts evolved in terms of logic and words. But though the non-logical, instinctive, subconscious part of the mind must play its part in his work, he also has a conscious mind which is not inactive. The artist works with a concentration of his whole personality, and the conscious part of it resolves conflicts, organises memories, and prevents him from trying to walk in two directions at the same time. (Ghiselin, 1952)

American poet Amy Lowell quite deliberately used 'incubation', describing how she would 'drop my subject into the subconscious, much as one drops a letter into a mailbox' and leave it undisturbed for a while. But she also acknowledged that intuition was 'a most temperamental ally':

> Often he will strike work at some critical point, and not another word is to be got out of him. Here is where the conscious training of the poet comes in, for

he must fill in what the subconscious has left … he must have knowledge and talent enough to 'putty' up his holes. (Ghiselin, 1952)

Recognition of the intricate ways in which intuition and intellect, reason and reflection, experience and explanation, balance and complement each other challenges theorists of professional development to come up with a rather more sophisticated model of adult professional learning than we have at present.

Smart and Stupid Organizations

A smart organization is one which understands the multifaceted nature of intelligence, which is hospitable to all those facets, and which is genuinely, cumulatively interested in discovering when and how each of those facets works best. A stupid organization is one which is deaf to new information about how to be smart, and which maintains a rigid adherence to rationalistic, spread-sheet thinking in all situations. There is a neurological condition called 'neglect' in which people come to 'disown' perfectly functional parts of their body: they see one of their own legs as 'alien', and keep trying to throw it out of bed, for example. Though they have two good legs, the belief makes them lame – not just hypothetically, but really. The belief that clear, fast, conscious, analytical thinking is the only form of intelligence worth using – when it is installed not just in individual minds but in a workplace culture – makes people collectively stupid, not just hypothetically but really.

Cleverness is often loud and self-confident, and in a culture of cleverness, other forms of smart can find it hard to be heard, and may slide underground, to the detriment of intelligent functioning as a whole. Non-clever intelligence needs both situational and psychological conditions to support it. The outer, contextual conditions include a conducive physical environment. Though stillness and solitariness are often quoted as being conducive to creativity, for example, such conditions are personal and idiosyncratic – some people have to smoke, or pace about, or look out (as Sartre did) onto an urban roof-scape. A smart culture encourages people to find out what their optimal environment is, and to develop the disposition to seek and create these conditions. In a smart culture, the pressures for accountability are balanced, to quote Westcott (1968), by factors that 'encourage looseness of reaction, speculation, non-analytic functioning and random association'.

Such an environment, of course, is one that is convivial, playful, co-operative and non-judgemental, as well as being purposeful and professional. Prince (1975), in a review of the conditions of creativity, concludes: 'Any reaction that results in the offerer of an idea feeling defensive will tend to reduce not only his speculation but that of others in the group … The victim of the win-lose or competitive posture is always speculation, and therefore idea production and problem-solving. When one speculates he becomes vulnerable. It is too easy to make him look like a loser.' Indeed, pressure and stress of any kind, whether competitive or not, are anathema to intuition, as they tend to focus perception and cognition on a predetermined range of strategies and information – those that are 'obvious' or 'normal' – and thus to remove the breadth and open-mindedness of vision which may be required to uncover a false assumption or a creative analogy (Easterbrook, 1959). (People in the business world are fond of quoting the old proverb: 'When you are up to your arse in alligators, it's hard to think about draining the swamp.')

Intuition also requires a conducive inner, psychological environment, one that is characterised by certain dispositions and tolerances. The foremost of these is what the poet John Keats referred to as 'negative capability', which he described as 'when a man is capable of being in uncertainties, mysteries and doubts without any irritable reaching after fact and reason'. If intuition may emerge as knowledge without comprehension, one must be able to tolerate that lack of mental clarity. If intuition takes time to develop, one must be prepared to wait – to resist the desire to end the discomfort of gestation by forcibly inducing the birth of understanding. In a classic study of creativity in artists, Getzels and Csikszentmihalyi (1976) found that the best still-life pictures were produced by those painters who played more slowly and creatively with the different elements of the composition, and who delayed foreclosing on their idea of what the painting was going to be, even until they were already part of the way through painting it.

The importance of 'daring to wait' can hardly be overstated (Claxton, 1997). As we have already seen, adults who are willing to enter a state of confusion learn a complex skill faster than those who insist on seeking theories and explanations; and insight problems are solved better by those who can think slowly. Finally, we might note the value of cultivating the skill of 'catching the inner gleam' which was mentioned earlier; and of developing the disposition to look for the unspoken assumptions – especially one's own – that may be dissolved in the very way in which a problematic situation seems to present itself.

Conclusion

Intelligence refers to a loose-knit clan of 'ways of knowing', some of which are less articulate and explicit than normal reasoning and discourse. This sub-family has tended to be ignored, marginalized, romanticized or denigrated in mainstream managerial cultures, partly because of its historical association with claims for its validity that seem grandiose or mystical; and partly because we have, until recently, lacked a cognitive psychology which makes scientific sense of its nature and its value. The members of this family include the ability to function fluently and flexibly in complex domains without being able to describe or theorize one's expertise; to extract intricate patterns of information that are embedded in a range of seemingly disparate experiences; to make subtle and accurate judgements based on experience without accompanying justification; to detect and extract the significance of small, incidental details of a situation that others may overlook; to take time to mull over problems in order to arrive at more insightful or creative solutions; and to apply this perceptive, ruminative, inquisitive attitude to one's own perceptions and reactions – 'reflection'.

Smart cognition manifests in a variety of different ways: as emotions; as physical sensations; as impulses or attractions towards certain goals or courses of action; as images and fantasies; as faint hunches and inklings; and as aesthetic responses to situations. Some intuitions are holistic interpretations of situations based on analogies drawn from a largely unconscious experiential database. They integrate (in an image or an impulse) a great deal of information, but may also incorporate assumptions or beliefs that may be invalid or inappropriate. Thus intuitions are instructive but fallible hypotheses which are valuable when taken as such. The intuitive mental modes are not subversive of or antagonistic to more explicit, verbal, conscious ways of knowing; they complement and interact productively with them. People vary in their facility with intuition, and in their ability to create both the inner and outer conditions which are conducive to intuition. These skills, dispositions and tolerances are acquired through both informal life experience, and in the course of formal education. Professional education and training thus have the opportunity, both through explicit instruction and modelling, and through the epistemological culture which they embody either to enable people to harness and develop their intuition, or to neglect it, and so allow it to atrophy.

Note

The solution: Call the steaks A, B and C and the two sides of each 1 and 2. Cook A1 and B1. Then cook A2 and C1. Finally cook B2 and C2. Total 9 minutes. If you do A1 + B1; A2 + B2; C1; C2, it takes 12 minutes.

References

Bechara, A., Damasio, H., Tranel, D. and Damasio, A.R. (1997) Deciding advantageously before knowing the advantageous strategy. *Science*, *275*, 1293–5.

Berry, D.C. and Dienes, Z. (1993) *Implicit Learning: Theoretical and Empirical Issues*. Hove, Sussex: Lawrence Erlbaum.

Bowers, K.S., Regehr, G., Balthazard, C. and Parker, K. (1990) Intuition in the context of discovery. *Cognitive Psychology*, *22*, 72–110.

Bruner, J.S. and Clinchy, B. (1972) Toward a disciplined intuition. In J.S. Bruner, *The Relevance of Education*. London: George Allen and Unwin.

Claxton, G.L. (1997) *Hare Brain, Tortoise Mind: Why Intelligence Increases When You Think Less*. London: Fourth Estate; San Francisco: HarperCollins.

Coulson, M. (1996) 'The cognitive function of confusion', paper presented to the British Psychological Society Conference, London, December.

Csikszentmihalyi, M. (1990) *Flow: The Psychology of Optimal Experience*. New York: Harper & Row.

Csikszentmihalyi, M. and Sawyer, K. (1996) Creative insight: the social dimension of a solitary moment. In R.J. Sternberg and J.E. Davidson (Eds), *The Nature of Insight*. Cambridge, MA: Bradford/MIT Press.

Damasio, A.R. (1994) *Descartes' Error: Emotion, Reason and the Human Brain*. New York: Putnam.

Davidson, J.E. (1995) The suddenness of insight. In R.J. Sternberg and J.E. Davidson (Eds), *The Nature of Insight*. Cambridge, MA: Bradford/MIT Press.

Dijksterhuis, A. (2003) Think different: the merits of unconscious thought in preference development and decision making, *Journal of Personality and Social Psychology*, 2003.

Dreyfus, H.L. and Dreyfus, S.E. (1986) *Mind over Machine: The Power of Human Intuition and Expertise in the Era of the Computer*. Oxford: Blackwell.

Easterbrook, J.A. (1959) The effect of emotion on cue utilization and the organization of behavior, *Psychological Review*, *66*, 183–201.

Fensham, P.J. and Marton, F. (1992) What has happened to intuition in science education? *Research in Science Education*, *22*, 114–22.

Fitzgerald, F. Scott (1934) *Tender is the Night*. New York: Scribner.

Getzels, J.W. and Csikszentmihalyi, M. (1976) *The Creative Vision: A Longitudinal Study of Problem-Finding*. New York: Wiley.

Ghiselin, B. (1952) *The Creative Process*. Berkeley, CA: University of California Press.

Hughes, T. (1967) *Poetry in the Making*. London: Faber and Faber.

Lewicki, P., Hill. T. and Czyzewska, M. (1992) Nonconscious acquisition of information. *American Psychologist*, *47*, 796–801.

Mangan, B. (1993) Taking phenomenology seriously: the 'fringe' and its implications for cognitive research, *Consciousness and Cognition*, *2*, 89–108.

Metcalfe, J. and Wiebe, D. (1987) Intuition in insight and noninsight problem solving. *Memory and Cognition*, *15*, 238–46.

Pierce, C.S. and Jastrow, J. (1884) On small differences in sensation. *Memoirs of the National Academy of Science*, *3*, 75–83.

Polanyi, M. (1958) *Personal Knowledge*. London: Routledge and Kegan Paul.

Prince, G.M. (1975) Creativity, self and power. In I.A. Taylor and J.W. Getzels (Eds), *Perspectives in Creativity*. Chicago: Aldine.

Rowan, R. (1986) *The Intuitive Manager*. Boston: Little, Brown.

Schooler, J., Ohlsson, S. and Brooks, K. (1993) Thought beyond words: when language overshadows insight. *Journal of Experimental Psychology: General*, *122*, 166–83.

Smith, S.M. (1995) Fixation, incubation and insight in memory and creative thinking. In S.M. Smith and T.B. Ward and R.A. Finke (Eds), *The Creative Cognition Approach*. Cambridge, MA: Bradford/MIT Press, 135–56.

Snodgrass, M., Shevrin, H. and Kopka, M. (1993) The mediation of intentional judgments by unconscious perceptions: the influence of task strategy, task preference, word meaning and motivation. *Consciousness and Cognition*, *2*, 169–93.

Wallas, G. (1926) *The Art of Thought*. New York: Harcourt Brace.

Westcott, M.R. (1968) *Toward a Contemporary Psychology of Intuition*. New York: Holt, Rinehart and Winston.

Wilson, T.D. and Schooler, J. (1991) Thinking too much: introspection can reduce the quality of preferences and decisions. *Journal of Personality and Social Psychology*, *60*, 181–92.

Organizational Knowledge Creation

Ikujiro Nonaka and Hirotaka Takeuchi

The distinctive approach of Western philosophy to knowledge has profoundly shaped the way organizational theorists treat knowledge. The Cartesian split between subject and object, the knower and the known, has given birth to a view of the organization as a mechanism for 'information processing'. According to this view, an organization processes information from the external environment in order to adapt to new circumstances. Although this view has proven to be effective in explaining how organizations function, it has a fundamental limitation. When organizations innovate, they do not simply process information, from the outside in, in order to solve existing problems and adapt to a changing environment. They actually create new knowledge and information, from the inside out, in order to redefine both problems and solutions and, in the process, to re-create their environment.

To explain innovation, we need a new theory of organizational knowledge creation. Like any approach to knowledge, it will have its own 'epistemology' (the theory of knowledge), although one substantially different from the traditional Western approach. The cornerstone of our epistemology is the distinction between tacit and explicit knowledge. The key to knowledge creation lies in the mobilization and conversion of tacit knowledge. And because we are concerned with organizational knowledge creation, as opposed to individual knowledge creation, our theory will also have its own distinctive 'ontology', which is concerned with the levels of knowledge-creating entities (individual, group, organizational and inter-organizational). Figure 5.1 presents the epistemological and ontological dimensions in which a knowledge-creation 'spiral' takes place.

We present the four modes of knowledge conversion that are created when tacit and explicit knowledge interact with each other. These four modes – which we refer to as socialization, externalization, combination and internalization – constitute the

Source: I. Nonaka and H. Takeuchi (1995) Edited extract from *The Knowledge Creating Company*. Oxford: Oxford University Press.

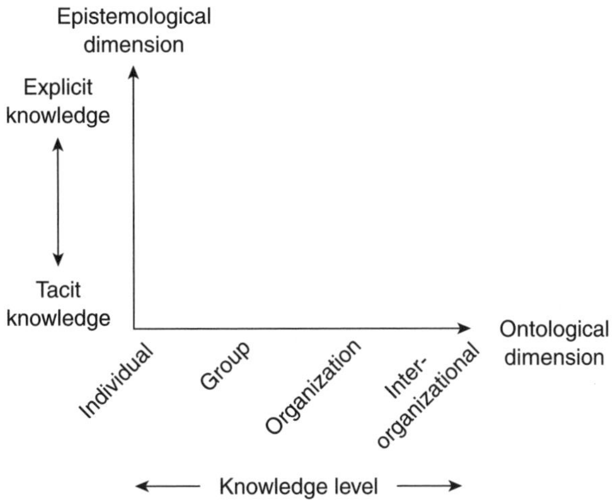

Figure 5.1 *Two dimensions of knowledge creation*

'engine' of the entire knowledge-creation process. These modes are what the individual experiences. They are also the mechanisms by which individual knowledge gets articulated and 'amplified' into and throughout the organization.

Knowledge and Information

Knowledge is similar to and different from information. First, knowledge, unlike information, is about *beliefs* and *commitment*. Knowledge is a function of a particular stance, perspective, or intention. Second, knowledge, unlike information, is about *action*. It is always knowledge 'to some end'. And third, knowledge, like information, is about *meaning*. It is context-specific and relational.

While traditional epistemology emphasizes the absolute, static and non-human nature of knowledge, typically expressed in propositions and formal logic, we consider knowledge as *a dynamic human process of justifying personal belief toward the 'truth'*.

Information is a flow of messages, while knowledge is created by that very flow of information, anchored in the beliefs and commitment of its holder. This understanding emphasizes that *knowledge is essentially related to human action*. We focus attention on the active, subjective nature of knowledge represented by such terms as 'commitment' and 'belief' that are deeply rooted in individuals' value systems.

Finally, both information and knowledge are context-specific and relational in that they depend on the situation and are created dynamically in social interaction among people. Berger and Luckmann (1966) argue that people interacting in a certain historical and social context share information from which they construct social knowledge as a reality, which in turn influences their judgment, behavior and attitude. Similarly, a corporate vision presented as an equivocal strategy by a leader is organizationally constructed into knowledge through interaction with the environment by the corporation's members, which in turn affects its business behavior.

Two Dimensions of Knowledge Creation

Although much has been written about the importance of knowledge in management, little attention has been paid to how knowledge is created and how the knowledge-creation process is managed. In a strict sense, knowledge is created only by individuals. An organization cannot create knowledge without individuals. The organization supports creative individuals or provides contexts for them to create knowledge. Organizational knowledge creation, therefore, should be understood as a process that 'organizationally' amplifies the knowledge created by individuals and crystallizes it as a part of the knowledge network of the organization. This process takes place within an expanding 'community of interaction', which crosses intra- and inter-organizational levels and boundaries.[1]

As for the epistemological dimension, we draw on Michael Polanyi's (1966) distinction between *tacit knowledge* and *explicit knowledge*. Tacit knowledge is personal, context-specific, and therefore hard to formalize and communicate. Explicit or 'codified' knowledge, on the other hand, refers to knowledge that is transmittable in formal, systematic language. Polanyi contends that human beings acquire knowledge by actively creating and organizing their own experiences. Thus, knowledge that can be expressed in words and numbers represents only the tip of the iceberg of the entire body of knowledge. As Polanyi (1966) puts it, 'We can know more than we can tell' (p. 4).[2]

In traditional epistemology, knowledge derives from the separation of the subject and the object of perception; human beings as the subject of perception acquire knowledge by analyzing external objects. In contrast, Polanyi contends that human beings create knowledge by involving themselves with objects, that is, through self-involvement and commitment, or what Polanyi called 'indwelling'. To know something is to create its image or pattern by tacitly integrating particulars. In order to understand the pattern as a meaningful whole, it is necessary to integrate one's body with the particulars. Thus indwelling breaks the traditional dichotomies between mind and body, reason and emotion, subject and object, and knower and known. Therefore, scientific objectivity is not a sole source of knowledge. Much of our knowledge is the fruit of our own purposeful endeavors in dealing with the world.[3]

Tacit knowledge includes cognitive and technical elements. The cognitive elements center on what Johnson-Laird (1983) calls 'mental models', in which human beings create working models of the world by making and manipulating analogies in their minds. Mental models, such as schemata, paradigms, perspectives, beliefs, and viewpoints, help individuals to perceive and define their world. On the other hand, the technical element of tacit knowledge includes concrete know-how, crafts, and skills. It is important to note here that the cognitive elements of tacit knowledge refer to an individual's images of reality and visions for the future, that is, 'what is' and 'what ought to be'. The articulation of tacit mental models, in a kind of 'mobilization' process, is a key factor in creating new knowledge.

Some distinctions between tacit and explicit knowledge are shown in Table 5.1. Features generally associated with the more tacit aspects of knowledge are listed on the left, while the corresponding qualities related to explicit knowledge are shown on the

Table 5.1   *Two types of knowledge*

Tacit Knowledge (subjective)	Explicit Knowledge (objective)
Knowledge of experience (body)	Knowledge of rationality (mind)
Simultaneous knowledge (here & now)	Sequential knowledge (there & then)
Analog knowledge (practice)	Digital knowledge (theory)

right. For example, knowledge of experience tends to be tacit, physical, and subjective, while knowledge of rationality tends to be explicit, metaphysical, and objective. Tacit knowledge is created 'here and now' in a specific, practical context and entails what Bateson (1973) referred to as 'analog' quality. Sharing tacit knowledge between individuals through communication is an analog process that requires a kind of 'simultaneous processing' of the complexities of issues shared by the individuals. On the other hand, explicit knowledge is about past events or objects 'there and then' and is oriented toward a context-free theory.[4]

Knowledge Conversion: Interaction Between Tacit and Explicit Knowledge

The history of Western epistemology can be seen as a continuous controversy about which type of knowledge is more truthful. While Westerners tend to emphasize explicit knowledge, the Japanese tend to stress tacit knowledge. However, tacit knowledge and explicit knowledge are not totally separate but mutually complementary entities. They interact with and interchange into each other in the creative activities of human beings. Our dynamic model of knowledge creation is anchored to a critical assumption that human knowledge is created and expanded through social interaction between tacit knowledge and explicit knowledge. We call this interaction 'knowledge conversion'. It should be noted that this conversion is a 'social' process *between* individuals and not confined *within* an individual.[5] According to the rationalist view, human cognition is a deductive process of individuals, but an individual is never isolated from social interaction when he or she perceives things. Thus, through this 'social conversion' process, tacit and explicit knowledge expand in terms of both quality and quantity (Nonaka, 1990).

The idea of 'knowledge conversion' may be partially consonant with [certain models] in cognitive psychology. The hypothesis that for cognitive skills to develop, all declarative knowledge, which corresponds to explicit knowledge in our theory, has to be transformed into procedural knowledge, which corresponds to tacit knowledge, used in such activities as riding a bicycle or playing the piano.[6] Proponents of this model consider knowledge transformation as mainly unidirectional from declarative (explicit) to procedural (tacit), whereas we argue that the transformation is interactive and spiral.

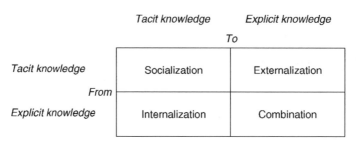

Figure 5.2   *Four modes of knowledge conversion*

Four Modes of Knowledge Conversion

The assumption that knowledge is created through the interaction between tacit and explicit knowledge allows us to postulate four different modes of knowledge conversion. They are as follows: (1) from tacit knowledge to tacit knowledge, which we call socialization; (2) from tacit knowledge to explicit knowledge, or externalization; (3) from explicit knowledge to explicit knowledge, or combination; and (4) from explicit knowledge to tacit knowledge, or internalization.[7] Three of the four types of knowledge conversion – socialization, combination, and internalization – have been discussed from various perspectives in organizational theory. For example, socialization is connected with the theories of group processes and organizational culture; combination has its roots in information processing; and internalization is closely related to organizational learning. However, externalization has been somewhat neglected.[8] Figure 5.2 shows the four modes of knowledge conversion. Each of these four modes of knowledge conversion will be discussed in detail below, along with actual examples.

Socialization: From Tacit to Tacit

Socialization is a process of sharing experiences and thereby creating tacit knowledge such as shared mental models and technical skills.[9] An individual can acquire tacit knowledge directly from others without using language. Apprentices work with their masters and learn craftsmanship not through language but through observation, imitation and practice. In the business setting, on-the-job training uses basically the same principle. The key to acquiring tacit knowledge is experience. Without some form of shared experience, it is extremely difficult for one person to project her- or himself into another individual's thinking process. The mere transfer of information will often make little sense, if it is abstracted from associated emotions and specific contexts in which shared experiences are embedded. The following three examples illustrate how socialization is employed by Japanese companies within the product development context.

The first example of socialization comes from Honda, which set up 'brainstorming camps' (*tama dashi kai*) – informal meetings for detailed discussions to solve difficult problems in development projects. This kind of brainstorming camp is not unique to Honda but has been used by many other Japanese firms. It is also not unique to developing new products and services but is also used to develop managerial systems or corporate strategies. Such a camp is not only a forum for creative dialogue but also a medium for sharing experience and enhancing mutual trust among participants.[10] It is particularly effective in sharing tacit knowledge and creating a new perspective. It reorients the mental models of all individuals in the same direction, but not in a forceful way. Instead, brainstorming camps represent a mechanism through which individuals search for harmony.

The second example, which shows how a tacit technical skill was socialized, comes from the Matsushita Electric Industrial Company. A major problem at the Osaka-based company in developing an automatic home bread-making machine in the late 1980s centered on how to mechanize the dough-kneading process, which is essentially tacit knowledge possessed by master bakers. Dough kneaded by a master baker and by a machine were x-rayed and compared, but no meaningful insights were obtained. Ikuko Tanaka, head of software development, knew that the area's best bread came from the Osaka International Hotel. To capture the tacit knowledge of kneading skill, she and several engineers volunteered to apprentice themselves to the hotel's head baker. Making the same delicious bread as the head baker's was not easy. No one could explain why. One day, however, she noticed that the baker was not only stretching but also 'twisting' the dough, which turned out to be the secret for making tasty bread. Thus she socialized the head baker's tacit knowledge through observation, imitation, and practice.

Socialization also occurs between product developers and customers. Interactions with customers before product development and after market introduction are, in fact, a never-ending process of sharing tacit knowledge and creating ideas for improvement. The way NEC developed its first personal computer is a case in point. The new-product development process began when a group from the Semiconductor and IC Sales Division conceived of an idea to sell Japan's first microcomputer kit, the TK-80, to promote the sales of semiconductor devices. Selling the TK-80 to the public at large was a radical departure from NEC's history of responding to routine orders from Nippon Telegraph and Telephone (NTT). Unexpectedly, a wide variety of customers, ranging from high school students to professional computer enthusiasts, came to NEC's BIT-INN, a display service center in Akihabara district of Tokyo, which is famous for its high concentration of electronic goods retailers. Sharing experiences and continuing dialogues with these customers at the BIT-INN resulted in the development of NEC's best-selling personal computer, the PC-8000, a few years later.

Externalization: From Tacit to Explicit

Externalization is a process of articulating tacit knowledge into explicit concepts. It is a quintessential knowledge-creation process in that tacit knowledge becomes explicit, taking the shapes of metaphors, analogies, concepts, hypotheses, or models. When we attempt to conceptualize an image, we express its essence mostly in language – writing is an act of converting tacit knowledge into articulable knowledge (Emig, 1983). Yet expressions are often inadequate, inconsistent, and insufficient. Such discrepancies and gaps between images and expressions, however, help promote 'reflection' and interaction between individuals.

The externalization mode of knowledge conversion is typically seen in the process of concept creation and is triggered by dialogue or collective reflection.[11] A frequently used method to create a concept is to combine deduction and induction. Mazda, for example, combined these two reasoning methods when it developed the new RX-7 concept, which is described as 'an authentic sports car that provides an exciting and comfortable drive.' The concept was *deduced* from the car maker's corporate slogan: 'create new values and present joyful driving pleasures' as well as the positioning of the new car as 'a strategic car for the US market and an image of innovation.' At the same time, the new concept was *induced* from 'concept' trips, which were driving experiences by development team members in the United States as well as from 'concept clinics', which gathered opinions from customers and car experts. When we cannot find an adequate expression for an image through analytical methods of deduction or induction, we have to use a non-analytical method. Externalization is, therefore, often driven by metaphor and/or analogy. Using an attractive metaphor and/or analogy is highly effective in fostering direct commitment to the creative process. Recall the Honda City example. In developing the car, Hiroo Watanabe and his team used a metaphor of 'Automobile Evolution'. His team viewed the automobile as an organism and sought its ultimate form. In essence, Watanabe was asking, 'What will the automobile eventually evolve into?'

I insisted on allocating the minimum space for mechanics and the maximum space for passengers. This seemed to be the ideal car, into which the automobile should evolve ... The first step toward this goal was to challenge the 'reasoning of Detroit', which had sacrificed comfort for appearance. Our choice was a short but tall car ... spherical, therefore lighter, less expensive, more comfortable, and solid.[12]

The concept of a tall and short car – 'Tall Boy' – emerged through an analogy between the concept of 'man-maximum, machine-minimum' and an image of a sphere that contains the maximum volume within the minimum area of surface, which ultimately resulted in the Honda City.

The case of Canon's Mini-Copier is a good example of how an analogy was used effectively for product development. One of the most difficult problems faced by the development team was producing at low cost a disposable cartridge, which would eliminate the necessity for maintenance required in conventional machines. Without a disposable cartridge, maintenance staff would have to be stationed all over the country, since the copier was intended for family or personal use. If the usage frequency were high, maintenance costs could be negligible. But that was not the case with a personal copier. The fact that a large number of customers would be using the machine only occasionally meant that the new product had to have high reliability and no or minimum maintenance. A maintenance study showed that more than 90 percent of the problems came from the drum or its surrounding parts. Aimed at cutting maintenance costs while maintaining the highest reliability, the team developed the concept of a disposable cartridge system in which the drum or the heart of the copier is replaced after a certain amount of usage.

The next problem was whether the drum could be produced at a cost low enough to be consistent with the targeted low selling price of the copier. A task force assigned

Table 5.2   *Metaphor and/or analogy for concept creation in product development*

Product (Company)	Metaphor/Analogy	Influence on Concept Creation
City (Honda)	'Automobile Evolution' (metaphor)	Hint of maximizing passenger space as ultimate auto development 'Man-maximum, machine minimum' concept created
	The sphere (analogy)	Hint of achieving maximum passenger space through minimizing surface area 'Tall and short car (Tall Boy)' concept created
Mini-Copier (Canon)	Aluminum beer can (analogy)	Hint of similarities between inexpensive aluminum beer can and photosensitive drum manufacture 'Low-cost manufacturing process' concept created
Home Bakery (Matsushita)	Hotel bread (metaphor)	Hint of more delicious bread
	Osaka International Hotel head baker (analogy)	'Twist dough' concept created.

to solve this cost problem had many heated discussions about the production of conventional photosensitive drum cylinders with a base material of aluminum-drawn tube at a low cost. One day Hiroshi Tanaka, leader of the task force, sent out for some cans of beer. Once the beer was consumed, he asked, 'How much does it cost to manufacture this can?' The team then explored the possibility of applying the process of manufacturing the beer can to manufacturing the drum cylinder, using the same material. By clarifying similarities and differences, they discovered a process technology to manufacture the aluminum drum at a low cost, thus giving rise to the disposable drum.

These examples within Japanese firms clearly show the effectiveness of the use of metaphor and analogy in creating and elaborating a concept (see Table 5.2). As Honda's Watanabe commented, 'We are more than halfway there, once a product concept has been created.' In this sense, the leaders' wealth of figurative language and imagination is an essential factor in eliciting tacit knowledge from project members.

Among the four modes of knowledge conversion, externalization holds the key to knowledge creation, because it creates new, explicit concepts from tacit knowledge. How can we convert tacit knowledge into explicit knowledge effectively and efficiently? The answer lies in a sequential use of metaphor, analogy and mode. As Nisbet (1969) noted, 'much of what Michael Polanyi has called "tacit knowledge" is expressible – in so far as it is expressible at all – in metaphor' (p. 5). Metaphor is a way of perceiving or intuitively understanding one thing by imaging another thing symbolically. It is most often used in abductive reasoning or non-analytical methods for creating radical concepts (Bateson, 1973). It is neither analysis nor synthesis of common attributes of associated things. Donnellon et al. (1986) argue that 'metaphors create novel inter-pretation of experience by asking the listener to see one thing in terms of something else' and 'create new ways of experiencing reality' (pp. 48, 52). Thus, 'metaphors are one communication mechanism that can function to reconcile discrepancies in mean-ing' (p. 48).[13]

Moreover, metaphor is an important tool for creating a *network* of new concepts. Because a metaphor is 'two thoughts of different things ... supported by a single word, or phrase, whose meaning is a resultant of their interaction' (Richards, 1936, p. 93), we can continuously relate concepts that are far apart in our mind, even relate abstract concepts to concrete ones. This creative, cognitive process continues as we think of the similarities among concepts and feel an imbalance, inconsistency, or contradiction in their associations, thus often leading to the discovery of new meaning or even to the formation of a new paradigm.

Contradictions inherent in a metaphor are then harmonized by analogy, which reduces the unknown by highlighting the 'commonness' of two different things. Metaphor and analogy are often confused. Association of two things through metaphor is driven mostly by intuition and holistic imagery and does not aim to find differences between them. On the other hand, association through analogy is carried out by ratio-nal thinking and focuses on structural/functional similarities between two things, and hence their differences. Thus analogy helps us understand the unknown through the known and bridges the gap between an image and a logical model.[14]

Once explicit concepts are created, they can then be modeled. In a logical model, no contradictions should exist and all concepts and propositions must be expressed in systematic language and coherent logic. But in business terms, models are often only rough descriptions or drawings, far from being fully specific. Models are usually gen-erated from metaphors when new concepts are created in the business context.[15]

Combination: From Explicit to Explicit

Combination is a process of systemizing concepts into a knowledge system. This mode of knowledge conversion involves combining different bodies of explicit knowledge. Individuals exchange and combine knowledge through such media as documents, meetings, telephone conversations, or computerized communication networks. Reconfiguration of existing information through sorting, adding, combining and cate-gorizing of explicit knowledge (as conducted in computer databases) can lead to new knowledge. Knowledge creation carried out in formal education and training at schools usually takes this form. An MBA education is one of the best examples of this kind.

In the business context, the combination mode of knowledge conversion is most often seen when middle managers break down and operationalize corporate visions, business concepts, or product concepts. Middle management plays a critical role in creating new concepts through networking of codified information and knowledge. Creative uses of computerized communication networks and large-scale databases facilitate this mode of knowledge conversion.[16]

At Kraft General Foods, a manufacturer of dairy and processed foods, data from the POS (point-of-sales) system of retailers is utilized not only to find out what does and does not sell well but also to create new 'ways to sell', that is, new sales systems and methods. Kraft successfully manages its product sales through supermarkets by controlling four elements of the 'category management' methodology – consumer and category dynamics, space management, merchandizing management, and pricing management.[17]

At the top management level of an organization, the combination mode is realized when mid-range concepts (such as product concepts) are combined with and integrated into grand concepts (such as a corporate vision) to generate a new meaning of the latter. Introducing a new corporate image in 1986, for example, Asahi Breweries adopted a grand concept dubbed 'live Asahi for live people'. The concept stood for the message that 'Asahi will provide natural and authentic products and services for those who seek active minds and active lives.' Along with this grand concept, Asahi inquired into the essence of what makes beer appealing, and developed Asahi Super Dry beer based on the new-product concept of 'richness and sharpness'. The new-product concept is a mid-range concept that made the grand concept of Asahi more explicitly recognizable, which in turn altered the company's product development system. The taste of beer was hitherto decided by engineers in the production department without any participation by the sales department. The 'richness and sharpness' concept was realized through co-operative product development by both departments.

Other examples of interaction between grand concepts and mid-range concepts abound. For example, NEC's 'C&C' (computers and communication) concept induced the development of the epoch-making PC-8000 personal computer, which was based on the mid-range concept of 'distributed processing'. Canon's corporate policy, 'Creationof an excellent company by transcending the camera business' led to the development of the Mini-Copier, which was developed with the mid-range product concept of 'easy maintenance'. Mazda's grand vision, 'Create new values and present joyful driving', was realized in the new RX-7, 'an authentic sports car that provides an exciting and comfortable drive'.

Internalization: From Explicit to Tacit

Internalization is a process of embodying explicit knowledge into tacit knowledge. It is closely related to 'learning by doing'. When experiences through socialization, externalization, and combination are internalized into individuals' tacit knowledge bases in the form of shared mental models or technical know-how, they become valuable assets. All the members of the Honda City project team, for example, internalized their experiences of the late 1970s and are now making use of that know-how and leading R&D projects in the company. For organizational knowledge creation to take place, however, the tacit knowledge accumulated at the individual level needs to be socialized with other organizational members, thereby starting a new spiral of knowledge creation.

For explicit knowledge to become tacit, it helps if the knowledge is verbalized or diagrammed into documents, manuals, or oral stories. Documentation helps individuals internalize what they experienced, thus enriching their tacit knowledge. In addition, documents or manuals facilitate the transfer of explicit knowledge to other people, thereby helping them experience the experiences of others indirectly (i.e. 're-experiencing' them). GE, for example, documents all customer complaints and inquiries in a database at its Answer Center in Louisville, Kentucky, which can be used, for example, by members of a new-product development team to 're-experience' what the telephone operators experienced. GE established the Answer Center in 1982 to process questions, requests for help and complaints from customers on any product 24 hours a day, 365 days a year. Over 200 telephone operators respond to as many as 14,000 calls a day. GE has programmed 1.5 million potential problems and their solutions into its computerized database system. The system is equipped with an on-line diagnosis function utilizing the latest artificial intelligence technology for quick answers to inquiries; any problem-solution response can be retrieved by the telephone operator in two seconds. In case a solution is not available, 12 specialists with at least four years of repair experience think out solutions on site. Four full-time programmers put the solutions into the database, so that the new information is usually installed into the system by the following day. This information is sent to the respective product divisions every month. Yet, the product divisions also frequently send their new-product development people to the Answer Center to chat with the telephone operators or the 12 specialists, thereby 're-experiencing' their experiences.

Internalization can also occur even without having actually to 're-experience' other people's experiences. For example, if reading or listening to a success story makes some members of the organization feel the realism and essence of the story, the experience that took place in the past may change into a tacit mental model. When such a mental model is shared by most members of the organization, tacit knowledge becomes part of the organizational culture. This practice is prevalent in Japan, where books and articles on companies or their leaders abound. Freelance writers or former employees publish them, sometimes at the request of the companies. One can find about two dozen books on Honda or Soichiro Honda in major bookstores today, all of which help instil a strong corporate culture for Honda.

An example of internalization through 'learning by doing' can be seen at Matsushita when it launched a companywide policy in 1993 to reduce yearly working time to 1,800 hours. Called MIT'93 for 'Mind and Management Innovation Toward 1993', the policy's objective was not to reduce costs but to innovate the mindset and management by reducing working hours and increasing individual creativity. Many departments were puzzled about how to implement the policy, which was clearly communicated as explicit knowledge. The MIT'93 promotion office advised each department to experiment with the policy for one month by working 150 hours. Through such a bodily experience, employees got to know what working 1,800 hours a year would be like. An explicit concept reducing working time to 1,800 hours, was internalized through the one-month experience.

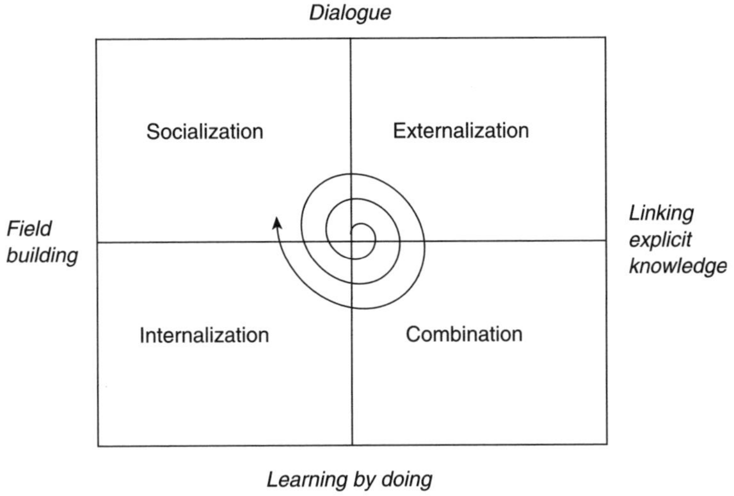

Dialogue

Figure 5.3   *Knowledge spiral*

Contents of Knowledge and the Knowledge Spiral

Organizational knowledge creation is a continuous and dynamic interaction between tacit and explicit knowledge. This interaction is shaped by shifts between different modes of knowledge conversion, which are in turn induced by several triggers (see Figure 5.3).

First, the socialization mode usually starts with building a 'field' of interaction. This field facilitates the sharing of members' experiences and mental models. Second, the externalization mode is triggered by meaningful 'dialogue or collective reflection', in which using appropriate metaphor or analogy helps team members to articulate hidden tacit knowledge that is otherwise hard to communicate. Third, the combination mode is triggered by 'networking' newly created knowledge and existing knowledge from other sections of the organization, thereby crystallizing them into a new product, service, or managerial system. Finally, 'learning by doing' triggers internalization.

The content of the knowledge created by each mode of knowledge conversion is naturally different (see Figure 5.4). Socialization yields what can be called 'sympathized knowledge', such as shared mental models and technical skills. The tacit skill of kneading dough in the Matsushita example is a sympathized knowledge. Externalization outputs 'conceptual knowledge'. The concept of 'Tall Boy' in the Honda example is a conceptual knowledge created through the metaphor of 'Automobile Evolution' and the analogy between a sphere and the concept of 'man-maximum, machine-minimum'. Combination gives rise to 'systemic knowledge', such as a prototype and new component technologies. The micro-merchandizing program in the Kraft General Foods example is a systemic knowledge, which includes retail management methods as its components. internalization produces 'operational knowledge' about project management, production

	Tacit knowledge	Explicit knowledge
		To
Tacit knowledge	Socialization (Sympathized knowledge)	Externalization (Conceptual knowledge)
Explicit knowledge	Internalization (Operational knowledge)	Combination (Systemic knowledge)

From (appears on left between the two rows)

Figure 5.4   *Contents of knowledge created by the four modes*

process, new-product usage, and policy implementation. The bodily experience of working 150 hours a month in the Matsushita case is an operational knowledge of policy implementation.

These contents of knowledge interact with each other in the spiral of knowledge creation. For example, sympathized knowledge about consumers' wants may become explicit conceptual knowledge about a new-product concept through socialization and externalization. Such conceptual knowledge becomes a guideline for creating systemic knowledge through combination. For example, a new-product concept steers the combination phase, in which newly developed and existing component technologies are combined to build a prototype. Systemic knowledge (e.g. a simulated production process for the new product) turns into operational knowledge for mass production of the product through internalization. In addition, experience-based operational knowledge often triggers a new cycle of knowledge creation. For example, the users' tacit operational knowledge about a product is often socialized, thereby initiating improvement of an existing product or development of an innovation.

Thus far, we have focused our discussion on the epistemological dimension of organizational knowledge creation. As noted before, however, an organization cannot create knowledge by itself. Tacit knowledge of individuals is the basis of organizational knowledge creation. The organization has to mobilize tacit knowledge created and accumulated at the individual level. The mobilized tacit knowledge is 'organizationally' amplified through four modes of knowledge conversion and crystallized at higher ontological levels. We call this the 'knowledge spiral', in which the interaction between tacit knowledge and explicit knowledge will become larger in scale as it moves up the ontological levels. Thus, organizational knowledge creation is a spiral process, starting at the individual level and moving up through expanding communities of interaction, that crosses sectional, department, divisional and organizational boundaries.

This process is exemplified by product development. Creating a product concept involves a community of interacting individuals with different backgrounds and mental models. While the members from the R&D department focus on technological potential, those from the production and marketing departments are interested in other issues. Only some of those different experiences, mental models, motivations and intentions can be expressed in explicit language. Thus, the socialization process of sharing tacit knowledge is required. Moreover, both socialization and externalization are necessary for linking individuals' tacit and explicit knowledge. Many Japanese companies have adopted brainstorming camps as a tool for that purpose.

The product created by this collective and co-operative process will then be reviewed for its coherence with mid-range and grand concepts. Even if the newly created product has superior quality, it may conflict with the divisional or organizational goals expressed by the mid-range and grand concepts. What is required is another process at a higher level to maintain the integrity of the whole, which will lead to another cycle of knowledge creation in a larger context.

Enabling Conditions for Organizational Knowledge Creation

The role of the organizational knowledge-creation process is to provide the proper context for facilitating group activities as well as the creation and accumulation of knowledge at the individual level. In this section we will discuss five conditions required at the organizational level to promote the knowledge spiral.[18]

Intention

The knowledge spiral is driven by organizational intention, which is defined as an organization's aspiration to its goals. Efforts to achieve the intention usually take the form of strategy within a business setting. From the viewpoint of organizational knowledge creation, the essence of strategy lies in developing the organizational capability to acquire, create, accumulate, and exploit knowledge. The most critical element of corporate strategy it to conceptualize a vision about what kind of knowledge should be developed and to operationalize it into a management system for implementation.

Autonomy

The second condition for promoting the knowledge spiral is autonomy. At the individual level, all members of an organization should be allowed to act autonomously as far as circumstances permit. By allowing them to act autonomously, the organization may increase the chance of introducing unexpected opportunities. Autonomy also increases the possibility that individuals will motivate themselves to create new knowledge. Moreover, autonomous individuals function as part of the holographic structure, in which the whole and each part share the same information. Original ideas emanate from autonomous individuals, diffuse within the team, and then become organizational ideas. In this respect, the self-organizing individual assumes a position that may be seen as analogous to the core of a series of nested Russian dolls. From the viewpoint of knowledge creation, such an organization is more likely to maintain greater flexibility in acquiring, interpreting, and relating information. It is a system in which the 'minimum critical specification' principle (Morgan, 1986) is met as a prerequisite for self-organization, and therefore autonomy is assured as much as possible.

Fluctuation and Creative Chaos

The third organizational condition for promoting the knowledge spiral is fluctuation and creative chaos, which stimulate the interaction between the organization and the external environment. Fluctuation is different from complete disorder and characterized by 'order without recursiveness.' It is an order whose pattern is hard to predict at the beginning (Gleick, 1987). If organizations adopt an open attitude toward environmental signals, they can exploit those signals' ambiguity, redundancy, or noise in order to improve their own knowledge system.

Redundancy

Redundancy is the fourth condition that enables the knowledge spiral to take place organizationally. To Western managers who are preoccupied with the idea of efficient information processing or uncertainty reduction (Galbraith, 1973), the term 'redundancy', may sound pernicious because of its connotations of unnecessary duplication, waste, or information overload. What we mean here by redundancy is the existence of information that goes beyond the immediate operational requirements of organizational members. In business organizations, redundancy refers to intentional overlapping of information about business activities, management responsibilities, and the company as a whole.

Requisite Variety

The fifth condition that helps to advance the knowledge spiral is requisite variety. According to Ashby (1956), an organization's internal diversity must match the variety and complexity of the environment in order to deal with challenges posed by the environment. Organizational members can cope with many contingencies if they possess requisite variety, which can be enhanced by combining information differently, flexibly, and quickly, and by providing equal access to information throughout the organization. To maximize variety, everyone in the organization should be assured of the fastest access to the broadest variety of necessary information, going through the fewest steps (Numagami et al., 1989).

Summary

Knowledge conversion takes place between tacit knowledge and explicit knowledge. Four modes of this conversion – socialization, externalization, combination and internalization – were discussed. These modes are not independent of each other, but their interactions produce a spiral when time is introduced as the third dimension. We introduced five organizational conditions – intention, fluctuation/chaos, autonomy, redundancy and requisite variety – that enable the four modes to be transformed into a knowledge spiral.

Knowledge created by individuals is transformed into knowledge at the group and organizational levels. These levels are not independent of each other, but interact with each other iteratively and continuously. The five-phase process of organizational knowledge creation [involves] sharing tacit knowledge, creating concepts, justifying concepts, building archetypes and cross-leveling knowledge.

Notes

1　Brown and Duguid's (1991) work on 'evolving communities of practice' shows how individuals' actual ways of working and learning might be very different from relatively rigid, official practices specified by the organization. In reality, informal groups evolve among individuals seeking to solve a particular problem or pursuing other commonly held objectives. Membership in these groups is decided by individuals' abilities to trade practically valuable information. Orr (1990) argues that members exchange ideas and share narratives or 'war stories', thereby building a shared understanding out of conflicting and confusing information. This knowledge creation includes not only innovation but also learning that can shape and develop approaches to daily work.

2　For example, we recognize our neighbor's face without being able to explain how to do so in words. Moreover, we sense others' feelings from their facial expressions, but explaining them in words is more difficult. Put another way, while it is virtually impossible to articulate the feelings we get from our neighbor's face, we are still aware of the overall impression. For further discussion on tacit knowledge, see Polyani (1958) and Gelwick (1977).

3　Michael Polyani was a renowned chemist and rumored to be very close to the Nobel Prize until he turned to philosophy at the age of 50.

4　Brown (1992: 3) argues that 'The organizations of the future will be "knowledge refineries" in which employees will synthesize understanding and interpretations from the sea of information that threatens to flood them from all sides.' In a knowledge refinery, he continues, workers need to collaborate with both the past and the present. While collaboration with the present is about sharing tacit knowledge, collaboration with the past draws on experiences gained from previous ways of doing things.

5　According to Maturana and Varela (1980: xxiv, 41), 'The linguistic domain as a domain of orienting behavior requires at least two interacting organisms, so that a cooperative system of consensual interactions may be developed. The central feature of human existence is its occurrence in a linguistic cognitive domain. This domain is constitutively social.'

6　This model is consonant with Ryle's (1949) categorization of knowledge into knowing that something 'exists' and knowing 'how' it operates. Squire (1987) listed contending taxonomies with more than a dozen labels, such as 'implicit' vs. 'explicit' and 'skill memory' vs. 'fact memory'.

7　A survey of 105 Japanese middle managers was conducted to test the hypothesis that the knowledge creation construct is comprised of four knowledge conversion processes – socialization, externalization, combination and internalization. Factor loading from first-order and second-order factor analyses empirically validated the existence of these four conversion processes. For details, see Nonaka et al. (1994).

8　For a limited analysis of externalization from a viewpoint of information creation, see Nonaka (1987).

9　Cannon-Bowers et al. (1993: 228) define 'shared mental models' as 'knowledge structures held by members of a team that enable them to form accurate explanations and expectations for the task, and in turn, to coordinate their actions and adapt their behavior to demands of the task and other team members', based upon their extensive review of the literature on the shared mental model and their research on team decision-making.

10　Condon (1976) argues that communication is a simultaneous and contextual phenomenon in which people feel a change occurring, share the same sense of change, and are moved to take action. In other words, he says, communication is like a wave that passes through people's bodies and culminates when everyone synchronizes with the wave.

11 Graumann (1990) views dialogue as multiperspective cognition. As noted before, language is inherently related to action. Dialogue, therefore, may be seen as a collective action. Moreover, according to Kant, creating concepts is creating the world.

12 Interviewed on 25 January 1984.

13 These authors emphasize the importance of creating shared meaning for organized action. According to Rosch (1973), we understand things not through theory attributes but through better examples of them, or what she called 'prototypes.'

14 The following famous episode illustrates the process. F.A. Kekule, a German chemist, discovered the chemical structure of benzene – a hexagonal ring of carbon atoms – through a dream of a snake gripping its own tail. In this case, the snake pattern was a metaphor, and possible combinations of the pattern became analogies of other chemical compounds. Thus, Kekule developed the structural model of organic chemistry.

15 According to Lakoff and Johnson (1980: 3), 'metaphor is pervasive in everyday life, not just in language but in thought and action'.

16 Information and communications technologies used for this purpose include VAN (Value-Added Network), LAN (Local Area Network), E-Mail (Electronic Mail), POS (Point-Of-Sales) system, 'Groupware' for CSCW (Computer Supported Cooperative Work), and CAD/CAM (Computer-Aided Design/Manufacturing).

17 In the triad database system, data from the Market Metrics' Supermarket Solutions system, which integrates POS data from supermarkets nationwide, is hooked to customized data on shopping behaviors provided by Information Resources, and lifestyle data from Equifax Marketing Decision System's Microvision database. For more information, see 'micro-Merchandizing with KGF', *Food and Beverage Marketing*, 10(6) 1991; 'Dawn of Brand Analysis', *Food and Beverage Marketing*, 10(10) 1991; and 'Partnering', *Supermarket Business*, 46(5) 1991.

18 See original article for examples of each of these enabling conditions.

References

Ashby, W.R. (1956) *An Introduction to Cybernetics*. London: Chapman and Hall.

Bateson, G. (1973) *Steps to an Ecology of Mind*. London: Paladin.

Berger, P.L. and Luckmann, T. (1996) *The Social Construction of Reality*, Garden City, NY: Doubleday.

Brown, J.S. (1992) *Reflections on the Document*. Mimeograph: Xerox Palo Alto (CA) Research Center.

Brown, J.S. and Duguid, P. (1991) 'Organizational Learning and Communities-of-practice: towards a unified view of working, learning and innovation. *Organizational Science*, 2(1), 40–57.

Cannon-Bowers, J.A., Salas, E. and Converse, S. (1993) Shared mental models in expert team decision making. In N.J. Castellan (Ed.) *Individual and Group Decision Making*. Hillsdale, NJ: Lawrence Erlbaum, pp. 221–46.

Condon, W.S. (1976) An analysis of behavioural organization. *Sign Language Studies*, 13.

Donnellon, A., Gray, B. and Bougon, G. (1986) Communication, meaning and organized action. *Administrative Science Quarterly*, *31*, pp. 43–55.

Emig, J. (1983) *The Web of Meaning*. Upper Montclair, NJ: Boynton/Cook.

Galbraith, J. (1973) *Designing Complex Organizations*. Reading, MA: Addison-Wesley.

Gelwick, R. (1977) *The Way of Discovery*. Oxford: Oxford University Press.

Gleick, J. (1987) *Chaos: Making a New Science*. New York: Viking.

Graumann, C.F. (1990) Perspectival structure and dynamics in dialogues. In I. Markova and K. Foppa (Eds) *The Dynamics of Dialogue*. New York: Harvester Wheatsheaf.

Johnson-Laird, P.N. (1983) *Mental Models*. Cambridge: Cambridge University Press.

Lakoff, G. and Johnson, M. (1980) *Metaphors We Live By*. Chicago, IL: University of Chicago Press.

Maturana, H.R. and Varela, F.J. (1980) *Autopoesis and Cognition*. Dordrecht, Holland: Reidel.

Morgan, G. (1986) *Images of Organization*. Beverly Hills, CA: Sage.

Nisbet, R.A. (1969) *Social Change and History*. London: Oxford University Press.

Nonaka, I. (1987) Managing the firm as information creation process. Working Paper, Institute of Business Research, Hitotsubashi University.

Nonaka, I. (1990) *A Theory of Organizational Knowledge Creation*. Tokyo: Nihon-Keizeai-Shimbunsha (in Japanese).

Nonaka, I., Byosiere, P., Boruki, C. and Komo, N. (1994) Organizational Knowledge Creation Theory Test. *International Business Review*, Special Issue.

Numagami, T., Ohta, I. and Nonaka, T. (1989) *Case Study SMIP 91 16 CN* (Japanese text). Tokyo: Nomura School of Advanced Management.

Orr, J.E. (1990) Sharing Knowledge, Celebrating Identity. In D. Middleton and D. Edwards, (Eds) *Collective Remembering*. Newbury Park, CA: Sage. (pp. 169–189).

Polyani, M. (1958) Personal Knowledge: Towards a Post-critical philosophy. London: Routledge and Kegan Paul.

Polyani, M. (1966) *The Tacit Dimension*. London: Routledge.

Richards, I.A. (1936) *The Philosophy of Rhetoric*. Oxford: Oxford University Press.

Rosch, E.H. (1973) Natural categories. *Cognitive Psychology*, 4, 328–50.

Ryle, G. (1949) *The Concept of Mind*. London: Hutchinson.

Squire, L.R. (1987) *Memory and Brain*. New York: Oxford University Press.

Beyond Sense-making:
Emotion, Imagery and Creativity

John Sparrow

Weick (1995) highlighted the importance of appreciating that it is the 'sense' that people make of their work environment that determines their decisions and actions, rather than the organization's or people's 'objective' properties. People at work clearly engage on an ongoing basis in sense-making. The appreciation that organizations 'benefit' from employees securing and deploying their understanding effectively has led to an acceptance that time spent reflecting on (Seibert and Daudelin, 1999) and in (Schon, 1991) action is key to work practice. The conscious use of reasoning undoubtedly helps us explain some aspects of our world. Since meaning making is not simply a psychological process that takes place in individuals' minds, the social nature of work means that we can explore and create shared meaning. Stahl sees shared meaning as an 'essentially social activity that is conducted jointly – collaboratively – by a community, rather than by individuals who happen to be co-located' (2003: 523). Meaning is socially produced and situationally interpreted. But do our intrapsychic and social efforts to *explain* occupy an exaggerated position in our accounts of work? This chapter explores evidence of the potential to move beyond rationality and understanding in work settings and considers why such potential is resisted within organizations.

In examining decisions and actions at work we see many other facets of people than their semantic understanding and their reasoning processes. Analysis of work practices in terms of a more comprehensive framework suggests that there are many features of thinking that appear to be relegated in our accounts or even largely denied (Sparrow, 1998). I argue that it is 'only through the broad elicitation of all of these aspects that organizations can achieve the comprehensive self-insight in practitioners, and mutuality of insight, that modern and future organizational decision-making requires' (1998: 44). A possible framework is presented in Figure 6.1. This framework brings together three key features of thinking.

First, it highlights the levels of consciousness at which different kinds of thinking occur. At the conscious level is our semantic understanding (i.e. knowledge and models of the world) and our episodic memories (information that is held together in our

Conscious thought	Semantic understanding
	Episodic memory
Subconscious thought	Skilled actions
	Tacit understanding
	Unconscious leanings
Types of thought	Propositional language
	Image based
Direction	Reasoned direction
	Fluid and tangential
	Circular and emotion-tagged

Figure 6.1   *Basic forms of thought*

mind, as a sequence of events as occurred in the experience itself). So we may know that London is the capital city of England or that Trafalgar Square is in London. We may also recall our walk to Trafalgar Square from Leicester Square as an episodic memory. Both semantic understanding and episodic memories are mental material that we can consciously access and process.

Some of our mental processes operate at a sub-conscious level. When we use the term 'skilled' at using a computer keyboard, we note that the person's decisions and actions are not consciously controlled but have become 'automatized'. Skills entail the use of mental material that has been learned and over time has become so automatic that we don't have to think much about it. Similarly, we often find ourselves manifesting another aspect of sub-conscious thinking: operating upon a tacit feel for a situation. The use of the term tacit knowledge in this regard means the use of a deep sense of a situation that has not been arrived at through conscious reasoning, nor reflected upon during skill acquisition, but is the product of pure experiential learning and acquired latently. Some people use the term intuition to refer to this kind of knowledge. Some psychologists argue that there is a level of consciousness below the sub-conscious level, where unconscious interpretation occurs. Jung, for example, suggested that we develop deep-seated thinking preferences combining two personality attitudes (introversion and extraversion) and four functions or modes of orientation (thinking, sensation, intuition and feeling). Jung (1921) noted that 'For complete orientation all four functions should contribute equally: thinking should facilitate cognition and judgment, feeling should tell us how and to what extent a thing is important or unimportant to us, sensation should convey concrete reality to us through seeing, hearing, tasting etc. and intuition should enable us to divine the hidden possibilities in the background' (par 900). He highlighted how the four functions are not equally at one's disposal and that the thinking preferences not brought into frequent use operate 'in a more or less primitive and infantile state' (par 955).

The framework depicted in Figure 6.1 secondly contrasts the propositional form of thought with an imagistic form of thought. Our linguistic accomplishments as a species mean that much of our thinking occurs through language (propositional thought), but clearly we also use mental imagery. We have, in our minds, mental representations that have a form that resembles the object they represent. In effect, we may have a 'picture' of somebody's face in our mind rather than some propositional statements about the position of her nose in relation to her eyes and ears.

Third, the framework suggests that we can distinguish different types of thinking. For example, we may reason and in a sense think in a direction. Sometimes we might think of this as thinking in straight lines. Sometimes we are less engaged with 'reality' and think more fluidly. We might think of this as thinking tangentially. Finally, we may find our thought affected by our mood, i.e. in a flow of thought that aligns with emotion. If we are depressed, then depressing thoughts may come more readily to mind and we may maintain depressive thinking, by ruminating in circles.

Many relatively distinct facets of thinking may be operating in parallel. Several may be operating upon different cycle times (Claxton, 1997). The argument in this chapter is that in acknowledging sense-making, organizations have essentially only acknowledged the role of reasoning with conscious material in a propositional form. In exploring more closely the ways in which types of thinking and forms of thought operate, it seeks to extend March's (1994) conception of *biases* in decision-making to reveal the partial role that reasoning necessarily makes in decision-making.

Emotion as a Quality of Performance

Conventional wisdom depicts emotion as something that 'takes over' rational thinking. An NBC4 news item on 28 October 2003 (NBC4 TV, 2003) for example, recounted how in the course of describing a fire for a newscast, the reporter 'was so overcome with emotion, that at one point, the seasoned reporter walked away from the camera'. Artists and poets have highlighted the qualitative difference in task performance associated with performance in particular mood states. Here we can consider two example emotional facets of particular actions: tasks performed lovingly and fearfully. In acknowledging a loving execution of a task, Louisa May Alcott (in describing Beth's piano playing in the book *Little Women*) writes, 'So Beth tried it; and every one pronounced it the most remarkable piano ever heard. It had evidently been newly tuned and put in apple-pie order; but, perfect as it was, I think the real charm of it lay in the happiest of all happy faces which leaned over it, as Beth lovingly touched the beautiful black and white keys'. Contrast this with a statement such as 'can play tunes on a piano' that might be written in a task analysis. Nathaniel Hawthorne in *Lady Eleanore's Mantle*, writes, 'With such anticipations, he stole reverentially to the door at which the physician stood, but paused upon the threshold gazing fearfully into the gloom of the darkened chamber'. This is more than 'go to see the doctor'. Writings such as these reveal the depth of impact that emotion has upon perception, decisions and actions. Not solely in a 'heat of the moment' impassioned sense, but as background and context for behaviour and as a quality of performance.

In the study of work behaviour even where there is an acknowledgement of emotion at work, there has been an emphasis upon feelings *about* work (e.g. job satisfaction) rather than the feeling *of* working (Fineman, 1993). The 'virtues' of commitment and motivation, for example, have been acknowledged. Whilst there has been an emphasis upon the importance/value of emotions that serve as positive assets for the organization therefore, the recognition of the *integral* role that all emotional tones can play has been less discussed. There have been some notable examples of 'insider' accounts of working from some of the more literary researchers. These accounts have revealed how large a role emotional considerations play in work life. There are also accounts from employees themselves. In writing about an organization that one might surmise would epitomise the impersonal precision of a bureaucratic machine – the British Civil Service – Bridges (1950) reveals how a civil servant 'feels with the fiercest intensity for those things which he has learned to cherish' (1950: 31) and highlights the importance of these feelings in maintaining effective organizational performance. Cracknell (1998) in reflecting on his own experiences of creative departments in marketing, notes how 'Emotion and passion are essential. So are heat and passion and inflammation and abrasion ... Often, the brilliant breakthrough is achieved by the bloody-minded will of one person' (1998: 5). He also suggests that climates where 'confrontation' and 'the heat' are removed or censured have 'taken out the brilliance, originality and creativity' required for creative work (ibid). It is, of course possible for creativity to operate as a stolid process, but Cracknell suggests that heat and passion may be facilitative. Post industrial jobs require workers to spend most of their time interacting with people rather than machines. In management, interpersonal and self-perception of emotional aspects of work are central. Decision-making and leadership processes are pregnant with emotional facets. Peters and Austin describe how a vision for an organization 'must be felt passionately before it is published' (1986: 287) and prescribe 'commitment, passion, zest, energy, care, love and enthusiasm' (1986: 292) as emotions to be celebrated in the individual. Sparrow and Bentley (2000) highlight the importance of the emotional tone of the small business entrepreneurial environment (predominated by expressions of feelings of threat, bravery, battling etc.) within the risk assessment and decision-making actions of small business owner-managers. Albrow (1997) goes on to suggest that entrepreneurs do not therefore 'rest with a strictly impersonal relationship' with employees, for 'converts, followers, disciples provide more reassurance and replenish the store of confidence more effectively than the payment of wages to casual workers' (1997: 117). Baron reports that strategic decision-making within top management teams may start 'as a rational exchange of opposing views' but may become 'an emotion-laden interchange ... in which negative feelings are aroused' (1984: 272). Amason and Sapienza highlight the management challenge of how outcomes such as 'decision quality, consensus and affective acceptance can be realised simultaneously' (1997: 495). As well as studying the practices of individuals as they manifest emotion in their own knowledge (decisions and actions), we can also see instances of where individuals develop the skills/knowledge to adapt their behaviour appropriately (perceptively) to the emotional behaviours/consequences of others (e.g. Goleman, 1995). Managing the interplay of emotions is difficult. Sparrow (2000) conducted an analysis of the emotions in play amongst managers in small and medium-sized enterprises. The following extract highlights the thinking and practice of a manager upon their management of training.

> And then the training – I don't know, I don't know ... we talk about
> up-training and getting them – but the same again, the pressure on
> performance doesn't allow you the time to take the people out to train
> them ... but what is going to be put on one side while you do it, that is the
> decision – what you leave while you are doing that – because people want
> this, this, and this ... unfortunately your own need probably has more of an
> impact on what you need to do ... you can't find time to do it.

The pressures of work mean that the manager performs this task *frustratedly*, but does not abandon hope however. A sense of *guilt* provokes a determination to continue to try. The approach towards training needs to be understood as it is conducted *determinedly, empathically, frustratedly and guiltily*. The manager knows how to train in this way. The consequences of this flow from the qualities of the approach and not from some abstract concept/practice of training, per se. Albrow (1997) argues 'Manual labour may be performed alertly, enthusiastically, vigorously, resentfully, steadily, carelessly, heedlessly, effortlessly, painfully, lackadaisically. Mental labour may be performed imaginatively, with concentration, with dour determination, haphazardly, painstakingly, with excitement, passionately', and that the lists are interchangeable (1997: 118–119). Feelings 'about' work (i.e. separation of emotion from cognition in decisions and action) can be contrasted with those of 'feelings of' working. Similarly, conceptions of emotions 'interfering with' individual or group work and learning can be contrasted with those where emotion is 'part of' work and learning.

Emotion in Decisions and Social Performance

Emotion is infused in decision-making. Experiences associated with the affect 'fear' may be associated with risk avoidance (Bagozzi, 1992). If feelings experienced in the course of decision-making are positive then decisions continue with the objectives, criteria and process initially construed, whilst feelings such as 'anxiety/fear' may be associated with restarting a decision (Kemdal and Montgomery, 1997). Decisions with elements of belief-value correlation (e.g. wishful thinking etc.) are 'speeded up', as desirable aspects of a decision are bolstered and undesirable aspects are dampened (Brickman, 1987).

Mood is not simply an intrapsychic physiological phenomenon but has appraisal, action, activation and *expressive* factors (Parkinson, 1995) and is *situated* in a particular discourse (i.e. is both a product and determinant of social action). The 'plots' and 'storylines' that organizational actors use to frame organizational events enable and constrain the expression (and possession) of 'emotion'. Nussbaum (2001) suggests that all that distinguishes emotions from other thoughts is that they refer to events or states in the world that directly relate to what she terms the *individual's own self-flourishing*. We may gain more insight into human behaviour if we integrate the performative nature of 'emotional' behaviour into our accounts.

Emotion and Consciousness

How might emotional cognition operate. In considering semantic understanding, Schiemann notes how mental models determine the way that people 'cognitively map inferences about probable states of the world, and hence likely outcomes given different actions, from available empirical evidence, including new information that raises in the course of the interaction' (2002: 20). Leichtman et al. (1992) highlighted how events with high emotional valence can direct attention in information collection. DeSteno et al. (2004) demonstrated that the persuasiveness of material is enhanced when it matches a user's current emotional state. Muramatsu and Hanoch (2005) conclude that emotions can enhance decision-making under certain conditions by priming specific decision-making heuristics such as focusing attention on important aspects of a decision, altering one's goals, shaping cost–benefit assessments, and quickly filtering many options without the need for complex processing of each option.

Episodic memory also has some important associations with emotion. Remembering negative events in our past when feeling depressed is an example. Clore and Gasper (2000) highlight how episodic memories that are compatible with our emotional sensations combine with our semantic knowledge to constitute our beliefs and actions. Our emotions are often a response to episodic memory, which in turn is influenced by our emotions relating to that particular episode.

Langan-Fox et al. (2002) suggest that since one function of emotion is to trigger or modulate self-awareness or control functions (i.e. a signal for attention, alertness, and scanning of the environment) that negative mood can impact upon skilled performance. They cite Ellis and Ashbrook's (1988) resource allocation model which proposes that negative affective states are likely to reduce the cognitive resources that can be allocated to a given task. This is because mood-congruent thoughts, possibly induced by the task itself, intrude into consciousness and may induce reflection about one's current mood state, bodily sensations, and sources of one's mood. Chronic negative affect can be associated with greater self-focused attention and self-monitoring which may involve attempts at self-understanding that require the investment of attentional resources. Beilock and Carr (2005) suggest that skilled performance is achieved because of superior attentional allocation capacities in working memory and that it is the more highly skilled who can be susceptible to disruption from negative emotion when such attentional capacity is compromised. It may also be hypothesized that when information might lead to interpretations or meanings that are not consistent with the person's skilled model of 'reality', we are more likely to see an emotional response.

Bolte et al. defined intuition as 'the ability to make above-chance judgments about properties of a stimulus on the basis of information that is not consciously retrieved' (2003: 416). They demonstrated that a positive mood improved participants' ability to make intuitive coherence judgements. Specifically, participants could make more accurate judgements about the coherence of sets of three words in the absence of conscious knowledge of the 'linking' word. The authors argue that an increase in positive affect promotes a *holistic* processing mode whilst negative affect promotes an *analytic* processing mode. The holistic mode is the product of activation of wide semantic fields including weak or remote associates. Whilst the analytic mode is characterised by a more restricted spread of activation to close and dominant associates. In tasks requiring implicit learning, 'positive mood promotes the activation of widespread associative networks, whereas negative mood restricts the spread of activation, such that remote associates are not sufficiently activated to guide intuitive coherence judgments' (Bolte et al., 2003: 420). These results align with general conclusions about the impact of positive affect upon managerial decision-making by Tran (2004): 'enhancing a broader search for information and a more thorough consideration of alternatives' though sometimes leading to 'quick and suboptimal decision-making because of the use of heuristics and hunches' (2004: 56). Here, the term suboptimal refers to 'logical' rigour. It is recognized that the use of intuition is known to be a primary tool for senior managers (Isenberg, 1984) and that a bedrock for intuitive decision-making is confidence in one's own understanding of the world. Indeed it can easily be argued that 'facts' are highly contextual in many respects, and therefore that they are no better than – or even worse than – heuristics for making decisions since they may lead to unjustified confidence in the correctness of ones decision (Einhorn and Hogarth, 1978).

Sayegh et al. (2004) discuss the role of emotion in intuitive decision-making for managers in crisis situations. They note how decision-makers may, on occasion, experience 'an unpleasant gut feeling when a negative outcome connected with a particular response option fleetingly comes to mind' and how such subconscious 'emotional responses help the decision-maker by providing an automated detection system to focus in on only the most relevant components of the decision scenario' (2004: 195).

Research and practice in the psychotherapeutic tradition has long maintained that emotions can operate at the unconscious level. Indeed, it is argued that the mind expends considerable waking and sleeping effort to 'manage' the impact of unconscious emotion. Research in the cognitive psychology tradition has identified the importance of a conscious 'appraisal' component in emotion, and, whilst acknowledging troublesome emotions including automatic negative thoughts (Neenan and Dryden, 2002), has focused attention upon conscious considerations. More recently, research has suggested that we can identify changes in experience, thought, or action that are attributable to one's emotional state, independent of conscious awareness of that state. Winkielman and Berridge demonstrate how, through the use of subliminal stimulation, one can create 'affect that is powerful enough to alter behavior, but that people are simply not aware of, even when attending to their feelings.' (2004: 122).

Overall, it seems clear that emotion impacts upon thinking at various levels of consciousness and has clear effects upon decisions and actions.

Emotion and Creativity

There is also a strong tradition of systematic use of reasoning as a type of thinking to identify potential (e.g. Zwicky, 1969). There is a history of over 50 years between fluidity in thinking and the formal study of creative outcomes (e.g. Osborne, 1953). 'Releasing' people from the dictates and linearity of rationality can lead to idea generation beyond logical thinking. There are also some well-established relationships between emotional states (mood) and memory (Ellis and Ashbrook, 1988).

The 'Pollyanna principle' reveals that people recall words in descending order of pleasantness. In general therefore, cursory recall of the past may paint us a rosy future. Mood congruence effects mean that people learn material in line with their mood at the time more efficiently. If we feel threatened we will 'see' and 'understand' threats more readily. Mood-state dependence means that it is easier to recall items/events encountered during mood states in line with current mood. If we are depressed we can conjure up many reasons for us to be depressed. How has emotion been considered in relation to creativity? Research into the structure of emotions and moods has demonstrated the existence of two orthogonal dimensions that account for the majority of the shared variance. The basic model of mood distinguishes between positive and negative feelings and different levels of arousal (Watson and Tellegen, 1985). Warr (1990) highlights a set of indicative states associated with the combination of these two dimensions. In the higher arousal/positive affect quadrant one might include emotions such as surprised, excited, full of energy, delighted, cheerful, happy, glad, pleased. The positive affect lower arousal emotions might be comfortable, satisfied, contented, calm, relaxed, tranquil, drowsy, sluggish. Negative affect lower arousal emotions include bored, fatigued, lacking energy, gloomy, sad, depressed, miserable and dejected. Negative affect higher arousal emotions include discouraged, dissatisfied, uneasy, anxious, tense, afraid, alarmed and aroused.

Fredrickson's (1998) 'broaden-and-build' theory of positive emotions suggests that positive emotions *broaden* individuals' thought-action repertoires enabling them to pursue a wider range of thoughts and actions than is typical. She also suggests that this effect has evolutionary adaptive value in that it *builds* physical resources (e.g. skills), intellectual resources (e.g. knowledge), social resources (e.g. networks) and psychological resources (e.g. resilience). Fredrickson and Branigan (2005) highlight how positive mood can broaden the scope of attention and thought-action repertoires, thus enhancing creativity. Other research has demonstrated that positive affect generally results in more divergent associations to neutral words (Isen, 1985) whilst negative mood may only enhance creativity in more specific circumstances (e.g. when perceived recognition and rewards for creative performance are high (George and Zhou, 2002). Prince (2003) suggests that a positive emotional 'climate' enhances creativity. There are instances however where mood may not affect divergent thinking (Clapham, 2001) and there is some evidence to suggest that a more qualified position needs to be adopted contrasting the effects concerning the quality and quantity of ideas (Vosburg, 1998). Kaufmann (2003: 134) concludes that there is a complex relationship between mood and creativity within different 'aspects of problem solving, such as problem definition, choice of strategy, type of process involved, as well as requirements of task solutions'.

The level of arousal within a particular mood state can affect creativity. Trait (chronic) high levels of arousal may enhance creativity (Carlsson, 2002) as may mild manic periods (Jamison, 1993). Lower levels of arousal in states such as relaxation are frequently conducive to primary process (associative) thinking with associated changes in cerebral levels of norepinephrine (Heilman et al., 2003), though again relaxation may not necessarily enhance creative thinking (Khasky and Smith, 1999). Sundararajan (2001) suggests that it can be 'background mood' (i.e. non-conscious 'inchoate' emotions) that contribute towards creativity and not just focal explicit emotional states. Indeed, the discussion earlier in this chapter of how emotion operates within thinking at different levels of consciousness suggests that creativity can have a emotional component. For example, Getz and Lubart (2001) demonstrate how idiosyncratic emotion-based associations can lie behind creativity.

Amabile et al. (2005) utilized a daily questionnaire technique with over 200 people over periods ranging from 9 to 38 weeks to explore relationships between reported emotions and 'daily creative thought' in work situations. They found that positive mood at the time was associated with higher levels of creativity. Qualitative reports of feelings in the course of creativity revealed 'enjoyment of and interest in the work itself, excitement about exercising or increasing competence, and satisfaction in feeling positively challenged' (2005: 389).

Emotion may also impact upon creativity indirectly through motivation. If we were to need to be able to span a gap, to find a solution to a problem, then we have a relevant motivation. Creativity may not be 'required' unless the eye of the beholder sees the need. A negative thinking person may be less inclined to see the need ... proclaiming for example 'what's the use of trying'.

Emotion as a Dimension of Creative Outcomes

Assessments of creativity have examined the conceptual diversity of ideas. The Torrance tests, for example, assess fluency, originality, elaboration, abstractness of titles, and resistance to closure. Clapham (2004) notes how additional dimensions of creativity interests might also usefully be assessed. Would it be possible to assess the emotional diversity of thinking? Simon (1977) argued that both scientific thinking in general and problem-solving in particular can be thought of as a search in a problem space. A problem space consists of all the possible states of a problem and all the operations that a problem-solver can use to get from one state to the next. According to this view, by characterizing the types of representations and procedures that people use to get from one state to another, it is possible to understand scientific creativity. Thus, scientific creativity can be characterized as a search in various problem spaces.

Boden (2000) identifies three types of creative activity involved in the development and exploration of what she terms conceptual space: (i) combinational activity, in which familiar elements within the space are combined in novel ways; (ii) exploratory activity, in which possibilities inherent in the structured conceptual space are explored; and (iii) transformational activity, in which the space and its possibilities are transformed through changing one of its basic dimensions or rules. Gardenfors (2000) has developed some models for cognition within conceptual space wherein most reasoning is done by evaluating the analog of a distance between two aspects of a perception. In essence, we find things to be similar if they are 'geometrically' (measurably) closer on some limited number of dimensional scales. The notion of multi-dimensional space can be extended to include emotional space. This would refer to the constellation of emotions that are associated with ideas in play.

There is a wider recognition that emotion can usefully be considered within integrative (multiple code) cognitive frameworks. In considering human problem-solving, creativity and decision-making therefore, one might usefully consider the scope of the emotional space in play. Some preliminary research has been undertaken in this regard. Sparrow (2005) reports increases in the range of emotions outlined by participants in a future visioning task when induced into different mood states within a guided imagery procedure. Earlier research (Brockmann and Anthony, 2002; Riquelme, 2000) in eliciting strategic visioning statements has tended to utilize creative thinking processes that operated in a 'narrow' emotional range, i.e. under conditions of low arousal along the positive affect dimension (e.g. calm, relaxed etc.). Furthermore, the statements were only analyzed in terms of the divergence of ideas and not their emotional range. In general, whilst there is recognition of the role of creative thinking in strategic visioning, little attention is paid to the emotions in play in the thinking process. Furthermore, the emphasis in considering the 'outcome' of a strategic visioning process is upon the *intellectual compellingness* of a vision rather than its overall comprehensiveness. Guided imagery entails a series of thoughts and suggestions that direct a person's imagination. Guided imagery takes participants through a process where participants can be supported to 'enter' into an imagined scene. Once participants are 'living' the scene, they can be given additional information or 'developments' and, because they are engaged in imagistic thinking, they may generate issues/possibilities that may not be afforded by propositional thinking. Wheatley et al. (1989) used guided imagery to enhance the creativity and imagination of strategic planners. They found that it was an effective method for getting individuals to entertain unique, diverse and radical alternative scenarios for organisations. Sparrow (2005) asked participants to indicate the range of possible students, sessions and physical environments for the university in positive and negative 'futures'. Mood induction procedures were used in the guided imagery session. Mood induction procedures have consistently been found to impact upon reported mood states, and influence memory retrieval (Lewis and Critchley, 2003), current cognitions (Siemer, 2005) and prospective memory (Kliegel et al., 2005). The study demonstrated a significantly higher number and range of emotional references when moods were induced. This may be because of the 'cognitive' explanation outlined above. An alternative explanation for the findings however needs to be borne in mind and relates to the performative aspects of emotion discussed earlier. The use of emotionally charged words may be felt to be 'appropriate' in a social situation that has been primed to be more receptive to them. A setting with a less defined emotional atmosphere may elicit a socially agreed 'performance' of manners and behaviours that exclude 'non-rational' language from discourse. Overall it seems clear that experienced emotion affects the emotional references within vision statements and potentially other creativity tasks, and that the emotional range of creative outputs can be considered.

Emotion, Imagery and Creativity

Creativity highlights the potential for imagistic thinking in decisions and actions, i.e. the ability to form mental images of things or events. Imagery relates closely to episodic memory in that visual imagery and visual perception draw on most of the same neural machinery (Ganis et al., 2004) and physical deficits in visual acuity and stereopsis can impact upon imagery ability and associated divergent thinking (Harland and Coren, 2001). Imagery also relates closely to skill. Experienced (skilled) designers are more able to benefit from the creative potential from images presented to them than less experienced designers. Bonnardel and Marmeche (2004: 183) suggest that 'experienced designers are able to take into account a multiplicity of aspects of suggested sources (functional, structural, aesthetic and so on)'. Imagery can relate to tacit aspects of cognition. General mindsets concerning self-worth, for example, can be influenced by imagistic thinking (Grant et al., (2004) and guided imagery has been found to have pervasive therapeutic effect in a range of emotion-related psychological conditions (Curwen et al., 2000). Intuitive imagery (Pehrson and Mehrtens, 1997) has been used in work contexts by managers to obtain insight into 'probable outcomes of different courses of action', thereby, 'enabling changes in strategy and tactics that make the business more viable' (1997: 61). Visual imagery has been used to work psychoanalytically with unconscious interpretations. Freud (1914: 212) highlights that through artistic creation we can encounter the 'emotional attitude' and 'mental constellation' behind intention. Bach (1999: 25) describes how a patient's 'picture language' can highlight considerations worthy of exploration. Segal describes how through art we can identify a person's 'necessity to recreate something that is felt to be a whole new world' (1991: 86).

Kosslyn (1994: 405) suggested that 'imagery appears to play a special role in representing emotionally charged material'. Hypotheses that imagery elicits emotion more readily than processing based on verbal language can be based on arguments including: emotional systems being particularly sensitive to imagery because other representational systems, such as language, evolved later than did basic emotions; and images appear to share properties with perceptual representations derived from direct sensory experience and specific emotional episodes may be stored in the form of images in autobiographical memory. Imagery can 'create' emotions more readily than listening to and rehearsing verbal descriptions of emotional events. Imagery has been found to be effective in preparing people to 'cope' with future emotionally-laden events. Stigler and Pokorny (2001) examined interrelationships between the degree of imagery, range of emotions and associated referential activity in analysing transcripts of psychotherapy sessions. They noted 'significantly more emotion vocabulary in imagery than in verbal sessions' (2001: 426). Imagery has been used extensively in management creativity contexts (e.g. Goodman, 1995; Henry, 1991; Morgan, 1993). Goodman (op cit) distinguishes between passive (e.g. relaxation, inspirational sound), bridging (e.g. metaphors, analogies and puns) and active (e.g. drawing, multimedia, guided imagery) utilization of imagery. The use of imagery in management contexts was promoted by Morgan (op cit) in his term 'imaginization'. The specific ways in which imagery relates to creativity have been explored. Finke (1996) outlines how creative mental images can operate as pre-inventive structures. Brainsketching was contrasted with brainstorming by van der Lugt (2002). The study found greater 'link density' with brainsketching and greater volume of ideas with brainstorming. The role that imagery can play in mediating contributions from different participants in design (e.g. customers and designers) is considered by Dahl et al. (1999). Holmes and Mathews (2005) report how imagery may influence the subjective experience of specific emotions but not necessarily impact upon judgement.

Barriers to Incorporation of Different Facets of Thinking

It seems clear that active consideration of emotion creativity and imagistic thought can contribute to work practice. There is, however, resistance to such consideration. Emotion is often considered to be an aspect of work performance that needs to be minimized. It has been seen as something that gets in the way of rational business practices. It has been acknowledged as a consequence (byproduct) of business practices (e.g. job satisfaction, organizational commitment) but treated as a separate 'issue' rather than incorporated in work practice. It may be 'suppressed' by organizations in their elevation of rationality as the only legitimate behaviour (Stearns, 1989). It has been seen as an essentially individual phenomenon that should be recognized, confronted and resolved (removed) from team/group interaction (e.g. Smith, 1980). This process has itself been described as 'tyrannical' (Sinclair, 1992), and a 'requirement' for effective working (van Maanen and Kunda, 1989). Emotion has been seen as a quality of performance only to the extent that it is a 'false' aspect of performance, performed as 'emotional labour', in particular interpersonal contexts. The 'containment' of emotion through 'feeling rules' has been argued to promote a deep sense of 'inauthenticity' within individuals (Hochschild, 1983). In essence, emotion at work is 'denied but present, ever potentially resurgent, never addressed as reality' (Linstead, 1997: 1115). Whilst it is true that the value of some emotions at work is acknowledged (e.g. a passion for excellence), there remains an uneasiness concerning emotional expression in general.

The use of creativity and imagery techniques raises its own obstacles. Techniques can highlight or create insights that 'everyday' thinking and encounter may omit. It is also possible, however, that the appreciation of the role of imagery in one's own thinking may not be perceived. Schwitzgebel (2002) highlights how people make 'gross and enduring errors about the nature of their visual imagery experiences'.

The take up of techniques in organizations can be lower than 'technical merit' might imply. Acceptance is subject to the perceived advantages and previous experience that those affected hold. Seeking to promote a single 'stand-alone' technique may be more problematic than an 'integrated' set of developments. An individual's response has to be more than intellectual acceptance of an approach. Techniques have to be assimilated into the behaviour of individuals. The opportunities for, and receptivity of, individuals to take up an innovation are subject to characteristics of individuals, top management support, the culture and infrastructure of the organization, characteristics of the industry, or indeed, national cultural considerations. Sparrow and Yeoman (1999) studied take up of visual techniques in decision-making within 18 case study organizations where a manager, familiar and acceptant of such techniques, served as an evangelist within their own organization. In comparing the initial and subsequent attitudes of managers in their own use of such techniques, the study identified statistically significantly more positive views of the potential of visual techniques after personal exposure.

The challenges for incorporating interplays of emotion with imagery and creativity within worklife are substantial. The potential contribution of acknowledgement of these factors may, nevertheless, win the day. Some aspects of the potential appear to have established some legitimacy. There is a groundswell of interest in positive psychology (Seligman and Csikszentmihalyi, 2000) and broad acceptance of the value of positive thinking. The value of positive work settings has been highlighted (Luthans, 2002). People involved in creative work frequently feel passionately involved with that work (Rae, 2004). It is a significant further step to acknowledge the contribution of other emotions at work and within the creative process. A greater appreciation of the interplay of emotion, imagery and cognition at work may enhance the possibility for harnessing tacit insights more readily into the creative process.

References

Albrow, M. (1997) *Do Organizations Have Feelings?* London: Routledge.

Amabile, T.M., Barsade, S.G., Mueller, J.S. and Staw, B.M. (2005) Affect and creativity at work. *Administrative Science Quarterly, 50,* 367–403.

Amason, A.C. and Sapienza, H.J. (1997) The effects of top management team size and interaction norms on cognitive and affective conflict. *Journal of Management, 23*(4), 495–517.

Bach, S. (1999) Small circles – closed early. In R. Goldstein (Ed.) *Images, Meanings and Connections: Essays in Memory of Susan R. Bach.* Einsiedeln, Switzerland: Daimon-Verlag.

Bagozzi, R.P. (1992) The self-regulation of attitudes, intentions and behaviour. *Social Psychology Quarterly, 55,* 178–204.

Baron, R.A. (1984) Reducing organizational conflict: An incompatible response approach. *Journal of Applied Psychology, 69,* 272–9.

Beilock, S.L. and Carr, T.H. (2005) When High-Powered People Fail: Working Memory and 'Choking under Pressure' in Math. *Psychological Science, 16*(2), 101–105.

Boden, M. (2000) Computer models of creativity. *The Psychologist, 13*(2), 72–6.

Bolte, A., Goschke, T. and Kuhl, J. (2003) Emotion and intuition: effects of positive and negative mood on implicit judgements of semantic coherence. *Psychological Science, 14*(5), 416–20.

Bonnardel, N. and Marmeche, E. (2004) Evocation processes by novice and expert designers: Towards stimulating analogical thinking. *Creativity and Innovation Management, 13*(3), 176–86.

Brickman, P. (1987) *Commitment, Conflict and Caring.* Englewood Cliffs, NJ: Prentice Hall.

Bridges, Lord Edward (1950) *Portrait of a Profession.* Cambridge: Cambridge University Press.

Brockmann, E.N. and Anthony, W.P. (2002) Tacit knowledge and strategic decision making. *Group and Organization Management, 27*(4), 436–55.

Carlsson, I. (2002) Anxiety and flexibility of defense related to high or low creativity. *Creativity Research Journal, 14*(3–4), 341–49.

Clapham, M.M. (2001) The effects of affect manipulation and information exposure on divergent thinking. *Creativity Research Journal, 13*(4), 335–50.

Clapham, M.M. (2004) The convergent validity of the Torrance Tests of Creative Thinking and creativity interest inventories. *Educational and Psychological Measurement, 64*(5), 828–41.

Claxton, G. (1997) *Hare Brain Tortoise Mind: Why intelligence increases when you think less.* London: Fourth Estate.

Clore, G.L. and Gasper, K. (2000) Feeling is believing: Some affective influences on belief. In N.H. Frijda, A.S.R Manstead and S. Bem (Eds) *Emotions and Beliefs: How Feelings Influence Thoughts*. Cambridge: Cambridge University Press. (pp. 10–44).

Cracknell, A. (1998) Confrontation is better for genius than a dull peace. *Marketing*, 10 Dec 1998, pp. 5–6.

Curwen, B., Palmer, S. and Ruddell, P. (2000) *Brief Cognitive Behaviour Therapy*. London: Sage.

Dahl, D.W., Chattopadhyay, A. and Gorn, G.J. (1999) The use of visual mental imagery in new product design. *Journal of Marketing Research*, 36(1), 18–28.

DeSteno, D., Petty, R.E., Rucker, D.D., Wegener, D.T. and Braverman J. (2004) Discrete emotions and persuasion: The role of emotion-induced expectancies. *Journal of Personality and Social Psychology*, 86(1), 43–56.

Einhorn, H.J. and Hogarth, R.M. (1978) Confidence in judgment: The persistence of the illusion of validity. *Psychological Review*, 85, 395–416.

Ellis, H.C. and Ashbrook, P.W. (1988) Resource allocation model of the effects of depressed mood states on memory. In K. Fiedler and J. Forgas (Eds) *Affect, cognition and social behaviour: New evidence and integrative attempts*. Toronto: Hogrefe. (pp. 25–43).

Fineman, S. (Ed.) (1993) *Emotion in Organizations*. London: Sage.

Finke, R.A. (1996) Imagery, creativity and emergent structure. *Consciousness and Cognition*, 5, 381–93.

Fredrickson, B.L. (1998) What good are positive emotions? *Review of General Psychology*, 2, 300–19.

Fredrickson, B.L. and Branigan, C. (2005) Positive emotions broaden the scope of attention and thought-action repertoires. *Cognition and Emotion*, 19(3), 313–32.

Freud, S. (1914) *The Moses of Michelangelo*. Volume 13 Standard Edition of the Complete Psychological Works of Sigmund Freud, Vintage Books.

Ganis, G, Thompson, W.L. and Kosslyn, S.M. (2004) Brain areas underlying visual mental imagery and visual perception: an fMRI study. *Cognitive Brain Research*, 20, 226–41.

Gardenfors, P. (2000) *Conceptual Spaces: The Geometry of Thought*. Boston: MIT Press.

George, J.M. and Zhou, J. (2002) Understanding when bad moods foster creativity and good ones don't: The role of context and clarity of feelings. *Journal of Applied Psychology*, 87(4), 687–97.

Getz, I. and Lubart, T.I. (2001) An emotional-experiential perspective on creative symbolic-metaphorical processes. *Consciousness and Emotion*, 1(2), 283–312.

Goleman, D. (1995) *Emotional Intelligence*. London: Bloomsbury Press.

Goodman, M. (1995) *Creative Management*. London: Prentice Hall.

Grant, A.M., Langer, E.J., Falk, E. and Capodilupo, C. (2004) Mindful creativity: Drawing to draw distinctions. *Creativity Research Journal*, 16(2/3), 261–5.

Harland, R.E. and Coren, S. (2001) Individual Differences in Divergent Thinking as a Function of Variations in Sensory Status. *Creativity Research Journal*, 13(3/4), 385–91.

Heilman, K.M., Nadeau S.E., Beversdorf, D.O. (2003) Creative innovation: Possible brain mechanisms. *Neurocase*, 9(5), 369–79.

Henry, J. (Ed.) (1991) *Creative Management*. London: Sage.

Hochschild, A.R. (1983) *The Managed Heart*. Berkeley, CA: University of California Press.

Holmes, E.A. and Mathews, A. (2005) Mental Imagery and Emotion: A Special Relationship? *Emotion*, 5(4), 489–97.

Isen, A. (1985) The asymmetry of happiness and sadness in effects on memory in normal college students. *Journal of Experimental Psychology: General*, 114, 388–91.

Isenberg, D.J. (1984) How senior managers think. *Harvard Business Review*, Nov–Dec, 81–90.

Jamison, K.R. (1993) *Touched with Fire: Manic-depressive illness and the artistic temperament*, Toronto, Canada: Free Press.

Jung, C.G. (1921) Psychological Types, Vol. 6 in *The Collected Works of C.G. Jung* (Bollingen Series XX) trans. R.F.C. Hull (Ed.) H. Read, M. Fordham, G. Adler, W. McGuire. Princeton: Princeton University Press, 1979.

Kaufmann, G. (2003) Expanding the mood-creativity equation. *Creativity Research Journal, 15*(2/3), 131–5.

Kemdal, A.B. and Montgomery, H. (1997) Perspectives and emotions in personal decision making. In R. Ranyard, W.R. Crozier and O. Svenson (Eds) *Decision Making: Cognitive Models and Explanations*. London: Routledge. (pp. 72–89).

Khasky, A.D. and Smith, J.C. (1999) Stress, relaxation states and creativity. *Perceptual and Motor Skills, 88*(2), 409–16.

Kliegel, M., Jäger, T., Phillips, L.H., Federspiel, E., Imfeld, A., Keller, M. and Zimprich, D. (2005) Effects of sad mood on time-based prospective memory, *Cognition and Emotion. 19*(8), 1199–213.

Kosslyn, S.M. (1994) *Image and brain: The resolution of the imagery debate*. Cambridge, MA: MIT Press.

Langan-Fox, J., Armstrong, K., Balvin, N. and Anglim, J. (2002) Process in Skill Acquisition: Motivation, Interruptions, Memory, Affective States, and Metacognition. *Australian Psychologist, 37*(2), 104–17.

Leichtman, M.D., Ceci, S.J. and Ornstein, P.A. (1992) The influence of affect on memory: Mechanism and Development. In Sven-Ake Christianson (Ed.) *The Handbook of Emotion and Memory: Research and Theory*. Hillsdale NJ: Lawrence Erlbaum Associates. (pp. 181–99).

Lewis, P.A. and Critchley, H.D. (2003) Mood-dependent memory. *Trends in Cognitive Science, 7*(10), 431–3.

Linstead, S. (1997) Abjection and organization: Men, violence and management, *Human Relations. 50*(9), 1115–45.

Luthans, F. (2002) Positive organizational behavior: developing and managing psychological strengths. *Academy of Management Executive, 16*(1), 57–62.

March, J.G. (1994) *A Primer on Decision-Making: How Decisions Actually Happen*. New York: The Free Press.

Morgan, G. (1993) *Imaginization: The Art of Creative Management*. Newbury Park, CA: Sage.

Muramatsu, R. and Hanoch, Y. (2005) Emotions as a mechanism for boundedly rational agents: The fast and frugal way. *Journal of Economic Psychology, 26*(2), 201–21.

NBC4 TV (2003) Firefighters Rescue Team, Take Them To Safety, News item posted 3:49 p.m. PST 28 October 2003, http://www.nbc4.tv/news/2589194/detail.html.

Neenan, M. and Dryden, W. (2002) *Life Coaching: A Cognitive-Behavioural Approach*. Hove: Routledge.

Nussbaum, M.C. (2001) *Upheavals of Thought: The Intelligence of Emotions*. Cambridge: Cambridge University Press.

Osborne, A.F. (1953) *Applied Imagination*. New York: Charles Scribners.

Parkinson, B. (1995) *Ideas and Realities of Emotion*. London: Routledge.

Pehrson, J.B. and Mehrtens, S.E. (1997) *Intuitive Imagery: A Resource at Work*. Boston, MA: Butterworth-Heinemann.

Peters, T. and Austin, N. (1986) *A Passion for Excellence*. London: Collins.

Prince, G.M. (2003) How the emotional climate (field) impacts performance. *Creativity and Innovation Management, 12*(4), 240–6.

Rae, D. (2004) Entrepreneurial learning: a practical model from the creative industries. *Education and Training, 46*(8/9), 492–500.

Riquelme, H. (2000) How to Develop More Creative Strategic Plans: Results from an Empirical Study. *Creativity and Innovation Management, 9*(1), 14–20.

Sayegh, L., Anthony, W.P. and Perrewé, L. (2004) Managerial decision-making under crisis: The role of emotion in an intuitive decision process. *Human Resource Management Review, 14*, 179–99.

Schiemann, J.W. (2002) History and Emotions, Beliefs and Mental Models: Toward a Hermeneutics of Rational Choice. Paper presented to American Political Science Association Meeting, Boston, http://alpha.fdu.edu/~schieman/research/mental-models.pdf.

Schon, D.A. (1991) *The Reflective Practitioner: How Professionals Think in Action*. Aldershot: Avebury.

Schwitzgebel, E. (2002) How well do we know our own conscious experience? The case of visual imagery. *Journal of Consciousness Studies, 9*(5/6).

Segal, H. (1991) *Dream, Phantasy and Art*. London: Routledge.

Seibert, K.W. and Daudelin, M.W. (1999) *The Role of Reflection in Managerial Learning: Theory, Research and Practice*. Greenwood Press.

Seligman, M.E.P. and Csikszentmihalyi, M. (2000) Positive psychology: An introduction. *American Psychologist*, *55*, 5–14.

Siemer, M. (2005) Mood-congruent cognitions constitute mood experience. *Emotion*, *5*(3), 296–308.

Simon, H.A. (1977) *Models of Discovery*. Dordrecht-Holland: D Reidel Publishing.

Sinclair, A. (1992) 'The tyranny of a team ideology'. *Organization Studies*, *13*(4), 611–26.

Smith, P.B. (1980) *Group Processes and Personal Change*. London: Harper and Row.

Sparrow, J. (1998) *Knowledge in Organizations: Access to Thinking at Work*. London: Sage.

Sparrow, J. (2000) *Recognising emotion in knowledge*. Birmingham: Knowledge Management Centre.

Sparrow, J. (2005) Incorporating mood within unlived scenarios, Paper presented to the *Institute of Reflective Practice Conference, Scenario-based learning: Reflection and action on lived and unlived experiences,* 23–4 June, Gloucester, UK.

Sparrow, J. and Bentley, P. (2000) Decision tendencies of entrepreneurs and small business risk management practices. *Risk Management: An International Journal*, *2*(1), 17–26.

Sparrow, J. and Yeoman, I. (1999) Factors in management use of visual thinking techniques in problem solving, *XIth World Productivity Congress*, Edinburgh, 3–6 October.

Stahl, G. (2003). Meaning and Interpretation in Collaboration. In B. Wasson, S. Ludvigsen and U. Hoppe (Eds) *Designing For Change in Networked Learning Environments*. Dordrecht: Kluwer Academic Publishers. (pp. 523–32).

Stearns, P.N. (1989) Suppressing unpleasant emotions: the development of a twentieth-century American. In A.E. Barnes and P.N. Stearns (Eds) *Social History and Issues in Human Consciousness*. New York: New York University Press.

Stigler, M. and Pokorny, D. (2001) Emotions and primary process in guided imagery psychotherapy: Computerised text-analytic measures. *Psychotherapy Research*, *11*(4), 415–31.

Sundararajan, L. (2001) Background-mood in emotional creativity: A microanalysis. *Consciousness and Emotion*, *1*(2), 227–43.

Tran, V. (2004) *The influence of emotions on decision making processes in management teams*. Unpublished PhD thesis. Faculty of Psychology and Education Sciences, University of Geneva.

van der Lugt, R. (2002) Brainsketching and how it differs from brainstorming. *Creativity and Innovation Management*, *11*(1), 43–54.

van Maanen, J. and Kunda, G. (1989) 'Real feelings': Emotional expression and organizational culture. *Research in Organizational Behavior*, *11*, 43–103.

Vosburg, S.K. (1998) Mood and the quantity and quality of ideas. *Creativity Research Journal*, *11*(4), 315–24.

Warr, P. (1990) The measurement of wellbeing and other aspects of mental health. *Journal of Occupational Psychology*, *63*(3), 193–210.

Watson, D. and Tellegen, A. (1985) Toward a consensual structure of mood. *Psychological Bulletin*, *98*, 219–235.

Weick, K.E. (1995) *Sensemaking in Organizations*. Thousand Oaks, CA: Sage.

Wheatley, W.J., Maddox, E.N. and Anthony, W.P. (1989) Enhancing creativity and imagination in strategic planners through the utilization of guided imagery. *Organizational Development Journal*, *110*(1), 33–9.

Winkielman, P. and Berridge, K.C. (2004) Unconscious emotion. *Current Directions in Psychological Science*, *13*(3), 120–3.

Zwicky, F. (1969) *Discovery, Invention, Research through the Morphological Approach*. New York: Macmillan.

Style

The way people think and behave is determined to quite a large degree by innate individual differences. There is increasing consensus that there are five key personality differences known as the Big Five – extraversion, openness, agreeableness, conscientiousness and emotional stability. Many personality tests can be related to these five factors.

In a short article, Hampson reviews thinking about personality, the prominence of the Big Five dimensions and implications for whether or not we can change. A number of commentators feel that at least 40% of the variance in the Big Five factors is accounted for by genetic inheritance. Test–retest scores over 3 to 30 years are about .65 for the Big Five measures, suggesting relatively little change in adult personality, though of course we may get much better at self-presentation and coping.

Historically, creativity in the West has been associated with the big break through – the radical innovation – but more recently the West has woken up to the importance of the hitherto somewhat neglected incremental creativity, the sort that builds on what has gone before. Through Adaption Innovation theory, Kirton has drawn attention to the idea of creative style, emphasizing that there are different ways of being creative – people who like to do things differently or innovatively and those that prefer to do things better or adaptively, and that both approaches are valuable. This offers a very different idea from the notion of testing for creative ability to try and differentiate between those who are creative and those who are not. Here Kirton describes Adaption Innovation theory and the implications for the way people behave. Adaption Innovation is related to the Big Five openness factor.

Management through people is now recognized as a, if not the, key management skill, but it is often approached from a largely cognitive angle, i.e deficient skills are analysed and training is seen as the magic bullet that will insert the missing competency into people's brains. Here Goleman gives prominence to the importance of Emotional Intelligence, a catchy phrase that draws together certain key personal and interpersonal skills, namely self-awareness, self-regulation, motivation, empathy and social skills. He argues that it is emotional intelligence that differentiates good and bad leadership and that these emotional skills can be learnt, but through a lengthy process of individualized coaching not short-term training.

7

State of the Art: Personality

Sarah Hampson

Back in the 1960s, normal personality was largely studied with some version of trait theory. Personality traits (e.g. extraversion) are relatively stable dispositions that give rise to characteristic patterns of behaviour (e.g. a preference for activities involving other people to being alone), and logically depend on evidence of behavioural consistency. Mischel (1968) compiled a seemingly devastating critique of traits in which he demolished the idea that people behave consistently regardless of situation. 30 years later personality is alive and well. Indeed, these days, personality research is popular and personality testing is profitable.

Units of Analysis

In the 1980s, a new generation of personality psychologists responded to the critique of traits by advocating different units of analysis (Buss and Cantor, 1989). A hierarchy of units of analysis of personality emerged, with the whole person at the apex branching down through middle-level units such as 'life tasks' to traits and behaviours at the base.

Middle-level units dealing with smaller chunks of life history, such as 'personal strivings' (e.g. 'be myself and not do things to please others') (Emmons, 1986), and 'life tasks' (e.g. 'maturing beyond my high school mentality') (Cantor and Kihlstrom, 1987). These middle-level units are personal goals that reflect elements of motivation and personality. That is, a first-year undergraduate with a strong need for affiliation (motivation) and who scores highly on extraversion (personality) might have a personal goal of 'having a thriving social life by the end of the first term'. This goal might be achieved via life tasks such as 'make at least one friend every week' and personal strivings such as 'become a more witty and entertaining person'. By focusing on middle-level units, personality psychologists have become interested in the processes involved in translating personality into goals, and goals into behaviour.

Source: S. Hampson (1999) Edited extract from *Psychologist, 12*(6), 284–8.

Norem (1989) described another kind of middle-level unit, the cognitive strategy of defensive pessimism, by which people protect themselves from the disappointment of failing to achieve a desired goal by playing through the 'worst-case' scenario. For example, a defensive pessimist who very much desires to get a first-class degree, and who has a track record of first-class marks, will nevertheless dwell on the possibility of failing the degree. Personality types are another form of middle-level approach.

Towards the base of the pyramid we have units on a scale at a similar level to traits, such as motives (wishes and desires) and values (aspects of life we deem especially important). At this level, the debates are about whether there is a real difference between traits and motives, or motives and values. For example, in an almost convincing study, Winter et al. (1998) argued that motives describe unique aspects of personality not captured by traits, and that both units of analysis are necessary for a complete understanding of personality. These alternative units do not rely on the same evidence for their validity as do traits, so the arguments and data marshalled against traits do not apply. Instead, they bring their own challenges, such as how they differ from traits and how they all fit together. There is no 'right' unit, but there is a large range to choose from depending on the scale of the research question.

The Big Five

Despite the alternatives to traits, a significant chunk of personality psychology is still built around the trait concept. The big debate of the 1990s has been about the structure of trait terms: in particular, how many broad traits are needed to provide a comprehensive description of personality.

Eysenck remained a strong advocate of three: extraversion, neuroticism and psychoticism (e.g. Eysenck, 1991), whereas Cattell believed in about 15 plus intelligence (Cattell et al. 1970). However, the winning number in this lottery is undoubtedly five, Digman (1990), Goldberg (1993), John (1990) and McCrae and Costa (1997) are all compelling advocates for a five-factor structure, composed of broad domains of personality known as the Big Five. The Big Five and their trait descriptors are summarized in Table 7.1.

One major advantage of the Big Five framework is that it can assimilate other structures. For example, Goldberg and Rosolack (1994) demonstrated empirically that Eysenck's three-factor system of extraversion, neuroticism and psychoticism can be integrated into the Big Five. Psychoticism is a combination of undesirable Big Five III (low conscientiousness) and undesirable Big Five II (low agreeableness), while Eysenck's extraversion is equivalent to Big Five I (also called extraversion) and Eysenck's neuroticism to Big Five IV (emotional stability, which is simply the desirable pole of neuroticism).

The Big Five makes a useful structure for organizing the large and confusing number of traits and their measures in vogue today. However, it remains, for the most part, a description of normal personality and therefore is not as useful in clinical applications as it is in other areas such as occupational psychology.

Table 7.1 *The Big Five personality domains and representative traits*

Domain	Desirable Traits	Undesirable Traits
extraversion (I)	outgoing, sociable, assertive	introverted, reserved, passive
agreeableness (II)	kind, trusting, warm	hostile, selfish, cold
conscientiousness (III)	organised, thorough, tidy	careless, unreliable, sloppy
emotional stability (IV)	calm, even-tempered, imperturbable	moody, temperamental, nervous
intellect or openness (V)	imaginative, intelligent, creative	shallow, unsophisticated, imperceptive

Personality Consistency

Mischel developed an alternative to traits, called social cognitive units. These units incorporate a person's cognitions, affect and action assessed in relation to the situations in which they occur (Mischel, 1973). The focus on what the person does cognitively, affectively and behaviourally, rather than on what the person has in terms of traits. They include cognitive activities, encoding strategies, expectancies, values, preferences and goals.

More recently, Mischel and his colleagues have developed these ideas into a cognitive-affective personality system that accounts for intra-individual consistency and predictable patterns of variability across situations (Mischel and Shoda, 1995, 1998). For example, a person may be shy in small groups but be an excellent public speaker. This pattern of behaviour would be cross-situationally inconsistent if viewed in purely trait terms. But if the difference in the psychological situation is taken into account, it becomes a meaningful and predictable pattern of responding: speaking to a large group does not require engaging personally with any one individual, whereas making conversation in a small group does.

An important feature of these developments is that they incorporate situational factors as a moderating influence on individual differences. This is a more sophisticated response to the critique of traits than pure situationism (in which behaviour is solely a function of situations) or mechanistic interactionism (in which behaviour is viewed as a function of independent situational factors and trait factors in an analysis of variance framework).

A moderator approach to personality allows for social cognitive units to operate in combination with traits. Moderator approaches attempt to explain why traits alone do not always predict behaviour reliably. The general principle behind such approaches is that consistency will not be found for all of the people for all of the time, and must instead be sought for certain types of behaviour of certain types of people in certain types of situation.

Several different ways of moderating traits (i.e. of determining under what conditions behavioural consistency will be found) have been proposed. For example, Biesanz et al. (1998) demonstrated that individuals with higher test–retest stability of their trait ratings had more self–other agreement on these ratings than those with less temporal stability. That is, people who regard themselves as more stable over time on a particular trait (e.g. punctuality) will also be rated more accurately by others on this trait.

Another approach to the consistency problem, which connects to the units of analysis issue, is to use personality measures at different levels of abstraction. Depending on the level of precision required for the given prediction task. The idea is that broad traits such as the Big Five serve to predict broad classes of behaviour, but will not be as good as narrower traits at predicting specific behaviours (Lay, 1997). For example, a measure of Big Five conscientious will predict whether or not a person will arrive for a meeting on time with less precision than a measure of the highly specific trait of punctuality.

When working with large units of analysis, such as entire life histories, inconsistencies become increasingly apparent. As novelists and laypeople have been telling us for hundreds of years, people are not consistent and descriptions of ourselves and others contain inconsistencies. We know we can be both hardworking and lazy, friendly and reserved. Studies of trait ratings indicate that we use more inconsistencies in trait descriptions of ourselves than of other people: I am more likely to describe myself as both hardworking and lazy than to describe a colleague in this way.

When we describe ourselves or another with two inconsistent traits, they are most likely to be from the Big Five domain of emotional stability (e.g. 'I am both relaxed and nervous'), whereas we are least likely to use two inconsistent traits from the domain of intellect (e.g. 'I am both deep and shallow') (Hampson, 1997). Inconsistencies can be a subtle way of signalling a negative evaluation of a disliked person by attributing both a desirable and an undesirable trait describing the same aspect of personality (e.g. 'my boss is both friendly and cold' is inconsistent on Big Five agreeableness) (Hampson, 1998).

Given that behaviour is not always stable across time and across situations, but can to some extent be understood and predicted, contemporary personality psychology is not so much concerned with consistency as with coherence. We recognize that people show cross-situational variability in their behaviour but that this can be understood when other factors are taken into account, such as the influence of moderator variables described earlier.

When trying to understand our own inconsistent behaviours, we often appeal to some form of situational account: 'I am usually a helpful person but this year I did not volunteer to organize the office party because I was too busy with other things.' Coherence recognizes that a person's behaviour can be understood, and perhaps even predicted, despite not necessarily being strictly consistent.

Personality Testing

While academic psychologists agonized about whether there was such a thing as personality, the personality testing business started to take off and is now enjoying huge success.

Although personality tests can contribute to the prediction of job performance (e.g. Barrick and Mount, 1991), their predictive power is relatively low compared with other types of assessments, such as that of cognitive abilities (Hunter and Hunter, 1984) and decisions to hire or fire based on personality test scores are being challenged in the courts.

The testing business depends on surrounding its tests with a degree of mystique. Consequently, published personality tests protected by copyright become fossilized. They do not undergo constant revision and improvement as a result of research by the scientific community at large. Producing new versions of tests and new methods of scoring them is expensive and annoying for customers, and does not happen very often. Meanwhile, research may have revealed serious limitations.

In response to the inherently unscientific nature of copyrighted tests, Goldberg has produced a website in which he places in the public domain over 1200 personality items which can be grouped into scales to create measures equivalent to those found in many of the well-known copyrighted tests (ipip.ori.org/). Goldberg provides the necessary statistics to demonstrate which personality constructs these alternative scales assess, and not infrequently the new scales outperform those on which they are modelled (Goldberg, in press).

This new development should improve the quality of personality tests, and may lead to a more equal and informed relationship between the tester and those tested as a result of test-takers having easy access via the internet to information about the purpose of a test and how it is scored.

Nature versus Nurture

Over the last 20 years, the pendulum has swung towards the nature side of the nature–nurture debate in personality development and, as with the behavioural consistency problem, the nature–nurture debate has become much more complicated. Behaviour is the result of the complex interplay of traits and situations. Similarly, behaviour is the result of the complex interplay of nature and nurture, with genes implicated in both (Plomin, 1994).

An accumulation of evidence from family, twin and adoption studies has led to the conclusion that approximately 40 per cent of the variation in personality is genetic (Plomin et al., 1990). Contrary to the wisdom encapsulated in newspaper headlines, personality traits are unlikely to each be determined by a single gene. It is much more likely that there are polygenic influences on personality. With advances in molecular genetics permitting the study of individuals' actual DNA, the variance attributed to genetic factors inferred from family, twin and adoption studies can now be studied at the physiological level.

Changing Personalities

The genetic foundation to personality suggests immutability, and, according to McCrae and Costa (1990) adult personality is stable and does not change after 30 years of age. However, others have evidence for the malleability of personality in adulthood (e.g. Helson and Wink, 1992).

Which is right? Is personality stable or does it change? The answer is: it depends what you mean by personality. Personality as defined by trait scores (e.g. the Big Five) appears to remain relatively stable in adulthood. The median correlation for measures of the Big Five assessed across time points of three to 30 years apart is $r = 0.65$ (Costa and McCrae, 1994).

Those who advocate different personality units, such as life tasks, personal strivings, or even the study of entire biographies, are more likely to assert that personality changes (McAdams, 1994). Genetics and life circumstances may place limits on personality, but within these limits there is room for growth and adaptation. Life events such as parenthood provide an opportunity for new facets of personality to emerge, such as playfulness or a sense of responsibility. On the negative side, an emotionally stable person may become more neurotic as a consequence of worrying about a problem child. Moreover, for those aspects of personality that are linked to self-presentation and are therefore socially constructed, such as friendliness or conformity, we have the power to influence how we appear to others by modifying this self-presentation (Hampson, 1998). For a deeper examination of these issues, an excellent airing of the various arguments concerning personality stability versus change is to be found in Heatherton and Weinberger (1994).

References

Ajzen, I. (1988) *Attitudes, Personality and Behaviour*. Milton Keynes: Open University Press.

Barrick, M.R. and Mount, M.K. (1991) The Big Five personality dimensions and job performance: a meta-analysis. *Personnel Psychology, 44*, 1–26.

Biesanz, J.C., West, S.G. and Graziano, W.G. (1998) Moderators of self-other agreement: Reconsidering temporal stability in personality. *Journal of Personality and Social Psychology, 75*, 467–77.

Block, J. (1995) A contrarian view of the Five-Factor approach to personality description. *Psychological Bulletin, 117*, 187–215.

Buss, D.M. and Cantor, N. (1989) *Personality Psychology: Recent Trends and Emerging Directions*. New York: Springer-Verlag.

Cantor, N. and Kihlstrom, J.K. (1987) *Personality and Social Intelligence*. New York: Prentice-Hall.

Cattell, R.B., Eber, H. and Tatsuoka, M.M. (1970) *Handbook for the Sixteen Personality Factor Questionnaire* (16PF). Champaign, IL: Institute for Personality and Ability Testing.

Costa, P.T. and McCrae, R.R. (1994) Set like plaster! Evidence for the stability of adult personality. In T.F. Heatherton and J.L. Weinbeiger (Eds) *Can Personality Change?* Washington, DC: American Psychological Association.

Digman, J.M. (1990) Personality structure: Emergence of the five-factor model. *Annual Review of Psychology, 41*, 417–46.

Emmons, R.A. (1986) Personal strivings: An approach to personality and subjective well-being. *Journal of Personality and Social Psychology, 51*, 1058–68.

Eysenck, H.J. (1991) Dimensions of personality: 16, 5, or 3? – Criteria for a taxonomic paradigm. *Personality and Individual Differences, 12*, 773–90.

Goldberg, L.R. (1993) The structure of phenotypic personality traits. *American Psychologist, 48*, 26–34.

Goldberg, L.R. (in press) A broad-bandwidth, public domain, personality inventory measuring the lower-level facets of several five-factor models. In I. Mervielde, I. Deary, F. De Fruyt and F. Ostendorf (Eds) *Personality Psychology in Europe*, vol. 7. Tilburg: Tilburg University Press.

Goldberg, L.R. and Rosolack, T.K. (1994) The Big Five factor structure as an integrative framework: An empirical comparison with Eysenck's P-E-N model. In C.F. Halverson jr., G.A. Kohnstamm and R.P. Martin (Eds) *The Developing Structure of Temperament and Personality from Infancy to Adulthood*. New York: Lawrence Erlbaum.

Hampson, S.E. (1997) Determinants of inconsistent personality description: Trait and target effects. *Journal of Personality, 65*, 250–90.

Hampson, S.E. (1998) When is an inconsistency not an inconsistency? Trait reconciliation in personality description and impression formation. *Journal of Personality and Social Psychology, 74*, 102–17.

Heatherton, T.F. and Weinberger, J.L. (Eds) (1994) *Can Personality Change?* Washington, DC: American Psychological Association.

Helson, R and Wink, P. (1992) Personality change in women from the early 40s to the early 50s. *Psychology and Ageing, 7*, 46–55.

Hogan, R., Johnson, J. and Briggs, S. (Eds) (1997) *Handbook of Personality Psychology*. San Diego CA: Academic Press.

Hunter, J.E. and Hunter, R.F. (1984) Validity and utility of alternative predictors of job performance. *Psychological Bulletin, 96*, 72–98.

John, O.P. (1990) The 'Big Five' taxonomy: Dimensions of personality in the natural language and in questionnaires. In L.A. Pervin (Ed.) *Handbook of Personality: Theory and Research*. New York: Guildford Press.

Lay, C.H. (1997) Explaining lower-order traits through higher-order factors: The case of trait procrastination, conscientiousness, and the specificity dimensions. *European Journal of Personality, 11*, 267–78.

McAdams, D.P. (1994) Can personality change? Levels of stability and growth in personality across the life span. In T.F. Heatherton and J.K. Weinberger (Eds) *Can Personality Change?* Washington, DC: American Psychological Association.

McAdams, D.P. (1996) Personality, modernity, and the storied self: A contemporary framework for studying persons. *Psychological Inquiry, 7*, 295–321.

McCrae, R.R. and Costa, P.T. (1990) *Personality in Adulthood*. New York: Guildford Press.

McCrae, R.R. and Costa, P.T. (1997) Personality trait structure as a human universal. *American Psychologist, 52*, 509–16.

Mischel, W. (1968) *Personality and Assessment*. New York: Wiley.

Mischel, W. (1973) Toward a cognitive social-learning reconceptualisation of personality. *Psychological Review, 80*, 252–83.

Mischel, W. and Shoda, Y. (1995) A cognitive-affective system theory of personality: Reconceptualising situations, dispositions, dynamics and invariance in personality structure. *Psychological Review, 102*, 246–68.

Mischel, W and Shoda, Y. (1998) Reconciling processing dynamics and personality dispositions. *Annual Review of Psychology, 49*, 229–58.

Nasby, W. and Read, N.W. (1997) The inner and outer vouages of a solo circumnavigator: An integrative case study. Special Issue. *Journal of Personality, 65*, 757–1116.

Norem, J.K. (1989) Cognitive strategies as personality: Effectiveness, specificity, flexibility, and change. In D.M. Buss and N. Cantor (Eds) *Personality Psychology: Recent Trends and Emerging Directions*. New York: Springer-Verlag.

Pervin, L.A. and John, O.P. (Eds) (in press) *Handbook of Personality Theory and Research*. Second edition. New York: Guildford Press.

Plomin, R. (1994) *Genetics and Experience: The Interplay between Nature and Nurture*. Thousand Oaks, CA: Sage.

Plomin, R., Chipur, H.M. and Loehlin, J.C. (1990) Behavioural genetics and personality. In L.A. Pervin (Eds) *Handbook of Personality Theory and Research.* New York: Guildford Press.

Winter, D.G., John, O.P., Stewart, A.J., Klohnen, E.C. and Duncan, L.E. (1998) Traits and motives: toward an integration of two traditions in personality research. *Psychological Review, 105,* 230–50.

York, K.L. and John, O.P. (1992) The four faces of Eve: A typological analysis of women's personality at midlife. *Journal of Personality and Social Psychology, 63,* 494–508.

Adaptors and Innovators: Why New Initiatives Get Blocked

Michael J. Kirton

Background

The Adaption–Innovation theory defines and measures two styles of decision making, (Kirton, 1976, 1977, 1980) clarifying earlier literature on problem-solving and creativity which concentrates more on defining and assessing *level* rather than *style*. This shift of emphasis has advantages in the practical world of business, commerce and administration.

According to the Adaption–Innovation theory, everyone can be located on a continuum ranging from highly adaptive according to their score on the Kirton Adaption–Innovation Inventory. The range of responses is relatively fixed and stable (Kirton, 1977),[1] and in the general population approaches the normal curve distribution. For the purpose of clarity the following descriptions characterize those individuals at the extreme ends of the continuum.

Adaptors characteristically produce a sufficiency of ideas,[2] based closely on, but stretching, existing agreed definitions of the problem and likely solutions. They look at these in detail and proceed within the established mores (theories, policies, practices) of their organizations. Much of their effort to change is in improving and 'doing better' (which tends to dominate management, e.g. Drucker, 1969).

Innovators, by contrast, are more likely in the pursuit of change to reconstruct the problem, separating it from its enveloping accepted thought, paradigms and customary viewpoints, and emerge with much less expected and probably less acceptable solutions (see Fig. 8.1). They are less concerned with 'doing things better' than with 'doing things differently'.

The development of the A–I theory began with observations made and the conclusions reached as a result of a study of management initiative (Kirton, 1961). The aim of this study was to investigate the ways in which ideas that had led to radical changes in the companies studied were developed and implemented.

In each of the examples of initiative studied the resulting changes had required the co-operation of many managers and others in more than one department.

Source: M.J. Kirton (1984) *Long Range Planning*, 17, 2, 137–43.

Numerous examples of successful 'corporate' initiative, such as the introduction of a new product or new accounting procedures, were examined, and this analysis highlighted the stages through which such initiative passed on the way to becoming part of the accepted routine of the company, i.e. perception of the problem, analysis of the problem, analysis of the solution, agreement to change, acceptance of change, delegation and finally implementation. The study also looked at what went wrong at these various stages, and how the development of a particular initiative was thus affected. From this, a number of anomalies were thrown up that at the time remained unexplained.

(1) Delays in introducing change

Despite the assertion of managers that they were collectively both sensitive to the need for changes and willing to embark on them, the time lag between the first public airing of most of the ideas studied, and the date on which an idea was clearly accepted as a possible course of action, was a matter of years – usually two or three. Conversely, a few were accepted almost immediately, with the bare minimum of in-depth analysis. (The size of proposed changes did not much affect this time scale, although all the changes studied were large.)

(2) Objections to new ideas

All too often, the new idea had been formally blocked by a series of well-argued and reasoned objections which were upheld until some critical event – a 'precipitating event' – occurred, so that none of these quondam, cogent contrary arguments (lack of need, lack of resource, etc.) was ever heard again. Indeed, it appeared at times as if management had been hit by almost total collective amnesia concerning past objections.

(3) Rejection of individuals

There was a marked tendency for the majority of ideas which encountered opposition and delays to have been put forward by managers who were themselves unacceptable to an 'establishment' group, not just before, but also after the ideas they advocated had not only become accepted, but even been rated highly successful. At the same time, other managers putting forward the more palatable ideas not only were themselves initially acceptable, but remained so, even if these ideas were later rejected or failed.

The A–I theory now offers a rational, measured explanation of these findings.

Adaptors and Innovators – Two Different Styles of Thinking

Adaptive solutions are those that depend directly and obviously on generally agreed paradigms, are more easily grasped intellectually, and therefore more readily accepted by most – by adaptors as well as the many innovators not so directly involved in the resolution of the problem under scrutiny. The familiar assumptions on which the solution depends are not under attack, and help 'butter' the solution advanced, making it more palatable. Such derived ideas, being more readily acceptable, favourably affect the status of their authors, often even when they fail – and the authors of such ideas are much more

Adaptor	Innovator
Characterized by precision, reliability, efficiency, methodicalness, prudence, discipline, conformity	Seen as undisciplined, thinking tangentially, approaching tasks from unsuspected angles
Concerned with resolving problems rather than finding them	Could be said to discover problems and discover avenues of solution
Seeks solutions to problems in tried and understood ways	Queries problems' concomitant assumptions; manipulates problems
Reduces problems by improvement and greater efficiency, with maximum of continuity and stability	Is catalyst to settled groups, irreverent of their consensual views; seen as abrasive, creating dissonance
Seen as sound, conforming, safe, dependable	Seen as unsound, impractical; often shocks his opposite
Liable to make goals of means	In pursuit of goals treats accepted means with little regard
Seems impervious to boredom, seems able to maintain high accuracy in long spells of detailed work	Capable of detailed routine (system maintenance) work for only short bursts; quick to delegate routine tasks
Is in authority within given structures	Tends to take control in unstructured situations
Challenges rules rarely, cautiously, when assured of strong support	Often challenges rules, has little respect for past custom
Tends to high self-doubt. Reacts to criticism by closer outward conformity. Vulnerable to social pressures and authority; compliant	Appears to have low self-doubt when generating ideas, not needing consensus to maintain certitude in face of opposition
Is essential to the functioning of the institution all the time, but occasionally needs to be 'dug out' of his or her systems	In the institution is ideal in unscheduled crises, or better still to help to avoid them, if he or she can be controlled
When collaborating with innovators: Supplies stability, order and continuity to the partnership	*When collaborating with adaptors:* Supplies the task orientations, the break with the past and accepted theory
Sensitive to people, maintains group cohesion and co-operation	Appears insensitive to people, often threatens group cohesion and co-operation
Provides a safe base for the innovator's riskier operations	Provides the dynamics to bring about periodic radical change, without which institutions tend to ossify

Orginally published in Kirton,1976

Figure 8.1 *Behaviour descriptions of adaptors and innovators*

likely to be themselves adaptors, characterized as being personally more acceptable to the 'establishment' with whom they share those underlying familiar assumptions (Kirton, 1976). Indeed, almost irrespective of their rank, they are likely to be part of that establishment, which in the past has led innovators to claim somewhat crudely that adaptors owe their success to agreeing with their bosses. However, Kirton (1977a) conducted a study in which KAI scores were compared with superior/subordinate identification in a sample of 93 middle managers. No connection was found between KAI scores and tendency to agree with one's bosses. Instead a more subtle relationship is suggested, i.e. that those in the upper hierarchy are more likely to accept the same paradigms as their adaptor juniors, and that there is, therefore, a greater chance of agreement between them on broad issues and on approved courses of action. Where they disagree on detail within the accepted paradigm, innovators may be inclined to attach less significance to this and view the broad agreements reached as simple conformity.

It can thus be seen how failure of ideas is less damaging to the adaptor than to the innovator, since any erroneous assumptions upon which ideas were based were also shared with colleagues and other influential people. The consequence is that such failure is more likely to be written off as 'bad luck' or due to 'unforeseeable events', thereby directing the blame away from the individuals concerned.

In stark contrast to this, innovative ideas, not being as closely related to the group's prevailing, relevant paradigms, and even opposing such consensus views, are more strongly resisted, and their originators are liable to be treated with suspicion and even derision. This rejection of individuals tends to persist even after their ideas are adopted and acknowledged as successful. (It should be noted that both these and the further descriptions to come are put in a rather extreme form (as heuristic device) and usually therefore occur in a somewhat less dramatic form.)

Differences in Behaviour

Evidence is now accumulating from a number of studies that *personality* is implicated in these characteristic differences between adaptors and innovators (Kirton, 1976, 1977, Carne and Kirton, 1982). Indeed it must be so, since the way in which one thinks affects the way in which one behaves, and is seen to behave, in much the same way as there are differences in personality characteristics between those who are left brain dominated and those who are right brain dominated – the former being described as tending towards methodical, planned thinking and the latter towards more intuitive thinking (there is a significant correlation between left–right brain preference scores and adaption–innovation, Torrance, 1982). The personality characteristics of adaptors and innovators that are part of their cognitive style are here described.

Innovators are generally seen by adaptors as being abrasive and insensitive, despite the former's denial of these traits. This misunderstanding usually occurs because the innovator attacks the adaptor's theories and assumptions, both explicitly when he feels that the adaptor needs a push to hurry him in the right direction or to get him out of his rut, and implicitly by showing a disregard for the rules, conventions, standards of behaviour etc. What is even more upsetting for the adaptor is the fact that the innovator does not even seem to be aware of the havoc he is causing. Innovators may also appear abrasive to each other, since neither will show much respect for the other's theories, unless of course their two points of view happen temporarily to coincide. Adaptors can also be viewed pejoratively by innovators, suggesting that the more extreme types are far more likely to disagree than collaborate. Innovators tend to see adaptors as stuffy and unenterprising, wedded to systems, rules and norms which, however useful, are too restricting for their (the innovators') liking. Innovators seem to overlook how much of the smooth running all around them depends on good adaptiveness but are acutely aware of the less acceptable face of efficient bureaucracy (Weber, 1970; Merton, 1957). Disregard of convention when in pursuit of their own ideas has the effect of isolating innovators in a similar way to Rogers' (1957) creative loner.

While innovators find it difficult to combine with others, adaptors find it easier. The latter will more rapidly establish common agreed ground, assumptions, guidelines and accepted practices on which to ground their collaboration. Innovators also have to do these things in order to fit at all into a company but they are less good at doing so, less concerned with finding out the anomalies within a system, and less likely to stick to the patterns they help form. This is at once the innovators' weakness and a source of potential advantage.

Where are the Innovators and the Adaptors?

Much of Kirton's earlier research was devoted to the description and classification of these two cognitive styles. More recently, attention has been focused on the issue of how they are distributed and whether any distinctive patterns emerge. It has been found from a large number of studies that KAI scores are by no means haphazardly distributed. Individuals' scores are derived from a 32-item inventory, giving a theoretical range of 32–160, and a mean of 96. The observed range is slightly more restricted, 46–146, based on over 1000 subjects; the observed mean is near to 95 and the distribution conforms almost exactly to a normal curve. The studies have also shown that variations by identifiable subsets are predictable, their means shifting from the population mean in accordance with the theory. However, the group's range of scores is rarely restricted – even smallish groups showing ranges of approximately 70–120 – a finding with important implications for change, against the background of differences found at cultural level, at organizational level, between jobs, between departments and between individuals within departments. This is a somewhat arbitrary grouping since norms of cognitive style can be detected wherever a group of people define themselves as differing or distinct from others, by whatever criteria they choose, be it type of work, religion, philosophy, etc. However, while allowing for a certain amount of overlap, the majority of research studies can be classified according to these groupings.

Innovators and Adaptors in Different Cultures

A considerable amount of research information has been accumulating regarding the extent to which mean scores of different samples shift from culture to culture. For example, published normative samples collected from Britain (Kirton, 1976, 1977, 1980; Kirton and Pender 1982), USA (Keller and Holland, 1978), Canada (Kirton, 1980), and New Zealand (Kirton, 1978) have all produced remarkably similar means. When the KAI was validated on a sample of Eastern managers from Singapore and Malaysia (Thomson, 1980) their mean scores of 95 were compatible with those of their Western counterparts (e.g. UK managerial sample had a mean of 97; compared to general UK samples which together yielded a mean of 95.3).

However, samples of Indian and Iranian managers yielded lower means (91) than similar samples in the UK, USA, Canada and Singapore (Dewan, 1982; Hossaini, 1981; Khaneja, 1982). More adaptive norms were also found in work still in progress in a sample of black South African business students (Pottas, unpublished). These differences may not simply be a split between Western and Chinese Western groups vs others, since tentative results from a sample of Flemish-speaking job applicants for professional posts in a leading Belgian pharmaceutical company (Peeters, unpublished) have yielded an even more adaptive mean (85.6) than that of the South African sample.[3] Clearly there may be cultural differences of adaptor–innovator norms.

There is also a further speculation put forward by Kirton (1978a) that people who are most willing to cross boundaries of any sort are likely to be more innovative, and the more boundaries there are and the more rigidly they are held, the higher the innovative score should be of those who cross. In the Thomson study, managers in Western-owned companies in Singapore scored higher in innovativeness then either those working for a private local company or those in the Civil Service, and those in this last category had the most adaptive scores of the triad. Further evidence for cultural differences emerges in work on Indian and Iranian managers (Dewan, 1982; Hossaini, 1981; Khaneja, 1982). Here, it was found that, as expected, entrepreneurs scored higher on the KAI than non-entrepreneurs (97.9 and 90.5 as opposed to 77.2 for Government Officers), but Indian women entrepreneurial managers were found to be even more innovative than their male counterparts. They had to cross two boundaries: they broke with tradition by becoming a manager in the first place, and they had succeeded in becoming a manager in a risky entrepreneurial business.

Innovators and Adaptors in Different Organizations

Organizations in general (Weber, 1970; Bakke, 1965; Mulkay, 1972) and especially organizations which are large in size and budget (Swatez, 1970, Veblen, 1928) have a tendency to encourage bureaucracy and adaptation in order to minimize risk. It has been said by Weber (1970), Merton (1957) and Parsons (1951) that the aims of a bureaucratic structure are precision, reliability and efficiency, and that the bureaucratic structure exerts constant pressure on officials to be methodical, prudent and disciplined, and to attain an unusual degree of conformity. These are the qualities that the adaptor–innovator theory attributes to the 'adaptor' personality. For the marked adaptor, the longer an institutional practice has existed, the more he feels it can be taken for granted. So when confronted by a problem, he does not see it as a stimulus to question or change the structure in which the problem is embedded, but seeks a solution within that structure, in ways already tried and understood – ways which are safe, sure, predictable. He can be relied upon to carry out a thorough, disciplined search for ways to eliminate problems by 'doing things better' with a minimum of risk and a maximum of continuity and stability. This behaviour contrasts strongly with that of the marked innovator. The latter's solution, because it is less understood and its assumption untested, appears more risky, less sound, involves more 'ripple-effect' changes in areas less obviously needing to be affected; in short, it brings about changes with outcomes that cannot be envisaged so precisely. This diminution of predictive certainty is unsettling and not to be undertaken lightly, if at all, by most people – but particularly by adaptors, who feel not only more loyal to consensus policy but less willing to jeopardize the integrity of the system (or even the institution). The innovator, in contrast to the adaptor, is liable to be less respectful of the views of others, more abrasive in the presentation of his solution, more at home in a turbulent environment, seen initially as less relevant in his thinking towards company needs (since his perceptions may differ as to what is needed), less concerned with people in the pursuit of his goals than adaptors readily tolerate. Tolerance of the innovator is thinnest when adaptors feel under pressure from the need for imminent radical change. Yet the innovators' very disadvantages to institutions make them as necessary as the adaptors' virtues in turn make them.

Every organization has its own particular 'climate', and at any given time most of its key individuals reflect the general outlook. They gradually communicate this to others in the organization, and in time due to recruitment, turn-over and such processes, the cognitive style will reflect the general organizational ethos. However, the range seems to remain unaffected, and this is critical when one wishes to consider who might be the potential agents for a change in the mode of the whole group.

Sufficient evidence has been collected to enable predictions to be made about not only the direction of, but the extent to which these shifts in KAI mean will occur from organization to organization. For example, Kirton (1977, 1980) hypothesized that the mean scores of managers who work in a particularly stable environment will incline more towards adaption, while the mean scores of those whose environment could be described as turbulent will tend towards innovation. This hypothesis was supported by Thomson (1980), whose study showed that a Singapore sample of middle-ranking Civil Servants were markedly adaptor-inclined (mean = 89) whereas the means of a sample of managers in multi-national companies were just as markedly innovator-inclined (mean = 107).

A dissertation by Holland (1982) suggests that bank employees are inclined to be adaptors; so are local government employees (Keller and Holland, 1978). Two of these studies support and refine the hypothesis that, given time, the mean KAI score of a group will reflect its ethos. Both Holland and Hayward and Everett found the groups of new recruits had means away from those of the established groups they were joining. However, within 3 years (Holland) or at most 5 years (Hayward and Everett), as a result of staff changes, the gaps between the means of the new groups and the established groups narrowed sharply.

If there are predictable variations between companies wherever selection has been allowed to operate for a sufficient length of time, then variations may be expected within a company as adaptors and innovators are placed in the parts of the organization which suit them best. It is unlikely (as well as undesirable), that any organization is so monolithic in its structure and in the 'demands' on its personnel that it produces a total conformity of personality profiles. This hypothesis was tested and supported by Kirton (1980) when adaptors were found to be more at home in departments of a company that must concentrate on solving problems which mainly emanate from within their departmental system (e.g. production) and innovators tend to be more numerous in departments that act as interfaces (e.g. sales, progress chasing). Studies by Keller and Holland (1978, 1978a, 1979) in American R&D departments found that adaptors and innovators had different roles in internal company communications: adaptors being more valued for communications on the workings of the company and innovators being more valued for communications on advanced technological information (Keller and Holland, 1979). Kirton (1980, 1980a) also found that managers who tend to select themselves to go on courses (i.e. selected) will have significantly different mean KAI scores from the managers on courses who were just sent as part of the general scheme (i.e. personally unselected), the former being innovator-inclined. Members of three groups of courses were tested: one British 'unselected', one British 'selected' and one Canadian 'selected'. The results (Kirton, 1980a) showed that the unselected managers scored significantly more adaptively than the selected groups. Among the Canadian sample of managers, there was sufficient information on their job titles to be able to divide them into two groups of occupations: those liable to be found in adaptor-oriented departments (e.g. line manager) and those liable to be found in innovator-oriented departments (e.g. personnel consultant). The latter group were found to be significantly more innovative than the former, having a mean of 116.4 for non-line managers as opposed to a mean of 100.14 for line managers.[4] These findings later led to a full-scale study (Kirton and Pender, 1982) in which data on 2375 subjects collected in 15 independent studies were cross-tabulated with reference to different occupational types and varying degrees of self-selection to courses. Engineering instructors and apprentices were studied as examples of occupations involving a narrow range of paradigms, thorough rigid training and closely structured environment, while research and development personnel were examined as examples of occupations involving a number of flexible paradigms and a relatively unstructured environment. The differences were large, significant and in the expected direction.

These variations which exist between companies and between occupational groups are also found within the relatively narrow boundaries of the job itself. For example, work in progress suggests that within a job there may be clear subsets whose tasks differ and whose cognitive styles differ, e.g. an examination of the job of quality control workers for a local government body revealed that the job contained two major aspects. One was the vital task of monitoring, and one was the task of solving anomalies which were thrown up in the system from time to time. The first of these tasks was carried out by an adaptive inclined group, and the second by an innovative one.

Such knowledge about jobs and who is inclined to do them could eventually lead to better integration of adaptors and innovators within a company.

Who are the Change Agents?

It has already been noted that the mean adaptor-innovator score of a group may shift quite considerably depending on the population in question, whilst the range remains relatively stable. This suggests that many a person is part of a group whose mean adaptor-innovator score is markedly different from his own. There are three possible reasons why these individuals should be caught up in this potentially stressful situation:

(a) they are in transit, for example, under training schemes
(b) they are trapped and unhappy and may soon leave (Holland, 1982; Haywood and Everett, 1983)
(c) they have found a niche which suits them and have developed a particular role identity

(These three categories should be regarded as fluid, since given a change in the individual's peer group, boss, department or even organizational outlook, he may well find himself shifting from one category to another.)

It is the identification of the third category which will most repay further investigation since it contains refinements of the A–1 theory which have considerable practical implications, though these are as yet speculations and work is currently being undertaken to explore their ramifications more fully.

The individual who can successfully accept and be accepted into an environment alien to his own cognitive style must have particular survival characteristics, and it is those characteristics which make him a potential agent for change within that particular group. In order to effect a change an individual must first have job 'know-how' which is also an important quality keeping him functioning as a valuable group member when major changes are not needed. He must also be able to gain the respect of his colleagues and superiors, and with this comes commensurate status, which is essential if he wants his ideas to be recognized. Lastly, if a person is embarked on a course of action for change, he will of course require the general capacity, e.g. leadership, management qualities, to carry out such a task. His different cognitive style gives him a powerful advantage over his colleagues in being able to anticipate events which others may not see (since due to their cognitive styles, they may not think to look in that direction).

Therefore, the agent for change can be seen as a competent individual who has enough skill to be successful in a particular environment (which he may in fact have made easier by selecting or being selected for tasks within the unit less alien to his or her cognitive style). At this point he plays a supportive role to the main thrust of the group with its contrasting cognitive style. Given a 'precipitating event' however (particularly if he has anticipated and prepared for it), the individual becomes at once a potential leader in a new situation. In order to be able to take advantage of this position, he must have personal qualities to bring to bear, management must have the insight to recognize the position, and management development must have also played its part. However, this may need to be reinforced by individual and group counselling which makes use of an understanding of Adaption–Innovation theory (Lindsay, unpublished; Davies, unpublished).

It should be emphasized here that the change agent can be either an adaptor or an innovator, and this is solely determined by the group composition, so that if it is an innovator group, the change agent will be an adaptor, and vice versa. This discovery challenges traditional assumptions that heralding and initiating change is the innovator's prerogative because a precipitating event could demand either an adaptive or innovative solution, depending on the original orientation of the group and the work. An example in which an adaptor is the change agent in a team of innovators might be where the precipitating event takes the form of a bank's refusal to give further financial support to a new business enterprise. At this stage the change agent (who may have been anticipating this event for months) is at hand with the facts, figures and a cost cutting contingency plan all neatly worked out. It is now that the personal qualities of know-how, respect, status and ability will be crucial for success. All this assumes that many groups will have means away from the centre. It seems likely that the more the mean is displaced in either direction, the harder it will be, the bigger the precipitating event needed, to pull the group back to the middle, which may be unfortunate both for the group and change agent. However, an 'unbalanced' team is what may be required at any particular time. To hold such a position and yet to be capable of flexibility is a key task of management to which this theory may make a contribution.

In a wider context, it is hoped that the Adaption–Innovation theory will offer an insight into the interactions between the individual, the organization and change. By using the theory as an additional informational resource when forward planning, it may also be possible to anticipate, and retain control in the face of changes brought about by extraneous factors. This hopefully will enable such changes to take place amid less imbalance and confusion, thereby rendering them more effective.

Notes

Throughout for he, him, his, read also she, her, hers.

1 Test–retest coefficients of 0.82 for 6th formers ($N = 412$) on one New Zealand study after 8 months (Kirton, 1978); South African study after 5 months on $N = 143$, means: 91.18, S.D. 9.31; and 91.10, S.D. 8.52 (Pottas, unpublished).

2 Factor analyses show that total adaptor–innovator scores are composed of three traits: sufficiency versus proliferation of originality; degree of (personal) efficiency; and degree of group-rule conformity. They are closely related respectively to Rogers' creative loner, and Weber's and Merton's typical bureaucratic behaviour.

3 Caution: based on a Dutch version of KAI which is still being tested.

4 Because of the nature of this course and selection system, both groups' means were displaced towards innovativeness; however, they retain their distance *vis-à-vis* each other.

References

Bakke, E.W. (1965) Concept of the social organisation. In M. Haire (Ed.) *Modern Organisation Theory*. Wiley: New York.

Carne, J.C. and Kirton, M.J. (1982) Styles of creativity: test score correlations between the Kirton Adaption–Innovation Inventory and the Myers-Briggs Type Indicator. *Psychological Reports, 50*, 31–6.

Davies, G.B. Unpublished data (in preparation) Cambridge Management Centre: UK.

Dewan, S. (1982) Personality characteristics of entrepreneurs, Ph.D. Thesis, Institute of Technology: Delhi.

Drucker, P.F. (1969) Management's new role. HBR Nov–Dec, 47, 6, 49–54. Harvard Business School Publishing.

Holland, P.A. (1982) Creative thinking: an asset of liability in employment, M.Ed. Dissertation, University of Manchester.

Hossaini, H.R. (1981) Leadership effectiveness and cognitive style among Iranian and Indian middle managers, Ph.D Thesis, Institute of Technology: Delhi.

Keller, R.T. and Holland, W.E. (1978) A cross-validation study of the Kirton Adaption–Innovation Inventory in three research and development organizations. *Applied Psychological Measurement, 2,* 563–570.

Keller, R.T. and Holland, W.E. (1978a) Individual characteristics of innovativeness and communication in research and development organisations. *Journal of Applied Psychology, 63,* 759–62.

Keller, R.T. and Holland, W.E. (1979) Towards a selection battery for research and development professional employees. *IEEE Transactions on Engineering Management, EM-26* (4) November.

Khaneja, D.K. (1982) Relationship of the adaption-innovation continuum to achievement orientation in entrepreneurs and non-entrepreneurs, Ph.D Thesis, Institute of Technology: Delhi.

Kirton, M.J. (1961) *Management Initiative.* Acton Society Trust: London.

Kirton, M.J. (1976) Adaptors and innovators; a description and measure. *Journal of Applied Psychology, 61,* 622–29.

Kirton, M.J. (1977) *Manual of the Kirton Adaption-Innovation Inventory.* National Foundation for Educational Research: London.

Kirton, M.J. (1977a) Adaptors and innovators and superior-subordinate identification. *Psychological Reports, 41,* 289–90.

Kirton, M.J. (1978) Have adaptors and innovators equal levels of creativity? *Psychological Reports, 42,* 695–98.

Kirton, M.J. (1978a) Adaptors and innovators in culture clash. *Current Anthropology, 19,* 611–12.

Kirton, M.J. (1980) Adaptors and innovators; the way people approach problems. *Planned Innovation, 3,* 51–4.

Kirton, M.J. (1980a) Adaptors and innovators in organizations. *Human Relations, 3,* 213–24.

Kirton, M.J. and Pender, S.R. (1982) The adaption–innovation continuum: occupational type and course selection. *Psychological Reports, 51,* 883–6.

Lindsay, P. Unpublished data (in press) Cambridge Management Centre: UK.

Merton, R.K. (Ed.) (1957) Bureaucratic structure and personality. In *Social Theory and Social Structure.* Free Press of Glencoe, New York.

Mulkay, M.S. (1972) *The Social Process of Innovation.* Macmillan: London.

Parsons, T. (1951) *The Social System.* Free Press of Glencoe: New York.

Peeters, L. Unpublished data, Janssen Pharmaceutical, Belgium.

Pottas, C.D. Unpublished data, University of Pretoria, South Africa.

Rogers, C.R. (1957) Towards a theory of creativity. In H.H. Anderson (Ed.) *Creativity And Its Cultivation.* Harper: New York.

Swatez, G.M. (1970) The Social Organisation of a University Laboratory. *Minerva, A Review of Science,* Learning and Policy, VIII, 1, January.

Thomson, D. (1980) Adaptors and innovators: a replication study on managers in Singapore and Malaysia. *Psychological Reports,* 47, 383–7.

Torrance, E.P. (1982) Hemisphericity and creative functioning. *Journal of Research and Development in Education, 15,* 29–37.

Veblen, T. (1928) *The Theory of the Leisure Class.* Vanguard Press: New York.

Weber, M. (1970). In H.H. Gerth and C.W. Mills (Eds and trans.) *From Max Weber: Essays in Sociology.* Routledge & Kegan Paul: London.

What Makes a Leader?

Daniel Goleman

Every business person knows a story about a highly intelligent, highly skilled executive who was promoted into a leadership position only to fail at the job. And they also know a story about someone with solid – but not extraordinary – intellectual abilities and technical skills who was promoted into a similar position and then soared.

Such anecdotes support the widespread belief that identifying individuals with the 'right stuff' to be leaders is more art than science. After all, the personal styles of superb leaders vary: some leaders are subdued and analytical; others shout their manifestos from the mountain tops. And just as important, different situations call for different types of leadership. Most mergers need a sensitive negotiator at the helm, whereas many turnarounds require a more forceful authority.

I have found, however, that the most effective leaders are alike in one crucial way: they all have a high degree of what has come to be known as *emotional intelligence*. It's not that IQ and technical skills are irrelevant. They do matter, but mainly as 'threshold capabilities'; that is, they are the entry-level requirements for executive positions. But my research, along with other recent studies, clearly shows that emotional intelligence is the sine qua non of leadership. Without it, a person can have the best training in the world, an incisive, analytical mind, and an endless supply of smart ideas, but he still won't make a great leader. In the course of the past year, my colleagues and I have focused on how emotional intelligence operates at work. We have examined the relationship between emotional intelligence and effective performance, especially in leaders. And we have observed how emotional intelligence shows itself on the job. How can you tell if someone has high emotional intelligence, for example, and how can you recognize it in yourself? In the following pages, we'll explore these questions, taking each of the components of emotional intelligence – self-awareness, self-regulation, motivation, empathy, and social skill – in turn.

Source: D. Goleman (1998) *Harvard Business Review*, November, 93–102.

Table 9.1   *The five components of emotional intelligence at work*

	Definition	**Hallmarks**
Self-awareness	The ability to recognize and understand your moods, emotions and drives, as well as their effect on others	Self-confidence, realistic self-assessment, self-depreciating sense of humour
Self-regulation	The ability to control or redirect impulses and moods The propensity to suspend judgement – to think before acting	Trustworthiness and integrity, comfort with ambiguity, openness to change
Motivation	A passion to work for reasons that go beyond money or status A propensity to pursue goals with energy and enthusiasm	Strong drive to achieve optimism, even in the face of failure, organizational commitment
Empathy	Ability in managing meaningful relationships and building networks Skill in treating people according to their emotional reactions	Expertise in building and retaining talent, cross-cultural sensitivity, service to clients and customers
Social skill	Proficiency in managing relationships and building networks An ability to find common ground and support	Effectiveness in leading change, persuasiveness, expertise in building and leading teams

Evaluating Emotional Intelligence

Most large companies today have employed trained psychologists to develop what are known as 'competency models' to aid them in identifying, training, and promoting likely stars in the leadership firmament. The psychologists have also developed such models for lower-level positions. And in recent years, I have analyzed competency models from 188 companies, most of which were large and global and included the likes of Lucent Technologies, British Airways, and Credit Suisse.

In carrying out this work, my objective was to determine which personal capabilities drove outstanding performance within these organizations, and to what degree they did so. I grouped capabilities into three categories: purely technical skills like accounting and business planning; cognitive abilities like analytical reasoning; and competencies demonstrating emotional intelligence such as the ability to work with others and effectiveness in leading change.

To create some of the competency models, psychologists asked senior managers at the companies to identify the capabilities that typified the organization's most outstanding leaders. To create other models, the psychologists used objective criteria such as a division's profitability to differentiate the star performers at senior levels within their organizations from the average ones. Those individuals were then extensively interviewed and tested, and their capabilities were compared. This process resulted in the creation of lists of ingredients for highly effective leaders. The lists ranged in length from 7 to 15 items and included such ingredients as initiative and strategic vision.

When I analyzed all this data, I found dramatic results. To be sure, intellect was a driver of outstanding performance. Cognitive skills such as big-picture thinking and long-term vision were particularly important. But when I calculated the ratio of technical skills, IQ, and emotional intelligence as ingredients of excellent performance, emotional intelligence proved to be twice as important as the others for jobs at all levels.

Moreover, my analysis showed that emotional intelligence played an increasingly important role at the highest levels of the company, where differences in technical skills are of negligible importance. In other words, the higher the rank of a person considered to be a star performer, the more emotional intelligence capabilities showed up as the reason for his or her effectiveness. When I compared star performers with average ones in senior leadership positions, nearly 90% of the difference in their profiles was attributable to emotional intelligence factors rather than cognitive abilities.

Other researchers have confirmed that emotional intelligence not only distinguishes outstanding leaders but can also be linked to strong performance. The findings of the late David McClelland, the renowned researcher in human and organizational behavior, are a good example. In a 1996 study of a global food and beverage company, McClelland found that when senior managers had a critical mass of emotional intelligence capabilities, their divisions outperformed yearly earnings goals by 20%. Meanwhile, division leaders without that critical mass underperformed by almost the same amount. McClelland's findings, interestingly, held as true in the company's U.S. divisions as in its divisions in Asia and Europe.

In short, the numbers are beginning to tell us a persuasive story about the link between a company's success and the emotional intelligence of its leaders. And just as important, research is also demonstrating that people can, if they take the right approach, develop their emotional intelligence. (See Box 9.1.)

Box 9.1   Can emotional intelligence be learned?

For ages, people have debated if leaders are born or made. So too goes the debate about emotional intelligence. Are people born with certain levels of empathy, for example, or do they acquire empathy as a result of life's experiences? The answer is both. Scientific inquiry strongly suggests that there is a genetic component to emotional intelligence. Psychological and developmental

(Continued)

research indicates that nurture plays a role as well. How much each perhaps will never be known, but research and practice clearly demonstrate that emotional intelligence can be learned.

One thing is certain: emotional intelligence increases with age. There is an old-fashioned word for the phenomenon: maturity. Yet even with maturity, some people still need training to enhance their emotional intelligence. Unfortunately, far too many training programs that intend to build leadership skills – including emotional intelligence – are a waste of time and money. The problem is simple: they focus on the wrong part of the brain.

Emotional intelligence is born largely in the neuro-transmitters of the brain's limbic system, which governs feelings, impulses, and drives. Research indicates that the limbic system learns best through motivation, extended practice, and feedback. Compare this with the kind of learning that goes on in the neocortex, which governs analytical and technical ability. The neocortex grasps concepts and logic. It is the part of the brain that figures out how to use a computer or make a sales call by reading a book. Not surprisingly – but mistakenly – it is also the part of the brain targeted by most training programs aimed at enhancing emotional intelligence. When such programs take, in effect, a neo-cortical approach, my research with the Consortium for Research on Emotional Intelligence in Organisations has shown they can even have a negative impact on people's job performance.

To enhance emotional intelligence, organizations must refocus their training to include the limbic system. They must help people break old behavioural habits and establish new ones. That not only takes much more time than conventional training programs, it also requires an individualized approach.

Imagine an executive who is thought to be low on empathy by her colleagues. Part of that deficit shows itself as an inability to listen; she interrupts people and doesn't pay close attention to what they're saying. To fix the problem, the executive needs to be motivated to change, and then she needs practice and feedback from others in the company.

A colleague or coach could be tapped to let the executive know when she has been observed failing to listen. She would then have to replay the incident and give a better response; that is, demonstrate her ability to absorb what others are saying. And the executive could be directed to observe certain executives who listen well and to mimic their behaviour.

With persistence and practice, such a process can lead to lasting results. I know one Wall Street executive who sought to improve his empathy – specifically his ability to read people's reactions and see their perspectives. Before beginning his quest, the executive's subordinates were terrified of working with him. People

(Continued)

> **Box 9.1** *(Continued)*
>
> even went so far as to hide bad news from him. Naturally, he was shocked when finally confronted with these facts. He went home and told his family – but they only confirmed what he had heard at work. When their opinions on any given subject did not mesh with his, they, too, were frightened of him.
>
> Enlisting the help of a coach, the executive went to work to heighten his empathy through practice and feedback. His first step was to take a vacation to a foreign country where he did not speak the language. While there, he monitored his reactions to the unfamiliar and his openness to people who were different from him. When he returned home, humbled by his week abroad, the executive asked his coach to shadow him for parts of the day, several times a week, in order to critique how he treated people with new or different perspectives. At the same time, he consciously used on-the-job interactions as opportunities to practice 'hearing' ideas that differed from his. Finally, the executive had himself videotaped in meetings and asked those who worked for and with him to critique his ability to acknowledge and understand the feelings of others. It took several months, but the executive's emotional intelligence was reflected in his overall performance on the job.
>
> It's important to emphasize that building one's emotional intelligence cannot – will not – happen without sincere desire and concerted effort. A brief seminar won't help; nor can one buy a how-to manual. It is much harder to learn to empathize – to internalize empathy as a natural response to people – than it is to become adept at regression analysis. But it can be done. 'Nothing great was ever achieved without enthusiasm,' wrote Ralph Waldo Emerson. If your goal is to become a real leader, these words can serve as a guidepost in your efforts to develop high emotional intelligence.

Self-awareness

Self-awareness is the first component of emotional intelligence – which makes sense when one considers that the Delphic oracle gave the advice to 'know thyself' thousands of years ago. Self-awareness means having a deep understanding of one's emotions, strengths, weaknesses, needs, and drives. People with strong self-awareness are neither overly critical nor unrealistically hopeful. Rather, they are honest – with themselves and with others.

People who have a high degree of self-awareness recognize how their feelings affect them, other people, and their job performance. Thus a self-aware person, who knows that tight deadlines bring out the worst in him, plans his time carefully and gets his work done well in advance. Another person with high self-awareness will be able to work with a demanding client. She will understand the client's impact on her moods and the deeper reasons for her frustration. 'Their trivial demands take us away from the real work that needs to be done,' she might explain. And she will go one step further and turn her anger into something constructive.

Self-awareness extends to a person's understanding of his or her values and goals. Someone who is highly self-aware knows where he is headed and why, so, for example, he will be able to be firm in turning down a job offer that is tempting financially but does not fit with his principles or long-term goals. A person who lacks self-awareness is apt to make decisions that bring on inner turmoil by treading on buried values. 'The money looked good so I signed on,' someone might say two years into a job, 'but the work means so little to me that I'm constantly bored.' The decisions of self-aware people mesh with their values; consequently, they often find work to be energizing.

How can one recognize self-awareness? First and foremost, it shows itself as candor and an ability to assess oneself realistically. People with high self-awareness are able to speak accurately and openly – although not necessarily effusively or confessionally – about their emotions and the impact they have on their work. For instance, one manager I know of was skeptical about a new personal-shopper service that her company, a major department-store chain, was about to introduce. Without prompting from her team or her boss, she offered them an explanation: 'It's hard for me to get behind the rollout of this service,' she admitted, 'because I really wanted to run the project, but I wasn't selected. Bear with me while I deal with that.' The manager did indeed examine her feelings; a week later, she was supporting the project fully.

Such self-knowledge often shows itself in the hiring process. Ask a candidate to describe a time he got carried away by his feelings and did something he later regretted. Self-aware candidates will be frank in admitting to failure – and will often tell their tales with a smile. One of the hallmarks of self-awareness is a self-deprecating sense of humor.

Self-awareness can also be identified during performance reviews. Self-aware people know – and are comfortable talking about – their limitations and strengths, and they often demonstrate a thirst for constructive criticism. By contrast, people with low self-awareness interpret the message that they need to improve as a threat or a sign of failure.

Self-aware people can also be recognized by their self-confidence. They have a firm grasp of their capabilities and are less likely to set themselves up to fail by, for example, overstretching on assignments. They know, too, when to ask for help. And the risks they take on the job are calculated. They won't ask for a challenge that they know they can't handle alone. They'll play to their strengths.

Consider the actions of a mid-level employee who was invited to sit in on a strategy meeting with her company's top executives. Although she was the most junior person in the room, she did not sit there quietly, listening in fearful silence. She knew she had a head for clear logic and the skill to present ideas persuasively, and she offered cogent suggestions about the company's strategy. At the same time, her self-awareness stopped her from wandering into territory where she knew she was weak.

Despite the value of having self-aware people in the workplace, my research indicates that senior executives don't often give self-awareness the credit it deserves when they look for potential leaders. Many executives mistake candor about feelings for 'wimpiness' and fail to give due respect to employees who openly acknowledge their shortcomings. Such people are too readily dismissed as 'not tough enough' to lead others.

In fact, the opposite is true. In the first place, people generally admire and respect candor. Further, leaders are constantly required to make judgment calls that require a candid assessment of capabilities – their own and those of others. Do we have the management expertise to acquire a competitor? Can we launch a new product within six months? People who assess themselves honestly – that is, self-aware people – are well suited to do the same for the organizations they run.

Self-regulation

Biological impulses drive our emotions. We cannot do away with them – but we can do much to manage them. Self-regulation, which is like an ongoing inner conversation, is the component of emotional intelligence that frees us from being prisoners of our feelings. People engaged in such a conversation feel bad moods and emotional impulses just as everyone else does, but they find ways to control them and even to channel them in useful ways.

Imagine an executive who has just watched a team of his employees present a botched analysis to the company's board of directors. In the gloom that follows, the executive might find himself tempted to pound on the table in anger or kick over a chair. He could leap up and scream at the group. Or he might maintain a grim silence, glaring at everyone before stalking off.

But if he had a gift for self-regulation, he would choose a different approach. He would pick his words carefully, acknowledging the team's poor performance without rushing to any hasty judgment. He would then step back to consider the reasons for the failure. Are they personal – a lack of effort? Are there any mitigating factors? What was his role in the debacle? After considering these questions, he would call the team together, lay out the incident's consequences, and offer his feelings about it. He would then present his analysis of the problem and a well-considered solution.

Why does self-regulation matter so much for leaders? First of all, people who are in control of their feelings and impulses – that is, people who are reasonable – are able to create an environment of trust and fairness. In such an environment, politics and infighting are sharply reduced and productivity is high. Talented people flock to the organization and aren't tempted to leave. And self-regulation has a trickle-down effect. No one wants to be known as a hothead when the boss is known for her calm approach. Fewer bad moods at the top mean fewer throughout the organization.

Second, self-regulation is important for competitive reasons. Everyone knows that business today is rife with ambiguity and change. Companies merge and break apart regularly. Technology transforms work at a dizzying pace. People who have mastered their emotions are able to roll with the change. When a new change program is announced, they don't panic; instead, they are able to suspend judgement, seek out information, and listen to executives explain the new program. As the initiative moves forward, they are able to move with it.

Sometimes they even lead the way. Consider the case of a manager at a large manufacturing company. Like her colleagues, she had used a certain software program for five years. The program drove how she collected and reported data and how she thought about the company strategy. One day, senior executives announced that a new program was to be installed that would radically change how information was gathered and assessed within the organization. While many people in the company complained bitterly about how disruptive the change would be, the manager mulled over the reasons for the new program and was convinced of its potential to improve performance. She eagerly attended training sessions – some of her colleagues refused to so – and was eventually promoted to run several divisions, in part because she used the new technology so effectively.

I want to push the importance of self-regulation to leadership even further and make the case that it enhances integrity, which is not only a person virtue but also an organizational strength. Many of the bad things that happen in companies are a function of impulsive behaviour. People rarely plan to exaggerate profits, pad expense accounts, dip into the till, or abuse power for selfish ends. Instead, an opportunity presents itself, and people with low impulse control just say yes.

By contrast, consider the behaviour of the senior executive at a large food company. The executive was scrupulously honest in his negotiations with local distributors. He would routinely lay out his cost structure in detail, thereby giving the distributors a realistic understanding of the company's pricing. This approach meant the executive couldn't always drive a hard bargain. Now, on occasion, he felt the urge to increase profits by withholding information about the company's costs. But he challenged that impulse – he saw that it made more sense in the long run to counteract it. His emotional self-regulation paid off in strong, lasting relationships with distributors that benefited the company more than any short-term financial gains would have.

The signs of emotional self-regulation, therefore, are not hard to miss: a propensity for reflection and thoughtfulness; comfort with ambiguity and change; and integrity – an ability to say no to impulsive urges.

Like self-awareness, self-regulation often does not get its due. People who can master their emotions are sometimes seen as cold fish – their considered responses are taken as a lack of passion. People with fiery temperaments are frequently thought of as 'classic' leaders – their outbursts are considered hallmarks of charisma and power. But when such people make it to the top, their impulsiveness often works against them. In my research, extreme displays of negative emotion have never emerged as a driver of good leadership.

Motivation

If there is one trait that virtually all effective leaders have, it is motivation. They are driven to achieve beyond expectations – their own and everyone else's. The key word here is achieve. Plenty of people are motivated by external factors such as a big salary or the status that comes from having an impressive title or being part of a prestigious company. By contrast, those with leadership potential are motivated by a deeply embedded desire to achieve for the sake of achievement.

If you are looking for leaders, how can you identify people who are motivated by the drive to achieve rather than by external rewards? The first sign is a passion for the work itself – such people seek out creative challenges, love to learn, and take great pride in a job well done. They also display an unflagging energy to do things better. People with such energy often seem restless with the status quo. They are persistent with their questions about why things are done one way rather than another; they are eager to explore new approaches to their work.

A cosmetics company manager, for example, was frustrated that he had to wait two weeks to get sales results from people in the field. He finally tracked down an automated phone system that would beep each of his salespeople at 5pm every day. An automated message then prompted them to punch in their numbers – how many calls and sales they had made that day. The system shortened the feedback time on sales results from weeks to hours.

That story illustrates two other common traits of people who are driven to achieve. They are forever raising the performance bar, and they like to keep score. Take the performance bar first. During performance reviews, people with high levels of motivation might ask to be 'stretched' by their superiors. Of course, an employee who combines self-awareness with internal motivation will recognize her limits – but she won't settle for objectives that seem too easy to fulfill.

And it follows naturally that people who are driven to do better also want a way of tracking progress – their own, their team's, and their company's. Whereas people with low achievement motivation are often fuzzy about results, those with high achievement motivation often keep score by tracking such hard measures as profitability or market share. I know of a money manager who starts and ends his day on the Internet, gauging the performance of his stock fund against four industry-set benchmarks.

Interestingly, people with high motivation remain optimistic even when the score is against them. In such cases, self-regulation combines with achievement motivation to overcome the frustration and depression that come after a setback or failure. Take the case of an another portfolio manager at a large investment company. After several successful years, her fund tumbled for three consecutive quarters, leading three large institutional clients to shift their business elsewhere.

Some executives would have blamed the nosedive on circumstances outside their control; others might have seen the setback as evidence of personal failure. This portfolio manager, however, saw an opportunity to prove she could lead a turnaround. Two years later, when she was promoted to a very senior level in the company, she described the experience as 'the best thing that ever happened to me; I learned so much from it.'

Executives trying to recognize high levels of achievement motivation in their people can look for one last piece of evidence: commitment to the organization. When people love their job for the work itself, they often feel committed to the organizations that make that work possible. Committed employees are likely to stay with an organization even when they are pursued by headhunters waving money.

It's not difficult to understand how and why a motivation to achieve translates into strong leadership. If you set the performance bar high for yourself, you will do the same for the organization when you are in a position to do so. Likewise, a drive to surpass goals and an interest in keeping score can be contagious. Leaders with these traits can often build a team of managers around them with the same traits. And of course, optimism and organizational commitment are fundamental to leadership – just try to imagine running a company with out them.

Empathy

Of all the dimensions of emotional intelligence empathy is the most easily recognized. We have all felt the empathy of a sensitive teacher or friend; we have all been struck by its absence in an unfeeling coach or boss. But when it comes to business, we rarely hear people praised, let alone rewarded, for their empathy. The very word seems unbusinesslike, out of place amid the tough realities of the marketplace.

But empathy doesn't mean a 'I'm okay you're okay' mushiness. For a leader, that is, it doesn't mean adopting other people's emotions as one's own and trying to please everybody. That would be a nightmare – would make action impossible. Rather, empathy means thoughtfully considering employees' feelings – along with other factors – in the process of making intelligent decisions.

For an example of empathy in action, consider what happened when two giant brokerage companies merged, creating redundant jobs in all their divisions. One division manager called his people together and gave a gloom speech that emphasized the number of people who would soon be fired. The manager of another division gave his people a different kind of speech. He was upfront about his own worry and confusion and he promised to keep people informed and treat everyone fairly.

The difference between these two managers was empathy. The first manager was too worried about his own fate to consider the feelings of his anxiety stricken colleagues. The second knew intuitively what his people were feeling, and he acknowledged their fears with his words. Is it any surprise that the first manager saw his division sink as many demoralized people, especially the most talented, departed. By contrast, the second manager continued to be a strong leader, his best people stayed, and his division remained as productive as ever.

Empathy is particularly important today as a component of leadership for at least three reasons – the increasing use of teams; the rapid pace of globalization; and the growing need to retain talent.

Consider the challenge of leading a team. As anyone who has ever been a part of one can attest, teams are cauldrons of bubbling emotions. They are often charged with reaching a consensus – hard enough with two people and much more difficult as the numbers increase. Even in groups with as few as four or five members, alliances form and clashing agendas get set. A team's leader must be able to sense and understand the viewpoints of everyone around the table.

129

That's exactly what a marketing manager at a large information technology company was able to do when she was appointed to lead a troubled team. The group was in turmoil, overloaded by work and missing deadlines. Tensions were high among the members. Tinkering with procedures was not enough to bring the group together and make it an effective part of the company.

So the manager took several steps. In a series of one-on-one sessions, she took the time to listen to everyone in the group – what was frustrating them, how they rated their colleagues, whether they felt they had been ignored. And then she directed the team in a way that brought it together: she encouraged people to speak more openly about their frustrations, and she helped people raise constructive complaints during meetings. In short, her empathy allowed her to understand her team's emotional makeup. The result was not just heightened collaboration among members but also added business, as the team was called on for help by a wider range of internal clients.

Globalization is another reason for the rising importance of empathy for business leaders. Cross-cultural dialogue can easily lead to miscues and misunderstandings. Empathy is an antidote. People who have it are attuned to subtleties in body language; they can hear the message beneath the words being spoken. Beyond that, they have a deep understanding of the existence and importance of cultural and ethnic differences.

Consider the case of an American consultant whose team had just pitched a project to a potential Japanese client. In its dealings with Americans, the team was accustomed to being bombarded with questions after such a proposal, but this time it was greeted with a long silence. Other members of the team, taking the silence as disapproval, were ready to pack and leave. The lead consultant gestured them to stop. Although he was not particularly familiar with Japanese culture, he read the client's face and posture and sensed not rejection but interest – even deep consideration. He was right: when the client finally spoke, it was to give the consulting firm the job.

Finally, empathy plays a key role in the retention of talent, particularly in today's information economy. Leaders have always needed empathy to develop and keep good people, but today the stakes are higher. When good people leave, they take the company's knowledge with them.

That's where coaching and mentoring come in. It has repeatedly been shown that coaching and mentoring pay off not just in better performance but also in increased job satisfaction and decreased turnover. But what makes coaching and mentoring work best is the nature of the relationship. Outstanding coaches and mentors get inside the heads of the people they are helping. They sense how to give effective feedback. They know when to push for better performance and when to hold back. In the way they motivate their protégés, they demonstrate empathy in action.

In what is probably sounding like a refrain, let me repeat that empathy doesn't get much respect in business. People wonder how leaders can make hard decisions if they are 'feeling' for all the people who will be affected. But leaders with empathy do more than sympathize with people around them: they use their knowledge to improve their companies in subtle but important ways.

Social Skill

The first three components of emotional intelligence are all self-management skills. The last two, empathy and social skill, concern a person's ability to manage relationships with others. As a component of emotional intelligence, social skill is not as simple as it sounds. It's not just a matter of friendliness, although people with high levels of social skill are rarely mean-spirited. Social skill, rather, is friendliness with a purpose: moving people in the direction you desire, whether that's agreement on a new marketing strategy or enthusiasm about a new product.

Socially skilled people tend to have a wide circle of acquaintances, and they have a knack for finding common ground with people of all kinds – a knack for building rapport. That doesn't mean they socialize continually; it means they work according to the assumption that nothing important gets done alone. Such people have a network in place when the time for action comes. Social skill is the culmination of the other dimensions of emotional intelligence. People tend to be very effective at managing relationships when they can understand and control their own emotions and can empathize with the feelings of others. Even motivation contributes to social skill. Remember that people who are driven to achieve tend to be optimistic, even in the face of setbacks or failure. When people are upbeat, their 'glow' is cast upon conversations and other social encounters. They are popular, and for good reason.

Because it is the outcome of the other dimensions of emotional intelligence, social skill is recognizable on the job in many ways that will by now sound familiar. Socially skilled people, for instance, are adept at managing teams – that's their empathy at work. Likewise, they are expert persuaders – a manifestation of self-awareness, self-regulation, and empathy combined. Given those skills, good persuaders know when to make an emotional plea, for instance, and when an appeal to reason will work better. And motivation, when publicly visible, makes such people excellent collaborators; their passion for the work spreads to others, and they are driven to find solutions.

But sometimes social skill shows itself in ways that the other emotional intelligence components do not. For instance, socially skilled people may at times appear not to be working while at work. They seem to be idly schmoozing – chatting in the hallways with colleagues or joking around with people who are not even connected to their 'real' jobs. Socially skilled people, however, don't think it makes sense to arbitrarily limit the scope of their relationships. They build bonds widely because they know that in these fluid times, they may need help someday from people they are just getting to know today.

For example, consider the case of an executive in the strategy department of a global computer manufacturer. By 1993, he was convinced that the company's future lay with the Internet. Over the course of the next year, he found kindred spirits and used his social skill to stitch together a virtual community that cut across levels, divisions, and nations. He then used this de facto team to put up a corporate Web site, among the first by a major company. And, on his own initiative, with no budget or formal status, he signed up the company to participate in an annual Internet industry convention. Calling on his allies and persuading various divisions to donate funds, he recruited more than 10 people from a dozen different units to represent the company at the convention.

Management took notice: within a year of the conference, the executive's team formed the basis for the company's first Internet division, and he was formally put in charge of it. To get there, the executive had ignored conventional boundaries, forging and maintaining connections with people in every corner of the organization.

Is social skill considered a key leadership capability in most companies? The answer is yes, especially when compared with the other components of emotional intelligence. People seem to know intuitively that leaders need to manage relationships effectively; no leader is an island. After all, the leader's task is to get work done through other people, and social skill makes that possible. A leader who cannot express her empathy may as well not have it at all. And a leader's motivation will be useless if he cannot communicate his passion to the organization. Social skill allows leaders to put their emotional intelligence to work.

It would be foolish to assert that good-old-fashioned IQ and technical ability are not important ingredients in strong leadership. But the recipe would not be complete without emotional intelligence. It was once thought that the components of emotional intelligence were 'nice to have' in business leaders. But now we know that, for the sake of performance, these are ingredients that leaders 'need to have.'

It is fortunate, then, that emotional intelligence can be learned. The process is not easy. It takes time and, most of all, commitment. But the benefits that come from having a well-developed emotional intelligence, both for the individual and for the organization, make it worth the effort.

D

Culture

The changing business environment is leading to different organizational forms. Here Ekvall outlines the openness that is characteristic of the climate of many creative organizations. Handy argues for a new relationship between employer and employee that reflects this and Semler advocates the merits of self-organization.

Ekvall describes a creative organizational climate, outlining the open characteristics associated with more innovative organizations and departments and contrasting these with the climate found in organizations and departments that lack these qualities. He goes on to differentiate between organizational characteristics that appear to be better suited for adaptive or incremental creativity and those appropriate for a setting where innovative or radical creativity is the goal, concluding that each thrives under slightly differing conditions.

Charles Handy, perhaps the foremost English business guru and social commentator, argues that it is time to redefine the relationship between the employer and employee, and that all staff are better seen as citizens of organizations. He suggests this approach would facilitate trust among core members, a trust needed if staff are ever to bond enough to be willing to share their intellectual property.

Management control procedures risk stifling creative endeavour with red tape, but until recently most Western managers assumed that the managerial paraphernalia of job descriptions, training, quality and planning departments were synonymous with good management. Semco is one of those companies demonstrating that a medium-sized organization can remove most of these monitoring devices to reveal a committed, motivated and responsible workforce. Here Semler, the majority shareholder in

Semco, originally a Brazilian equipment manufacturing company, champions the merits of a largely self-organizing workforce. Semler explains how Semco's practice of employee participation, profit-sharing and open information systems has led to a highly entrepreneurial business where the distinction between employee and contractor has been well and truly blurred. He explains how this philosophy has seen them though serious recession in Brazil and argues that openness breeds motivation, responsibility and an entrepreneurial spirit.

10

Organizational Conditions and Levels of Creativity

Göran Ekvall

Two levels of creativity can be identified whether we look at the concept from the product, the person or the process point of view. One is radical and revolutionary, the other adaptive and confirmatory. Some results are presented that indicate differing influences on higher and lower level creativity. It is argued that the issue of innovation in organizations harbours a couple of basic dilemmas which requires understanding of the psychology of creativity.

New Research Questions

The understanding of creative products, persons and processes, that have emerged through the research during the present century, provides a valid basis for formulating hypotheses about organizational structures, systems and processes that simulate or block creative acts. Conditions that restrict free and open communications, such as rigid bureaucratic rules and instructions, 'holy' hierarchies and detail controlling supervision keep creativity down, because new mental structures, new constellations, come into being when knowledge, experiences, ideas from widely differing and distinct domains meet. Such meetings can more easily appear when there are few restrictions to the members' possibilities to move mentally inside and outside the organization and be able to confront variety. As creative thinking questions established ways of doing things, conservative values, strategies and policies, that support the conventional, are blocking creativity. Those that ask for change stimulate it. As incubation phases and subconscious mental activities are elements of the creative problem-solving process, time for retreat, reflection and relaxation promotes the processes and subsequent time pressure, heavy work-load and stress reactions hamper them. As risk taking and anxiety are ingredients of creative acts, culture elements that make risk taking and failure less threatening and dangerous are promoting of creative behaviour, whereas in situations where creative

Source: G. Ekvall (1997) Edited extract from *Creativity and Innovation Management*, 6(4), 195–205.

initiatives are met with suspicion, defensiveness and aggression, the fear of failure becomes strong and holds creativity back.

Those propositions have support in research reports and in management textbooks on creativity and innovation in organizations (Amabile, 1988; Hage and Aiken, 1970; Hall, 1977; Peters and Waterman, 1982; Woodman, 1995). We have some solid knowledge about the organizational conditions that enhance and those that block creativity in general terms. There are also indications and hypotheses about differential influences related to the two levels, or if we prefer, the two kinds, of creativity (Ekvall, 1996).

Do some organizational characteristics promote lower, more adaptive, creative acts but impede more radical creativity? And do some conditions that stimulate the radical block the adaptive kind of creative acts? Two studies that shed light on these questions will now be presented.

A Study at a Chemical Company

This was a study of four divisions of a middle-sized Swedish industrial company, producing chemicals for other industries, i.e. paper, pulp, detergents and others. Each division had its own product development, marketing and sales. Three of them also had their own production facilities, whereas the fourth used one of the others as subcontractor. The study had a broad scope concerning the domains studied (history, strategies, philosophies, policies, structures, leadership, processes, climates, job-satisfaction, profits and innovations) and the research methods applied (document analysis, interviews, questionnaires, direct observations, group discussions).

The analyses are geared to the issue of differences in innovative achievements between the divisions and the organizational conditions influencing the innovative outcomes (Ekvall et al., 1987; Ekvall, 1988, 1991, 1996; Nyström, 1991).

The four divisions (we can call them A, B, C and D) showed fundamental differences in history, age, culture, strategies, leadership and innovative achievements.

Division A, the oldest, was a traditional process-plant, with its roots in the late 19th century. It produced some basic chemicals and had a given market share for those mature products. No development activities about products existed. The organization was of the traditional, hierarchical style and the leadership was patriarchal.

Division B produced a chemical that was of a later date than those of the A division. The prospects for the chemical were bright, the sales volume had grown substantially. These successes were the result of purposeful market-oriented development work. Project groups were established with customers in order to adapt the chemical to new applications and to meet the needs of the customer better. There prevailed a rational systematic, achievement-oriented culture, an administrative functioning style, stressing systems, procedures, goals. The leadership reinforced these values and principles.

The C division had about the same size and was of the same age as the B division. But in contrast to B, which was a one-product business, it contained several product lines and it had both mature and younger products and furthermore a lot of new

Table 10.1 *Mean scores on organizational indexes: White-collar and supervisory employees*

	Divisions		
Index	B	C	Diff.
Order/Structure/Plan	1.77	1.12	.65***
Goal clarity	1.73	1.56	.17+
Risk taking	1.37	1.92	−.55**
Freedom	1.95	2.33	−.38*
Playfulness/Humour	1.66	1.96	−.30*
Debates	.96	1.35	−.39*
Livefulness/Dynamism	1.68	2.05	−.37*

Scale 0–3. $^+p < .10$ * $p < .05$ ** $p < .01$ *** $p < .001$

product development projects were in progress. The leadership was democratic and relations-oriented and emphasized integration and synergies between old and new parts of the business. Values of creativity and flexibility were salient elements of the culture.

The D division was the youngest. At the time of the study it was a large product project for a new chemical system that had recently started to appear on the market. The concept had its roots in the C division. The leadership and the culture were of the typical entrepreneurial style. The product concept later became a great commercial success.

Comparison between the B and C divisions are feasible; they were of the same size and age, roughly. Both were complete plants with their own development, production, marketing and sales functions. They however differed considerably, in the case of creativity and innovation; the B division being a one-product business, striving to adapt its concept to new applications and new customers and the C division being a multi-product business with a mix of mature and young products and many new product development projects going on. The innovative activities at the B division were of a typical adaptive sort, whereas the C division presented a clear example of radical innovation strivings. These justify a proposition that adaptive, lower level creative acts were prevailing at the B division and radical, higher level, creative acts at the C division.

A questionnaire was handed out to all white-collar and supervisory personnel in the divisions. The items consist of statements about practice and behaviour patterns in the organization, which the respondent has to agree or disagree with. Examples:

- Tasks are clearly defined.
- Rules and principles are stressed.
- There is a clear tendency for risk-taking here.

In six of the 15 indexes there were statistically significant differences between B and C, shown in Table 10.1.

The indexes where no differences were observed belonged to three different domains: information and personnel policy; climate of challenge and achievement

Table 10.2   *Mean scores on items of the order/structure/plan index*

	Divisions		
Index	B	C	Diff.
The operations are strictly planned and organized	1.58	.82	.76***
One is exacting about plans being followed	1.85	1.13	.72***
Everyone knows what is expected of him/her	2.04	1.37	.67***

Scale 0–3. *** p<. 001

orientation; trust, openness and harmony in relations. Both B and C scored quite high in those domains.

Table 10.1 shows that B division scored higher than C on only two indexes, order/structure/plan and goal clarity. The differences on order/structure/plan are substantial, the largest of the differences.

In Table 10.2 the three items that carried the main part of the difference in this index are presented.

The results indicate that the strict, rational, structured culture and praxis prevailing in the B division appeared to promote adaptive creativity and the second-order innovations that characterized the product strategies and achievements. The C division with its looser structure, more freedom, higher risk-inclination and debating, dynamic and playful atmosphere tended to stimulate creative acts of the higher, first-order kind, that paved the way to new projects and products.

A Study at a Mechanical Company

This study was carried out in Sweden (Ljungkvist, 1993). The author used the Creative Climate Questionnaire (CCQ) (Ekvall, 1991 and 1996), to compare different parts of a multinational company that produces systems and machinery for packing food-stuffs and is very successful on the world-market.

The company's product development function is divided into two departments; the one working with design of new products, the other with improvements of old established products.

The CCQ is a 50-item questionnaire, covering ten dimensions: challenge, freedom, idea-support, trust, dynamism, playfulness, debates, conflicts, risk taking and idea time. All dimensions except conflicts are positively related to an organization's degree of creativity and innovativeness (Ekvall, 1996). The items are phrased in the same way as those in the questionnaire described in the previous example. The CCQ items are all about climate – the behaviours, attitudes and feelings – characterizing the life in the organization.

The study included two random samples of ten design engineers each, from the department for development of new products and from the department of product improvements. Table 10.3 shows the mean scores in the climate indexes for the two samples.

Table 10.3 *Mean scores in CCQ indexes for two departments*

| | Departments | | |
Index	New products	Improvements	Diff.
Challenge	2.26	1.98	.28 n.s.
Freedom	2.12	1.72	.40*
Idea support	2.12	1.70	.42*
Trust	2.02	1.82	.20 n.s.
Dynamism	2.06	1.64	.42*
Playfulness	2.08	1.90	.18 n.s.
Debates	1.08	1.64	.44*
Conflicts[1]	.76	1.18	−.42*
Risk taking	1.82	1.39	.43*
Idea time	1.80	1.43	.37*

Scale 0–3. * $p < .05$

[1]The conflict dimension, in the CCQ operationalized by items concerning ego and power tensions in the organization, has in all studies so far showed negative correlations with all the other dimensions, debates (tensions between ideas) included. Person collisions (conflicts) have come out as obstacles to creativity and innovation in the studies, as opposed to idea collisions (debates that have shown positive relations.

The results are evident. The designers in the new product department perceived a more creativity promoting and stimulating climate than the design engineers in the product improvement department did. The management of the R & D function declared that they 'accepted' a lower level of creativity in the product improvement department than in the new product department, from which they thus expected higher levels of creativity.

Both departments were living up to expectations, as the company is very successful with its product goals and strategies. This makes comparisons with other companies, whose creative achievements are known, apt.

In Table 10.4 the two departments' mean scores on the climate indexes are compared to mean scores of three other organizations (Ekvall, 1996).

(a) A large product development project in high-tech, lasting for three years and with 30 engineers working full time in the project. The climate was measured each third month with the CCQ. (The scores in Table 10.4 are means of these measurements.) The product, a new type of operator station for defence systems, was rated as comprising several original spearhead technical solutions. Creative acts of the 'higher' level were no doubt occurring in this project.

(b) The product development department of a large mechanical company operating in an old business line characterized by incremental product changes. The companies in this trade watch each other keenly and product changes of the same

Table 10.4 *CCQ mean scores for the two divisions compared to mean scores for other organizations*

	High-tech project	New product department	Mechanical company	Product improvement department	Five 'stagnated' organizations
Challenge	2.36	2.26	1.80	1.98	1.63
Freedom	2.00	2.12	1.70	1.72	1.53
Idea support	1.83	2.12	1.50	1.70	1.08
Trust	2.23	2.02	1.60	1.82	1.28
Dynamism	2.20	2.06	1.60	1.64	1.40
Playfulness	2.30	2.08	1.70	1.90	1.40
Debates	1.85	2.08	1.60	1.64	1.05
Conflicts	.30	.76	1.00	1.18	1.40
Risk taking	1.57	1.82	1.20	1.39	.53
Idea time	1.40	1.80	1.10	1.43	.97

Scale 0–3

kind tend to appear at the same time in their programmes. The adaptive kind of creativity might be the hallmark of this product development department (Ekvall, 1990).

(c) Five 'stagnated' organizations. Small companies or independent divisions of larger companies, all being in difficult economical circumstances, at the time of the study, due to lack of new products and/or updating their old products. It is reasonable to assume that these organizations were uncreative and had been so for a couple of years.

The climate pattern of the new products department is similar to that of the high-tech project. The pattern of the product improvement department is near the mechanical company's and is substantially deviated from the stagnated organizations', in the positive direction, which places its climate between the climates of highly creative and uncreative organizations. The climate picture as defined by the CCQ indexes seems to reflect the two levels of organizational creativity; the product improvement department can be assumed to expose a climate typical of organizations where adaptive creativity is practised, and the new products department can, in the same way, be assumed to show a climate representative of organizations where radical creative acts occur frequently.

Discussion

The data indicate that creative acts in companies are related to organizational variables. The relationships are, as usual in organizational settings, complex from the causality point of view. Climate aspects stimulate or hamper creativity, but creative outcomes then influence climate.

The CCQ data may be interpreted as indicating that the differences in organizational variables between the two levels of creativity is a matter of degree; the constructs are positive for both kinds of creativity, but more is required for radical creativity to occur than for adaptive, the exception being conflicts, where the case is reversed.

We can speculate about effects of 'too much' of some climate dimensions. For example: What will happen if risk taking and freedom are being stressed harder than previously by management in an organization working with incremental innovations and thus practising adaptive creativity? It is probable that highly creative people, those with an 'innovative style' in Kirton's terminology (1987), will be stimulated and respond by presenting more radical ideas and problem solutions than before. The 'adaptors', on the other hand, will be uneasy and lose energy and motivation to solve problems. It is not probable that persons who, due to personality dispositions, are adaptive problem solvers will turn into radical thinkers. The organizational effect will accordingly be that the adaptive creativity fades away and more innovative creative acts tend to appear, provided that the organization harbours some innovative thinkers, who respond to the new management signals and that recruiting more such employees is possible. If the strategy aims purely at exchanging adaptive innovations for radical innovations, the effects are adequate. If, however, the idea with the stronger push for risk taking and freedom is to reach a balance of adaptive and radical creativity and a mix of improvement and new product achievements, the decreasing motivation and morale among the adaptive problem solvers may become a problem. This dilemma of having 'innovators' and 'adaptors' understand and accept each other's ways of approaching and solving problems and working together is discussed by Kirton (1987). The case with the two different departments, one for product improvements and another for development of new products might be regarded as an attempt to manage the dilemma.

A still more intricate issue is that of organizational dimensions where high scores may block the radical creativity and innovation but promote the adaptive.

The study at the chemical company provides an indication that strict and clear structures, policies and rules are hindrances to higher level, innovative creativity and that more loose, vague and variable structures are prerequisites for such radical creative acts to be prevalent in the organization. The C division (with its radical innovation strategy and outcomes) showed low scores on items about order, structure, planning. The adaptively inclined B division, on the other hand, had high scores, which supports the assumption that its systematic, structured organizational functioning favoured the appearance of adaptive creative acts.

The reason that strict and plain organizational principles and practice hamper the radical, higher level creativity and promote the adaptive, lower level creativity is found in the nature of creative processes and of creative personalities. As creative processes consist in 'making new and valuable connections' and as the more apart the connected elements are at the outset, the more creative the outcome will be, it is reasonable to assume that organizational conditions that support meetings of ideas, knowledge, experiences and standpoints, which are highly different, prepare the way for radical creative processes to come up. A loose structure and elastic practice facilitates such encounters. That kind of structure allows the members of the organization to search for information and viewpoints freely and not be restricted to using only formal channels and contacts. Furthermore the lower stress laid on time schedules, strict planning and fixed role assignments entails time and freedom for initiatives, experimentation, reflection and 'incubation', which raises the chances for 'shifts in perception' to occur.

The radical problem solver is very content with a vague and loose structure. His/her ways of intellectual, motivational and emotional functioning are apt to such situations. Strict, rigid, formal organizational settings are experienced as uneasy and are resisted. Kirton (1987) has described the 'innovator' as a person who challenges rules, dislikes routine work and takes control in unstructured situations. The latter tendency implies that highly creative persons are stimulated by vague, unstructured situations because these present possibilities for them to make scope for their own new 'mental configurations'. Researchers of the creative personality have maintained that highly creative persons are characterized by 'tolerance of ambiguity' (Rogers, 1962; Stein, 1962). It might be that they are not only tolerant of the vagueness, they are even motivated by it.

The Adaptor personality as described by Kirton (1987) is the psychological pendant to the bureaucratic structure with its stress on precision, methods, stability and conformity. They are the kind of people who 'seek solutions to problems in tried and understood ways', who 'reduce problems by improvement and greater efficiency, with maximum of continuity and stability.' The Norwegian scholar Paul Moxnes has described this kind of personality as socio-structure dependent and found that they tend to become anxious in loose, vague, fluid situations (Moxnes, 1978). The Adaptor needs a clearly defined context in order to feel well and be able to utilize his/her capabilities at work. And when solving problems it becomes necessary to operate within that context and not put the safe frame at risk.

Goal clarity probably has similar effects on the creativity in the organization as structure and order, even if the results of the study at the chemical company were not strongly indicative.

The elaboration of the mission, goals and strategies of the company and proclaiming this to the members of the organization is a management principle and procedure aimed at consistency and guidance and at the same time supposed to engender meaning and commitment. The principle has been named MBO (management by objectives) in management philosophy. The energy, initiatives and problem-solving efforts of the employees are expected to be geared to the company's stated goals and support the goal attainment. Management by objectives has developed in opposition to bureaucratic management by strict rules and prescriptions to give more scope for discretion and initiatives to the members of the organization.

Clear mission statements, goals and strategies entail a structure different from the bureaucratic, but still a structure. The business lines, the expected achievements in different aspects and the main routes are laid out by top management. Inside this framework departments and teams are expected to use initiatives and discretion to have their work contribute to the goal attainment. This kind of structure supports creativity because of the amount of freedom it allows. Departments, teams and individuals have to organize their work and set their targets at their own discretion, inside the frames given, in order to promote the overall goal. It is, however, the adaptive kind of creativity that grows best in the MBO culture. It is a situation where the Adaptor feels at home and becomes productive as a problem solver. Steady improvements alongside the set avenues are expected. Some basic, governing values in the MBO culture are very much the same as in the bureaucratic culture: consistency, predictability, risk-avoidance. The main difference is the higher trust in people's capacities to take on responsibility characterizing MBO. The values that MBO have in common with the bureaucratic systems tend to make the scope for radical creativity on problems of work organization and methods more narrow than the general frame of goals and strategies would permit.

Elaborated goals and strategies that are clearly announced in the company are intended to work as fixed guiding stars and guideways for initiatives and plans. Highly creative individuals with their 'innovator style' of approaching problems are frustrated when things are settled and indisputable. Their drives are to question the established, to reformulate problems and goals, not to stay mentally inside frames that are given, traditional and accepted. The MBO principles do not permit much scope for such ambitions, especially not where the principles have been introduced in organizations with deep-rooted bureaucratic values.

The difficulties of generating innovations in large organizations have had growing attention during the 1980s and 1990s. The rigidity and gravity of large, bureaucratic systems are considered as the basic problem. The common conclusion is creative ideas are not taken care of in such systems. Some of the modern management trends such as MBO and decentralization can be assumed to promote creative acts, mainly of the adaptive kind, but other tendencies that are pushing pace, efficiency and productivity, like 'time management', 'lean production', 'just in time', 'reengineering' and 'cutting down product development time', might be pressing down even the lower (adaptive) kind of creativity and probably blocking the more radical (Mellström, 1995). Layoffs due to the rationalizations or to shrinking markets have deteriorating effects on the rate of creative behaviours (Amabile and Conti, 1995).

The TQM (total quality management) movement has introduced strict control systems and procedures not only in production but in almost all operations and functions. It has been argued that TQM implies a renaissance of Taylorism (Boje and Windsor, 1993). If this is so and quality has become a cardinal all-embracing light, approached by scientific management methods, there has come a second unconditional goal, besides efficiency, whose application has a similar complicated relation to creativity and innovation.

The fundamental problem with radical innovation in organizations can be described as consisting of a couple of inter-related dilemmas:

- The fact that creativity on the one hand and time pressure, speed and stress on the other are counteracting forces.
- The fact that organizational principles, systems and procedures aimed at structure and stability do shrink the scope for high-level creativity but allow adaptive creativity.

- The necessity of ample resources to bring forth radical innovations in modern high-tech industries implies large organizations with many people, frequent cooperation and joint ventures, where two or more companies are co-actors, which requires structures and procedures for co-ordination and control, i.e. the sort of organizational mechanisms that reduce the chances for radical creative acts to appear.
- The fact that companies in highly competitive markets must create the means for long-term development by having high efficiency in their operations, which brings in strategies, systems and structures which are problematic from the creativity point of view.
- The experiences of the difficulty of having Adaptors and Innovators co-operate because they challenge each other's beliefs and basic values.

The dilemmas have been observed and expressed not only by organization theorists but also by management people, who try to find ways to overcome them. There are still, however, plenty of managers who deny the problem and argue that radical innovations can be brought forth by strict planning and follow-up systems. There is even much material with that kind of message included in textbooks and courses on project management. The trend seems nevertheless to be towards a broadening awareness of the problem, which probably is a consequence of the constantly increasing requirements for innovations in the world of business.

These growing insights can be traced in strategic statements and policy documents. They are also revealed in metaphorical phrases flitting around in the organization as normative cultural elements, such as 'love and care for the kids as much as the grown-ups', 'don't shoot the skunks', 'stand the mavericks and wild cats'. Examples of organizational strategies to manage the dilemmas are of many kinds: special departments for evaluation of ideas and finding funding and promoters inside the company for the promising ideas – Kodak's 'office of innovation' for example (Rosenfeld and Servo, 1984). Giving R & D people time for 'free projects' as with 3M; establishing company funds for high-risk projects where departments and subsidiaries can apply for grants – the Perstorp system of a variety of funds being an example (Nordberg, 1983); starting separate subsidiaries for development of new products, where the structures, rules, administrative principles, policies and economic targets of the mother company are not applied – this being probably the most common strategy; running idea and innovation campaigns during a limited time and directed towards specified problems, like the Volfram campaign at Volvo (Ekvall, 1990).

There have been success stories as well as failures reported for all these kinds of strategies. The variance in outcomes is probably due to differences in the top managers' understandings of the basic character of the problem and the differences in ways to put the strategies into practice according to the diverging understandings.

The thesis of this article is that the problem of innovation in organizations is rooted in the nature of creative processes and creative persons and that the two different kinds of creativity that have been identified are differentially facilitated by organizational conditions. This creates organizational dilemmas. These dilemmas cannot be wiped out because creative processes and the creative personality are given. The dilemmas must, however, be managed as companies must have capacity for radical changes in different aspects in order to survive in the long run, and they must at the same time earn the money day by day by effective operations to make the resources for the development work. The keys to success in the inevitable balancing act are to be found in understanding and paying regard to the nature of creative processes and creative persons in the construction and application of the organizational strategies aimed at managing the dilemmas.

References

Amabile, T.M. (1988) A model of creativity and innovation in organizations, *Research in Organizational Behaviour, 10,* 123–67.

Amabile, M. and Conti, R. (1995) What down-sizing does to creativity, *Issues and Observations, 15*(3), Greensboro: Center for Creative Leadership.

Arieti, S. (1976) *Creativity: The Magic Synthesis,* New York: Basic Books.

Barron, F. (1969) *Creative Person and Creative Process,* New York: Holt, Reinehart and Winston.

Besemer, S.P. and O'Quin, K. (1987) Creative product analysis. Testing a model by developing a judging instrument. In S.G. Isaksen (Ed.), *Frontiers of Creativity Research,* Buffalo: Bearly Ltd.

Boje, D.M. and Windsor, R.D. (1993) The resurrection of Taylorism: total quality management's hidden agenda, *Journal of Organizational Change Management, 6*(4).

De Bono, E. (1971) *The Mechanism of Mind,* Middlesex: Penguin Books.

Ekvall, G. (1988) *Förnyelse och Friktion,* Stockholm: Natur and Kultur.

Ekvall, G. (1990) *Idéer, Organisationsklimat och Ledningsfilosofi,* Stockholm: Norstedts.

Ekvall, G (1991) The organizational culture of idea-management: a creative climate for the management of ideas. In J. Henry and D. Walker (Eds), *Managing Innovation,* London: Sage Publications.

Ekvall, G. (1996) Organizational climate for creativity and innovation, *European Journal of Work and Organizational Psychology, 5*(1), 105–23.

Ekvall, G., Arvonen, J. and Nyström, H. (1987) *Organisation och innovation,* Lund: Studentlitteratur.

Ghiselin, B. (1952) *The Creative Process,* New York: New American Library.

Ghiselin, B. (1963) Ultimate criteria for two levels of creativity. In C.W. Taylor and F. Barron (Eds), *Scientific Creativity,* New York: Wiley and Sons.

Guilford, J.P. (1967) *The Nature of Human Intelligence,* New York: McGraw-Hill.

Hage, J. and Aiken, M. (1970) *Social Change in Complex Organizations,* New York: Random Hansey, Inc.

Hall, R.H. (1977) *Organizations: Structure and Process* (2nd edn.), Englewood: Prentice-Hall, Inc.

Kaufmann, G. (1980) *Problemløsning og Kreativitet,* Oslo: Cappelens Forlag.

Kirton, M.J. (1987) Adaptors and innovators. Cognitive style and personality. In S.G. Isaksen (Ed.), *Frontiers of Creativity Research,* Buffalo: Bearly Ltd.

Koestler, A. (1964) *The Act of Creation,* New York: Dell.

Kris, E. (1952) *Psychoanalytical Explorations in Art,* New York: International Universities Press.

Ljungkvist, P. (1993) *Bolagiseringens Effekter på Innovationsklimat och Kommunikationsmönster,* Magisteruppsats: Högskolan i Halmstad.

Maslow, A.H. (1962) Emotional blocks to creativity. In S.J. Parnes and H.F. Harding (Eds), *A Source Book for Creative Thinking,* New York: Scribner's Sons.

Mellström, U. (1995) *Engineering Lives. Technology, Time and Space in a Male World,* University of Linköping.

Moxnes, P. (1978) *Angst og Organisasjon,* Oslo: Gyldendal Norsk Forlag.

Nordberg, S. (1983) *Perstorps Kretaive Bas – en unik väg mot förnyelse,* Konferens-paper, Liber Förlag.

Nyström, J. (1990) Organizational innovation. In M.A. West and J.L. Farr (Eds), *Innovation and Creativity at Work: Psychological and Organizational Strategies*, Chichester: Wiley.

Nyström, J. (1991) *Technological and Market Innovation – Strategies for Product and Company Development*, Chichester: Wiley and Sons.

Peters, T. and Waterman, R., Jr. (1982) *In Search of Excellence*, New York: Harper and Row.

Poincaré, H. (1970) Mathematical creation. In P. Vernon (Ed.), *Creativity*, London: Penguin Books.

Rogers, C.R. (1962) Towards a theory of creativity. In S.J. Parnes and H.F. Harding (Eds), *A Source Book for Creative Thinking*, New York: Scribner's Sons.

Rosenfeld, R. and Servo, J. (1984) Business and creativity. Making ideas connect. *The Futurist*, August.

Simonton, D.K. (1984) *Genius, Creativity and Leadership*, Cambridge: Harvard University Press.

Smith, G.J.W. (1981) Creation and reconstruction, *Psychoanalysis and Contemporary Thought*, 4, 275–86.

Smith, G. and Carlsson, I. (1990) The creative process. A functional model based on empirical studies from early childhood to middle age, *Psychological Issues*, 57.

Stein, M.I. (1962) Creativity as an intra- and inter-personal process. In S.J. Parnes, and H.F. Harding (Eds), *A Source Book for Creative Thinking*, New York: Scribner's Sons.

Wallas, G. (1926) *The Art of Thought*, London: Watts.

Wertheimer, M. (1945) *Productive Thinking*, New York: Harper.

Woodman, R.W. (1995) Managing creativity. In C.M. Ford and D.S.A. Gioia (Eds), *Creative Action in Organizations*, London: Sage Publications.

11

The Citizen Company

Charles Handy

Business and indeed all institutions, are communities not properties, and their inhabitants are to be more properly thought of as citizens rather then employees or human resources. What will this mean in practice?

Citizens in all democracies have the rights of residence, justice, free speech, a share of the wealth of society in some way, and a say, usually a vote, in the governance of their society. Most importantly, however, a citizen is entitled to life, liberty and the pursuit of happiness, as the Americans have it, in other words the right to make your own life, subject to the laws of the land. The essential freedom of the individual has been the driving force behind democracy down the ages. It is this force that organizations must now come to terms with as their individuals begin to expect from their work communities the same collection of freedoms, rights and responsibilities that they have in the wider society. People are property no more.

Translated into corporate terms, a citizen's right to residence means some guarantee of employment; not for life, because that would be unrealistic, but for a fixed period of years – a decade, for example. It is reasonable to substitute predictability for permanence in a more uncertain world, and few, anyway, of the citizen-calibre workers would want to sign a commitment for life. What is needed to restore commitment in the workplace is a rebalancing of power, so that those in control make commitments in order to win commitment. We will increasingly, I suggest, live our lives in five- to ten-year chunks, so that a ten-year commitment will be seen as a fair definition of guaranteed residence. Justice, free speech and a share of the wealth are all easy to translate into the corporate world, but not always delivered. A say in governance translates into a right to be consulted about major decisions affecting the future of the corporation.

This has all the feel of a trade union manifesto, and some unions are moving this way, wanting to make their members citizens of the employing organization. In 1997 two large British industrial groups agreed to a guarantee of four years' employment for their core workforce in return for a promise of flexible working. But citizenship is not just the outcome of negotiation or arbitration. It is more subtle than that, something that grows

---

Source: C. Handy (1997) Edited extract from *The Hungry Spirit*. New York: Random House, 179–204.

from a shared commitment, bits of which can be defined in writing, such as the length of residence and the share of the wealth, but much of which is more intangible. As long as trade unions have an adversarial relationship with the organization they will have little role in a citizen company, and the citizens will not want them.

Oddly, perhaps, the British are not citizens (except, by international convention, on their passports) but subjects, subjects of Her Majesty the Queen. Although this is an historical accident, the different words may have made a subconscious difference. There is no Bill of Rights in Britain and no written constitution. Citizens tend to expect these things, which are to be found in most other democracies. ... Citizen Companies will need written constitutions.

Partnership or associate are terms that fall more comfortably on British ears. They are also terms that are easier to apply to two other stakeholders – the suppliers and the customers. It is important for any company to win the trust and co-operation of the targets and most important of these groups, along with the most significant of their investors. Were citizenship to be formalized in any way, it would be appropriate to see these other stakeholders as associate citizens, with at least the right to be kept informed to be consulted whenever appropriate. This form of associate citizenship should help to bond these crucial players into the long-term aims of the organization and to build a degree of mutual trust by the sharing of information. To win trust you have first to give trust.

One way to give formal expression to the right of citizenship would be to resurrect the old idea of A shares and B shares – voting and non-voting shares. The A shares, with their votes, would be confined to the personal citizens of the business – the core employees, or a Trust representing their interests. To these could be added significant holders of the equity, being investors who could be presumed to have a long-term interest in the business. Citizen rights could also be extended to the larger suppliers if they held an equity stake (as suppliers tend to do in Japan). To involve the community it might be possible to create the equivalent of the 'golden share' which the British Government awarded themselves in some of the companies created by privatization. This would give the community a voice, and conceivably a veto, in specific areas to do with the environment.

The idea of non-voting shares has always been hotly contested by the investment community – for obvious reasons. The investors would lose much of their power. But it is this power that will have to be reduced if the real members of these wealth-creating communities, the people who work there, are to have more say over their destiny and if the business is going to be more than the property of its financiers. The change will not, however, be soon or sudden. It will happen as the newer businesses explore ways to enfranchise their important constituents. It is only when these new businesses become large in their turn that the stock markets of the world will notice that they have, in their turn, lost their power.

The emergence of completely new forms of organizations may, of course, make all the talk of ownership irrelevant. The Internet, probably the fastest growing organization of all time, is owned by no one. Visa, the credit card service, carries over 7 billion transactions a year, worth over $650 billion, but is 'owned', if that is the right word, by the financial institutions, well over 20,000 of them, who are its services. Organizations like the Internet and Visa are facilitating mechanisms rather than collections of assets. Few in number at the moment, they may set a pattern for the future as more and more independent operators look for Geoff Mulgan's mechanisms of connexity.

Federalism is an old idea for the combination of independents but one which, rethought for the information age, offers some clues to possible futures. The point of federalism is that too much power should never be in one place or in one function. The centre is the servant of the parts, a facilitating mechanism with powers delegated to it by those parts. In practical terms, ownership then resides with the parts even if the outside investors think that they own the whole. To equate federalism with a super-state ruled by a powerful centre is a uniquely British distortion, one that may come to haunt us in years to come if we turn our backs on what may well be the form of the future.

We recently installed a new kitchen in our home. The firm we went to implied that they would design, build and install the kitchen. In practice they did none of these things themselves. It was a hollow firm. All the functions were subcontracted. None of them worked as they should. There was little the original firm could do about it other than harass and cajole their subcontractors who held the real power. It would have worked better the other way round; if the subcontractors had owned the firm who first sold us the promise of the kitchen, because it was the subcontractors who had the real power, but needed help to deliver it.

It will happen that way, eventually. Effective ownership will gradually revert to those who hold the resources, who will employ those who previously employed them. Those on the outside who provide only one of the resources – finance – will inevitably see their effective power recede. It is called 'subsidiarity', the old idea that power should morally and rightly lie at the bottom not the top of things. Put more simply – stealing people's responsibilities is morally wrong and doesn't work in the end. It is a pleasing thought that, ultimately, the pressures of modern business will compel us to be moral.

Sometimes one has to wonder why we need the concept of ownership at all. Oxfam, that large non-governmental organization, was described to me as a community which belonged to no one and which was fuelled by belief. As business realizes that its best people are really volunteers, there because they want to be, not because they have to, the model of the voluntary agencies may become increasingly relevant.

The Herding of Cats

Citizenship is about autonomy, the freedom to run your own life. In return for this freedom, the corporate state can demand little, but hope for much. Citizens in a democracy are free to emigrate. You cannot stop anyone leaving. Nor can you demand commitment, only hope for it. Combining this freedom and these rights with the aim of the organization is the real challenge of the citizen company. Many managers would prefer not to accept the challenge, because organizing talented people is akin to the proverbial herding of cats – difficult by definition. We have to manage people whom we can't totally control. Instead we have to trust them, and they have to trust us. The principle is simple. The practicalities mean that it seldom happens.

For a start, organizations as well as individuals have to earn the right to be trusted. But in an atmosphere of downlayering and outsourcing, loyalty to the organization is today a rare commodity. Which is odd, because loyalty is worth money. Frederick Reichfield has put numbers on the Loyalty Effect, suggesting that *dis*loyalty from employees, investors and customers can stunt performance and productivity by up to 50%.

Once established, however, an organization with mutual trust at its core can be both creative and efficient. People obviously work better if they are not looking over their shoulders for the next job. They work more creatively if they respect the people around them and believe in what they are doing. Where they trust the organization, where they are committed to its goals and share in some way in the results of the business, they are more likely to accept relocation, reassignments, even temporary across-the-board pay cuts.

Who are these citizens? States, nowadays, require proof of talent and good behaviour from those who would apply to be their citizens. Some states would like to apply similar tests to those born into their citizenship, were there only some place else that they could dump them. Organizations are privileged in this respect. They can choose all their citizens, and would be wise to do so very carefully. Citizenship will certainly not be granted to all. In changing times no organization can make even ten-year commitments to too many people, but will keep their citizenship core as small as possible.

There will also be the necessary mercenaries, who could always turn into citizens, and there will be probationer citizens, who have to prove their worth and earn trust. The citizen core will be the proven 'trusties'. For an example of how such an organization works we only have to look at professional partnerships, in law, accountancy, consulting or architecture. The partners in a professional partnership are the full citizens of that organization, so much so that all the outcomes belong to them, bad as well as good. A public company with limited liability does not have to ask so much of its citizens, but, proportionately, the rewards and the commitment are probably lower.

Businesses could also look at universities, who have long struggled with the dilemma of tenure, or life citizenship. This dilemma is nicely put in the jibe that those who need tenure don't deserve it and those who deserve it don't need it. Tenure, which was once the guarantee that you could speak your mind without fear of dismissal, is now a guarantee of a job for life, a protection that the best should not need. Unfortunately, the best are not guaranteed to remain that way. The universities fear that they may get lumbered with unworthy citizens who cannot be expelled. Indefinite tenure then becomes expensive and demoralizing to the rest.

To prevent this deterioration the stakes have been raised in the initial tenure decision. It is now much harder to be accepted as a full citizen after the necessary probationary period. Tenure is also becoming more conditional, subject to periodic review or, even, to termination after due process and proper notice. Citizenship, in other words, is now more clearly seen to have responsibilities as well as rights. In business it was often the other way round – citizens, if one could call them such, had more responsibilities than rights. The worlds of academia and commerce are meeting each other halfway.

The payoff for a citizen company should be a shared commitment and mutual trust. But the trust has to be in the bloodstream, no matter how well the bone structure or the nervous system have been designed. In a world where work is where you are – in the car or plane, at the office or at home, on the client's premises or in a hotel – you will increasingly have to work with people whom you do not see. Organizations are drowning in communications, in e-mail, voice mail, faxes and telephones, but you can tell lies on e-mail and not be noticed, and who knows whether your fax or your e-mail has actually been read, not crumpled, lost or deleted. More than ever before we have to trust those with whom we work.

Trust sounds like a nice motherhood term, something no one could be against, all warm and woolly. In practice, however, it is difficult and tough. Management by trust depends upon some clear rules and principles, which will have to become the guidebook for a citizen company. There are seven cardinal principles of trust:

1 Trust Is Not Blind

It is unwise to trust people whom you do not know well, whom you have not observed in action over time, and who are not committed to the same goals. How many people do any of us know that well? In ordinary life there seems to be a rule of twelve. When asked how many people's death would affect them personally, or how many telephone numbers they can remember, it is seldom more than twelve. Work demands less stringent conditions. In practice, we can probably know a maximum of 50 people well enough to rely on them in ordinary circumstances. Those 50 can, in their turn, know another 50, and so on.

Large organizations are not, therefore, incompatible with the principle of trust, but they have to be made up of relatively constant and smaller groupings. Impossible? Asea Brown Boveri (ABB) has 225,000 employees working in 5,000 business units which operate in 142 different countries. Each unit has an average of 45 people working in its citizen core. The larger factories manage with 300, which is stretching it. The units combine with each other in an infinitely flexible way to create a powerful and fast-growing complex corporation, but the building blocks conform to the rule of fifty.

Make the groups larger, or change them too frequently, and the organization starts to replace trust with systems of control, because the people do not know each other well enough to develop trust. My title, in one large organization, was MKR/32. In this capacity I wrote memos to FIN/41 or PRO/23. I often knew no names and met no people behind these titles. I had no reason to trust them and, frankly, no desire to. I was a 'temporary role occupant' in the jargon of the time, a role occupant in an organization of command and control, based on the premise that no one could really be trusted, only the system. I left after a year, for such places can truly be a prison for the human soul, and in those prisons people seldom grow because there is no space to explore the truth about yourself. Worse, these prisons, boring though they may be, suck up energy, leaving little over for explanation outside. Role underload, studies show, can be more crippling than role overload.

2 Trust Needs Boundaries

Unlimited trust is, in practice, unrealistic. We trust our friends in some respects of life but not in all. A neighbour may be a great help in emergencies, but hopelessly unreliable when it comes to money. 'I would trust him with everything – except for my wife' one man wrote in a reference for an applicant to the programme I was running. We manage our young on a loose rein, but the rein is always there, getting longer and looser as we trust them more. It is no different in organizations.

By trust, organizations really mean confidence, a confidence in someone's competence, and in their commitment to the goal. Define that goal, and the trusted individual or team can be left to get on with it. Control is then exercised after the event, by assessing the results, rather than before the event, by granting permission. This freedom within boundaries works best, of course, when the work-unit is self-contained, with the capability to solve its own problems.

Trust-based organizations are redesigning their work, pulling back from the old reductionist models of organization, whereby everything was divided into component parts or functions, where everybody only did bits of things and seldom saw the whole. The new, holistic designs for the units of the organization look, at first, to be more expensive than the old functional types, because they often duplicate functions, maintaining separate accounting sections, for instance. The hope is that the energy and effectiveness released by the new freedom within boundaries more than compensates. Where we are trusted to find our own means to some agreed results we have the room to explore, to put our own signature on the work.

Unfortunately, this redesigning was called 're-engineering' – a word from the old world of machines. Re-engineering became a euphemism for getting rid of people, the sign of a manipulative management, never to be trusted. This is sad, because the redesigning was intended to be an outward and visible sign of trust. It is interesting to reflect that very old organizations, such as the Catholic Church, were structured on the principle of the microcosm: that each part should be a microcosm, a smaller mirror image, of the whole, with the ability to organize its own destiny. Perversely, it was because the centre could not communicate with the parts that the parts had to be trusted to look after themselves, bonded together only by a common ethos and tradition. Trust was then essential. These days, the abundance of our communication gets in the way of trust. It is too easy to find out what is going on.

3 Trust Requires Constant Learning

An organizational architecture made up of relatively independent and constant groupings, pushes the organization towards the sort of federal structure that is becoming more common everywhere. A necessary condition of constancy, however, is an ability to change. The constant groups must always be flexible enough to change when times, and customers, demand it. This, in turn, requires that the groups keep themselves abreast of change, forever exploring new options and new technologies, in order to create a real learning culture. The choice of people for these groups is, therefore, of crucial importance. Every individual has to be capable of self-renewal. The ability to search for oneself and to regard learning as a continuing part of life, which was the justification for trusting someone in the first place, becomes one of the keys to its success.

Learning, however, like trust, can be squashed by fear. No one will stick their neck out, or take the sort of initiatives which new situations require, if they are fearful of the consequences if they are wrong. Trust, like learning, requires unconditional support, and forgiveness for mistakes, provided always that the mistakes are learnt from.

4 Trust Is Tough

When trust proves to be misplaced, not necessarily because people are deceitful or malicious, but because they do not live up to expectations, or cannot be relied upon to do what is needed, then those people have, ultimately, to go, or have their boundaries severely curtailed. Trust is like glass: once broken it can never be the same again. Where you cannot trust, you have to check once more, with all the systems of control that involves. Therefore, for the sake of the bigger whole the individual must leave. Trust has to be ruthless. The pressures to perform, however, can be positive. Most of us need deadlines and targets to pull the best out of us. Where rules and checks predominate, on the other hand, satisficing, doing enough to get by, is the preferred behaviour. We settle for enough when enough, in the case of personal growth or creativity, is never enough.

5 Trust Needs Bonding

Self-contained units, responsible for delivering specified results, are the necessary building blocks of an organization based on trust, but long-lasting groups of trusties can create their problems, those of organizations within the organization. For the whole to work, the goals of the bits have to gel with the goals of the whole. The blossoming of Vision and Mission statements is one attempt to deal with this, as are campaigns for 'total quality' or 'excellence'. These well-meant initiatives can boomerang, however, if they are imposed from the top. They become the equivalent of the compulsory school song, more mocked than loved. In one organization where I worked, a memorandum was circulated from Head Office stating that with immediate effect the organization was committed to a Theory Y philosophy – a belief that individuals are self-motivating. The contrast between the medium and the message caused hilarity. Like morality, visions and missions are caught, not taught.

Anita Roddick holds her spreading Body Shop group together by what can best be called 'personal infection', pouring her energies into the reinforcement of her values and beliefs through every medium she can find. It is always a dangerous strategy to personalize a mission, in case the person themselves stumbles or falls, but organizations based on trust need this sort of personal statement from their leaders. Trust is not, and can never be, an impersonal commodity.

6 Trust Needs Touch

Visionary leaders, however, no matter how articulate, are not enough. A shared commitment still requires a personal contact to make the commitment feel real. Paradoxically, the more virtual an organization becomes the more people need to meet in person. The meetings, however, are different. They are more to do with process than task, more concerned that the people get to know each other than that they deliver. Video conferences are more task-focused, but they are easier and more productive if the individuals already know each other as persons, not just as images on the screen. Work and play, therefore, alternate in many of the corporate get-togethers which now fill the conference resorts out if season.

These are not perks for the privileged. They are the necessary lubricants of virtuality, occasions for not only getting to know each other, and for meeting the leaders, but for reinforcing corporate goals and rethinking corporate strategies. As one who delivers the occasional 'cabaret' at such occasions, I am always surprised to find how few of the participants have met each other in person, even if they have worked together before. I am then further surprised by how a common mood develops. You can almost watch the culture grow and you wonder how anyone could have worked effectively without it.

7 Trust Has To Be Earned

This principle is the most obvious and yet the most neglected. Organizations who expect their people to trust them, must first demonstrate that they are trustworthy. Organizations that break implied contracts through downsizing will find that those who are left will trust them even less. Individuals will not be trusted fully until they have proved they can deliver. Governments who promise to cut taxes but end up increasing them forfeit the trust of the voters.

These cultures of trust are easier to grow and to preserve within the bounds of a single organization. As organizations become semi-dismantled, as many more people find themselves outside the organization, then the issues become more difficult to deal with. Do you and your suppliers, or you and your clients, have the same goals? If not, then trust will be difficult because each will suspect the other of promoting their agenda rather then the joint one. Are the boundaries and the contracts clear and understood? How often have you met, and what sort of affinity is there between you? Are genuine mistakes acknowledged and forgiven? These questions are as important outside the organization as inside. If they can't be answered positively, business becomes adversarial, complicated and no fun.

Stories to Make a Point

St Luke's Advertising Agency

At the end of 1996 there were 55 names on their notepaper, because that was the number of staff they had then. They were on the notepaper because the agency is owned by all members of the staff, from receptionist to chairman.

The ownership is handled through a British device called a 'Quest' – a qualifying employee share ownership trust. The trust held all the shares initially, but then dispensed some of them to each employee. Every year there is another distribution so that those who stay longest get most shares. The company is valued every year and the trust buys back, at full value, the shares of anyone who is leaving, although not many are expected to leave, says Andy Law, the chairman. In fact, unusually for the advertising industry, only two of the original thirty-five members in 1995 have since left, one to be a deep sea diver.

Although everyone is an equal citizen, as far as their ownership entitlement goes, the normal operational hierarchies do still exist, but they are as flat as can be. There are also pay differentials and annual performance reviews. The office is modelled on a university, in the sense that the place is a resource centre rather than a working day apartment house. There is a refectory and a library, but no personal offices, and no one has a secretary, not even the chairman. Staff put their belongings in lockers and carry their work around in standard issue shoulder bags, borrowing an office or a desk when they need it. Each floor has computers where messages and diaries can be checked. The rooms are, in fact, allocated to clients rather than departments. Once a room has been allocated to a client, all meetings and data relevant to that client are held there. Andy Law tells clients, 'Here is a raw, boiling talent of creative people who are smart and have got the right resources. You tell us what you need and we'll change to fit the shape.'

Not to everyone's taste perhaps, but here is a new model of a citizenship company, where everyone is involved and committed to a common purpose, which is underlined by the physical layout. Why, after all, are we so fixated on having our private apartment at work? Most people work where the client is – teachers don't have private offices, nor do plumbers, electricians or almost anyone in the building trade. Shop assistants, restaurant staff, hairdressers, most journalists, actors, consultants most of the time, lorry drivers, gardeners and cooks, factory foremen and women – none of these feels the need for a private space which they can fill with their files and their family photographs. They find their privacy at home, if they need it.

More and more of us will be pressured into doing likewise as organizations begin to question the sense of having offices available for 168 hours a week but only used for 48 or so at most. We will turn the idea of the office upside down, as St Luke's have done, and make the office the client's room so that we work together where the client is, and on our own wherever we want to be.

Making Magic

As an experiment in executive development, the Arts Business Forum in London invited ten leading companies to nominate one of their executives to join an experimental programme of learning from the theatre.

Six of them went to the circus, as one of their chosen shows. [Afterwards] they said that they had seldom seen such an example of teamwork, discipline and commitment to excellence – better, said one, than anything in our company. One of them summed it up: 'That night, we saw ordinary people making magic,' and he added, 'I bet they are paid peanuts, while my bank pays people fortunes and we don't get anything like that standard of work out of them. What are we missing?'

What they were missing, the group agreed, was a dedication to an art form which mattered more to them than money, plus the nightly applause which was a constant recognition of their expertise and their 'magic'. Large pay packets and an annual appraisal do not always compensate for that intensity of commitment or the nightly 'high' for the whole team.

The circus is one example of what businesses can learn from other organizations who have long experience of harnessing individual talent to common purposes.

Professionalism, Projects, Passion and Pride seem to be the hallmarks of the organizations of talent. The theatre is another example, one where individuals become team members for a production, with a shared interest in its success. In like vein, the world of film and television is organized around projects and, at its best, draws on passion and pride as well as professionalism. Orchestras and jazz bands have also been cited as models for the new way of working. Few of these places would claim to be perfect, but they understand that at their best they are engaged in making magic.

The Great Game of Business

This is the title of a book written by Jack Stack, describing his experience at Springfield Re-Manufacturing company in Missouri. This company has now become as much an exhibition as a manufacturing business. More than 2,500 people have paid $1,250 each to go and see what Jack Stack and his colleagues have been doing in this un-high-tech business, reconditioning engines. The concept which they gave birth to and called 'open book management' may be the most important of the new managerial gizmos of recent times, with the added value that it corresponds with common sense and a respect for the average human being's capacity for good work if he or she is treated as a citizen.

In 1983 Stack and others bought out a unit of International Harvester when that company was going through hard times. They started with no money and lots of debt, to be precise, an 89:1 debt:equity ratio with interest at 18%. Stack's only priority, he says, was 'don't run out of cash'. To help with that aim it was important to help all the 119 people working at Springfield Re-Manufacturing to understand the firm's cash situation, so the management started to share all the numbers with everyone, right down to the doorman, and to provide bonus systems and share incentives to reward their efforts. Over 30% of the company is now owned by the workers. All obvious, really, but more difficult than one might think to do in practice. You have to walk your talk, as they say.

The process begins by giving people information regularly, every week, on company performance, as if they were confidential analysts looking at the business. Job counts, inventory levels, sales, expense ratios, bank balances, nothing is held back. The company then puts a great deal of effort into educating people to understand all these numbers. There are what they call 'huddles' to share views and to help work out the implications of the financial figures, a network of 'player coaches' and a big emphasis on self-management. Stack called it The Great Game of Business, on the grounds that business can be fun and personally rewarding, like a good game, but that to play it everyone needs to know all the rules, they need to be able to follow the action, and they have to have a stake in winning.

Denise Bedfeld remembers her first experience. She worked on the line building pumps, valves and cylinders. Jack asked her one day if she thought that she was making the company money. 'Sure,' she replied. 'Prove it,' said Jack. 'Then he gave me a two-hour lecture on how to determine costs. I took two weeks and scrabbled around, digging up information. I didn't know anything. I had to learn as I went along. Finally I proved that our section was making money, but not as much as I thought.

Transmissions were making more. They say numbers don't lie – and it was obvious from the numbers what we had to do. He armed us with the information we needed to make wise decisions.'

Some of the proof lies in the numbers. The share price rose from 10 cents to $18.60 in just ten years. The company now does over $100 million in sales, operates several different divisions, and employs nearly 800 people. Jack wrote his book about it all, and has now had more than 200 imitators. Treating people as responsible adults and citizens, trust and recognition, room to be yourself – it seems to work, for everyone.

The stories cited relate to relatively small organizations. At first sight it is hard to see how they might apply to the large supranationals discussed in the previous chapter. But, as ABB has proved, large organizations can be composed of flexible combinations of very small organizations, in each of which there can be a sense of partnership in a shared adventure, trust, recognition and a share in the rewards of success. The four Ps of Professionalism, Projects, Passion and Pride are not the exclusive property of new or creative businesses, but they seem to be the necessary elements of corporate citizenship. Given the mood of the times, and the hungry spirit which sits within each of us, there is no alternative but to give more space and more sense of partnership to the citizen core of any organization.

The practical implications are:

- a much greater emphasis on the selection of the citizens, to ensure that they are likely to be kindred spirits, as well as professionally competent;
- an explicit contract with each individual, laying down tenure limits and partnership rights, to demonstrate that the work is to the benefit of all and to make the commitment of the organization clear;
- a formal constitution which sets out rights and duties, so that the boundaries of trust are known;
- a clear understanding, not necessarily in writing, of the imperatives of the organization, what it stands for and what it seeks to achieve, above and beyond the monetary goals, to elicit some of that passion;
- control by results more than by procedures, as a demonstration of trust and a source of pride.

Those who qualify for the citizen core of any organization will no longer be content to be regarded as the instruments of that organization, no matter how well rewarded, because they will, mostly, be able to turn mercenary if they need to. The citizen company will, therefore, gradually become a necessary way to organize, difficult though it will always be to manage and to lead.

In *Organizing Genius*, Warren Bennis, philosopher of leadership and articulate observer of American organizations, has described the methods and the history of some of America's most famous creative groups, including the Manhattan Project which made the first atomic bomb, the Disney animation studio and Bill Clinton's campaign team for his first presidential election. As he analyzes these Great Groups, Bennis finds they had much in common despite their variety. They were all grouped around a specific and prestigious project and their members were all recognized as experts in their field. Those members had a consuming passion for their cause. They were careless of money or material comfort, often working in makeshift quarters for long hours with little pay, they were young (mostly under 30), had great camaraderie and were given as much space in their work as they could handle. Their pride in their membership and, eventually, their achievements was obvious. He doesn't call them citizens, but that is what, in effect, they were.

12

Why My Former Employees Still Work for Me

Ricardo Semler

I own a manufacturing company in Brazil called Semco, about which I can report the following curious fact: no one in the company really knows how many people we employ. When we walk through our manufacturing plants, we rarely know who works for us. Some of the people in the factory are full-time Semco employees; some work for us part-time; some work for themselves and supply Semco with components or services; some work for themselves under contract to outside companies (even Semco's competitors); and some of them work for each other. We could decide to find out which are which and who is who, but for two good reasons we never bother. First, the employment and contractual relationships are so complex that describing them all would take too much time and trouble. Second, we think it's all useless information.

Semco has long been a laboratory for unusual employment and management practices. What we're now engaged in might be called a radical experiment in unsupervised, in house, company-supported satellite productions of goods and services for sale to Semco itself and to other manufacturers by employees, part-time employees, ex-employees, and people who have never been connected with Semco whatsoever (but who work on our premises and on our equipment). This is not at all the same thing as outsourcing. This is a borderless system of short-term, non-contractual task assignment often using Semco's own fixed assets, some of it in Semco's own plants and some dispersed at a dozen sites that don't belong to the company.

This satellite program, as we call it, sounds chaotic, can be frustrating, and is in some ways uncontrollable. It requires daily leaps of faith. It has serious implications for corporate security. And, for three years it has been working very well. Since 1990, 28% of Brazilian capital goods manufacturers have gone bankrupt. In 1990, 1991 and 1992, Brazilian gross industrial product fell by 14%, 11%, and 9%, respectively. Capital goods output has fallen back to what it was in 1977. But in this same period, Semco's overall sales and profits have remained intact, and I attribute the indifference first and foremost to our satellite production.

Source: R. Semler (1994) *Harvard Business Review*, January, 64–74.

Ever since I took over the company 12 years ago, Semco has been unorthodox in a variety of ways. I believe in responsibility but not in pyramidal hierarchy. *I think that strategic planning and vision are often barriers to success.* I dispute the value of growth. I don't think a company's success can be measured in numbers, since numbers ignore what the end user really thinks of the product and what the people who produce it really think of the company. I question the supremacy of talent, too much of which is as bad as too little. I'm not sure I believe that control is either expedient or desirable.

I don't govern Semco – I own the capital, not the company – but on taking over from my father, I did try to reconstruct the company so that Semco could govern itself on the basis of three values: employee participation, profit sharing, and open information systems. We've introduced idiosyncratic features like factory-floor flexitime, self-set salaries, a rotating CEOship, and, from the owner to the newest, greenest maintenance person-only three levels of hierarchy.

You might say that what we practice is an extreme form of common sense: 'common' because there's nothing we do that thousands of other people didn't think of ages ago, 'extreme' because we actually do it. Another way of looking at Semco is to say that we treat our employees like responsible adults. We never assume that they will take advantage of our rules (or our lack of rules); we always assume they will do their level best to achieve the results beneficial to the company, the customer, their colleagues, and themselves. As I put it in an earlier article in HBR, participation gives people control of their work, profit sharing gives them a reason to do it better, information tells them what's working and what isn't.

With rare exceptions, this approach has been successful. We've had two or three strikes, but they were quickly settled, especially once the strikers saw that we would neither lock them out of the plant nor suspend their benefits during work stoppage. (They were able to plan outgoing strike tactics while eating lunch in the company cafeteria.) We've had a few employees take wholesale advantage of our open stockrooms and trusting atmosphere, but we were lucky enough to find and prosecute them without putting in place a lot of insulting watchdog procedures for the nine out of ten who are honest. We've seen a few cases of greed when the people set their own salaries too high. We've tried a few experiments that we later backed away from. We've had to accept occasional democratic decisions that management disliked, but we learned to swallow hard and live with them.

On the whole, as I say, our approach has worked. Loyalty is high, quality is excellent, and sales and profits are suprisingly good for a manufacturing company in one of the worlds most lunatic business environments. But in Brazil no state of the economy is permanent. Few last long enough to be called temporary. Surviving the ups and downs of the Brazilian economy is a little like riding a Brahma bull. It is even more like riding a Brahma bull in an earthquake. Some of the worst jolts come not from the bull but the landscape.

In 1990, the jolt that sent us into our present experiment came from the minister of finance, who, believing Brazil's inflation was simply the result of too much money being used for too much speculation, seized 80% of the country's cash and introduced an extended period of economic bedlam. Employers could not meet payrolls. Consumer spending vanished. Business spending shuddered to a halt. Bankruptcies soared. Industrial output plummeted.

At Semco, we had several months of zero sales. After all, what company was going to buy machinery with a ten months delivery when it didn't know if it could last out the week? Worse yet, back orders were cancelled, or we found that our customers had gone out of business. Our marine division alone had $1.5 million of receivables that we couldn't hope to collect and $4 million worth of products that shipbuilders could no longer pay for. We had to rent warehouse space just to store all the unsold goods.

We cut costs. We organised workers into teams and sent them out to sell replacement parts directly to ships and restaurants. We cut down on coffee breaks, locked up the copiers, cancelled orders for new uniforms, and turned off the lights we all could find, scrimped on telephone calls. None of it was enough, and anyway, I don't really believe in cost cutting. I like to think we don't waste money when we've got it. *And who can say how many sales we lose when we play Scrooge with the travel money or penny pinch the phone calls?*

Finally, we called the workers together in groups of 100 and discussed what we should do. They came up with lots of ideas, and we tried them without success until we reached a point where no one had anything else to propose and neither did we – except for two unhappy alternatives: cut pay or cut workforce. We thought we could avoid layoffs by cutting salaries 30% across the board until business picked up again. But a lot of people were already struggling with bills and rents and mortgages and wanted us to start laying people off instead, so those who stayed could at least survive. We went on searching desperately for a third way out.

And then suddenly the shop-floor committee came to us and said, 'Okay, we will take a 30% pay cut, but on three conditions.' The first was that we increase their profit sharing by 15%, from just under 24% to just under 39%, until they got back up to their former salary levels. The second was that management takes a 40% pay cut. And the third was that a member of the union committee would co-sign every cheque we wrote; because the workers wanted to be absolutely certain that their sacrifice would be worthwhile, they wanted to oversee each and every expenditure.

Well, at that moment, we *had* no profits to share, so there was nothing for us to lose and everything to gain. And by the second months, we were actually covering expenses. In their drive to save, the workers took on more and more of the former contract work. They did security and cleaning, drove trucks, even cooked the food in the cafeteria. No expense went unchallenged, and for four or five months, we made a small profit in the worst economic times any of us had ever seen.

But we kept on looking for a better solution.

In the first place, pure reduction has to be a temporary measure. What about training, research new product development, and all the seemingly peripheral activities that produce profits over the long haul? Those weren't responsibilities we could abdicate.

And what about those cheques? The dual-signature scheme was working at the moment, but management couldn't permanently yield its power of the purse to a person chosen by the union without management input or approval.

Yet the explosion of energy, inventiveness, and flexibility we'd been witnessing was hugely attractive. And when we then added in several other factors – the need to cut our standing labour costs, the demands of the Brazilian Labour law, the dynamic example of our own peculiar Nucleus of Technological Innovation, which I'll come back to in a moment – what began taking shape was a radically new principle of organization.

The Thinkodrome at the Free-for-All Corporation

Years ago, in the mid-1980s, three Semco engineers proposed a new kind of work unit. They wanted to take a small group of people raised in Semco's culture and familiar with its products and set them free. The new group would not have to worry about production problems, sales, inventory, equipment maintenance, delivery schedules or personnel. Instead. They would invent new products, improve old ones, refine marketing strategies, uncover production inefficiencies, and dream up new lines of business. They would have no boss, no subordinates. They would pick their own focus, set their own agenda, and have complete freedom to change their minds. Twice a year they'd report to senior management, which would decide whether or not to keep them on for another six months.

The three engineers suggested we call the new unit the Nucleus of Technological Innovation (NTI) and somewhat predictably proposed themselves as its first three members. We bought their odd idea, and then we worked out an odd form of compensation to go along with it. Their guaranteed salaries went down sharply, but they would now share in the proceeds of their inventions, innovations, and improvements. They would received a percentage of any savings they introduced, royalties on new products they devised, a share of the profits on their inventions, and would also be free to sell consulting services on the open market. They might have done better as truly independent entrepreneurs, but as NTI members, Semco would cushion them against disaster and give them the support of an established and well-equipped manufacturing operation.

By the end of their first six months, NTI had 18 projects under way, and over the next few years they uncorked such an array of inventions, changes, and refinements (one of my favourites is a scale that weighs freight trains moving at full speed) that NTI's members began to prosper mightily and Semco became unthinkable without their constant innovation and reform.

By 1990, we'd begun to feel that we'd like to NTI the entire company, liberate more creativity, tie compensation even more specifically to performance, loosen the ties that bound us all together, and scramble our overall structure. The 30% pay-cut-and-cost-reductions scheme had given us breathing space of several months, but with the Brazilian economy in a bucket and no imminent prospect of recovery, we *had* to become permanently leaner and more flexible. At the same time, of course, we had a commitment to our workforce that was central to the way we did business, that commitment had been our principle reason for trying to avoid layoffs.

For most other companies, there was another reason as well: Brazilian labour law protects laid-off workers by granting them several different forms of special compensation. The largest of these comes from an individual fund for each worker to which the employer contributes 8% of wages every month. When people are fired (or retire early), they collect all this accumulated money, plus interest, in the form of a lump sum. Less substantial – not, unlike the 8% fund, a great problem for many employers – is severance pay itself, which is paid on the spot out of current income which can amount to two years' salary in the case of workers with many years' seniority. By the end of 1990, a lot of Brazilian companies drifted slowly into bankruptcy rather than lay people off and go bankrupt overnight. With our finances still more or less intact, this widespread problem proved in our case to be an opportunity.

Semco's sales had gradually increased again, and we were making enough money to restore salaries to where they had been before the 30% cut. We took back our cheque signing privileges. We were surviving in a crisis economy, but only just, and we began to face the facts that we had to cut out permanent staff and contract more of our work. We looked hard for a way of doing it without destroying the support system that Semco people lived on. It was here that NTI's free-form structure suggested solution.

Instead of giving contracts out to strangers, we decided we could just as well give the contracts to our own employees. We would encourage them to leave the Semco payroll and start their own satellite enterprises, doing work, at least initially for Semco. Like NTL, these satellites could stay under our larger umbrella by leasing our machines, even working in our plant. Like NTI, they could also do work for other companies, again on our machines and in our factories. Like NTI, their compensation would take a variety of forms – contract payments, royalties, commissions, profit sharing, piece-work, whatever they could think up that we could both live with. And like NTI, they could have some beginning guarantees. In particular, we would offer all of them some contract work to cut their teeth in, and would defer the lease payments on all equipment and space for two full years.

This satellite program would have obvious advantages for Semco. We could reduce our payroll, cut inventory costs by spreading out raw materials and spare parts among our new suppliers, and yet enjoy the advantage of having subcontractors who knew our business and the idiosyncrasies of our company and our customers. Moreover, we would pick up the benefit of entrepreneurial motivation, because of our profit sharing, our employees already worked evenings and weekends when necessary, without any prompting from management, being in business for themselves ought to raise that sense of involvement higher still.

But what in heaven's name were the advantages for our workers, who'd be giving up a secure nest at Semco for the risks of small business? And in the midst of economic bedlam? To begin with, of course, they all had the chance to make many times what they could at Semco – if the economy straightened out. Of course that was a big *if*. And should the recession persist, they might make less. But only assuming they continued to have a job at Semco, which was becoming an even bigger *if* with every day that passed. The fact was, they had distressingly few choices. And so did we.

We eased the transition in every way we could. We created a team of executives to teach cost control, pricing, maintenance, inventory management. To provide seed money, we gave people lay off payments on top of severance pay and all the other legally required benefits. Many also made use of their 8% nest-egg funds. No one *had* to start a satellite. Some took their severance and left. Some managed to stay on the payroll for months or for good. But despite the difficulties, satellites sprang up quickly. White-collar workers were the first. Our tax accountants, human resources staffers, and computer programmers all went off on their own, then blue-collar workers in food services and refrigeration systems followed suit.

Today, about half the manufacturing we once did in-house has gone to satellites, and we think we can farm out another 10% to 20% in the coming years. Best of all, to this day only one satellite has failed. Some are expanding and looking for partners. The company has rehired some satellite workers, and a few had moved repeatedly back and forth between satellite and employee status as needs – theirs and ours – shifted. Some satellites have broadened their scope so greatly that most of their time – often right on our premises, remember – is spent with customers and production partners who have no other connection with Semco whatsoever.

In 1990, Semco had about 500 employees. Today, we have about 200, plus at least that many in our satellites, with another 50 or 60 people who work for a satellite and also work for us part-time. We have employees with fixed salaries. We have employees with variable salaries made up of royalties or bonuses based on self-set objectives like cash flow, sales, profits, production units, or any one of a dozen other measures. We have employees with both fixed and variable salaries. All our employees share in our profits.

On the satellite side, compensation may take the form of a fixed fee, an hourly stipend, a percentage of increased sales, a finder's fee, an honorarium, a retainer converting to an advance converting to a royalty, or even a simple win-or-lose commission. In one case, we had decided to kill a product-development project when one of our people picked it up from the table and said, 'I'll take it. If you give me $1,000 a month, which will just pay my expenses, plus a 7% royalty for the first five years if I can make it work – I'll take it.' So of course we gave it to him. The most we can lose is $1,000 a month, where we had been spending $10,000 to $15,000 a month and getting nowhere. The most he can make is something like half a million, I'd guess, with the other 93% coming to Semco.

Once we posted a job for one engineer and got 1,430 resumes. We took them home in packs of a hundred, and then we interviewed for five months. In the end, we invited several dozen final candidates to a one day seminar where we walked them through the entire company, opened our files, showed them everything we did, then asked them for proposals. We wound up hiring 41 engineers – one salaried employee and 40 satellite workers whom we paid on various forms of percentage-based commission.

In one of our plants, we've set aside a large room full of desks and computers to give everyone within our company sphere and, for all we know, a variety of guests and visitors from well beyond it, a place to sit and plan and ask questions and solve problems. We call it the Thinkodrome, and it's a busy place, quiet place. That Semco survived at all we owe in large part to surrounding ourselves with people who look at everything we do and ask why we can't do it better or cheaper or faster or in some entirely novel way.

Hunting the Free Market

Our ancestors laid out the ground rules of human teamwork several thousand generations ago, they go like this: the woman with the keen eyesight is Chief Mammoth Finder, the guy with the strong arm and the long spear is Head Mammoth Killer, and the tribal elder with the special feel for herbs and spices gets to be Grand Mammoth Cook. For now. All these positions are temporary and to some extent self-selecting. If you want to be Chief Finder go find some mammoths and the job is probably yours. But since everyone's well being depends on your success, your status is also highly situational. Fail to find, and the job will pass swiftly and naturally to someone else.

Generally speaking, Semco's production process works along similar lines, both for satellite operations and for the work we do in-house. All work, including some aspects of management, goes to people with proven track records who want the jobs and can compete for them successfully. Satellite as well as in-house business units rise and fall on their merits alone – at least in theory.

This commitment to free-market principles was put to the test about a year into the satellite program, when our marine division found itself with a good deal of idle capacity. Marine's strategy was built on quality, not price – low volume but high margins. A shipbuilder seeking the very best performance and dependability in, say, a propeller system, tended to come to us. But with the economy in a straightjacket, orders had nearly disappeared.

On the other hand, our biscuit division, which designs and builds turnkey cookie factories for global giants like Nabisco and Nestle, had two fairly big contracts in hand, for about $2 million, another for $5.5 million, and was going to need a lot of skilled subcontracting. The portion of this work that marine could do would keep it occupied for four or five months, and marine's top manager (called a counsellor at Semco) went ahead and figured the contracts from the biscuit division into his budget. But biscuit's purchasing people did not award the contracts to the marine division, which took too long to deliver, they said, and which charged too high a price for its exaggerated quality. They gave the contracts instead to satellite producers and outside contractors, including one of the marine's archcompetitors. The fight that triggered was a bitter one, and the attempts of the interdepartmental management meeting to act as a go-between did not make things easier. We were of two minds ourselves.

On the one hand, we were going to pay marine employees to sit around on their hands while another division paid outsiders to do work the marine employees could have done. And on the other hand, how could we ask biscuit employees, who share in their division's profits, to subsidise a business in trouble? Moreover, wouldn't the subsidy just postpone marine's inevitable reckoning with its own strategic predicament? In the end, we let biscuit have its way and endorsed the need to be as unforgiving toward our own business units as we would to outsiders. It was the right decision, of course. We finished the cookie factories on schedule, and the marine division – which decided to stick with its high-quality, high-margin strategy but to eliminate a number of products whose quality and cost were too high for the market – cut its staff by 70%, began farming out a lot of its work to satellites, and recovered its profitability.

Control

At the centre of Semco are a group of six so-called counsellors, and all of us take a six-month turn as acting CEO. We also do six month as opposed to yearly budgeting, because an annual budget tempts managers to postpone unpleasant decisions to the third and fourth quarters.

The budget cycles are January to June and July to December, but the CEO cycles begin in March and September. In other words, we avoid what other companies and shareholders think they want – responsibility nailed down to a single man or woman. Our CEOs don't wear themselves out trying to meet quarterly financial goals, and there's no one person to blame if the company goes down the drain. When financial performance is one person's problem then everyone else can relax. In our system, no one can relax. You get to pass on the baton, but it comes back again two and a half years later.

One consequence of this system is that we need to keep each other informed, which we do as regular divisional meetings and biweekly interdivisional meetings. All these meetings are open and optional, and those who attend make decisions that those who don't may simply have to live with.

This self-selecting element in decision making is another consequence of the deliberate fragmentation of responsibility. Like our predecessors the mammoth hunters, the people who get responsibility are the people who seek it out and meet it. In fact, the actual, ad hoc control structure we work with from day to day builds on this principle and on two others that, together, create a kind of invisible order from the apparent chaos that characterizes the Semco environment.

The first principle holds that information is the ultimate source of virtually all power. For this reason, we try to make all of it available to everyone. All meetings are open. Designs and specifications are shared. The company's books are open for inspections by employees and for auditing by their unions. In short, we try to undercut and so eliminate the process of filtering and negotiating information that goes on in so many corporations. The person who knows most about the subject under discussion rather than by the person who has the highest declared status chairs meetings by apparent income.

The second principle is that the responsibility for any task belongs to the person who claims it.

The third is that profit sharing for employees and success-orientated compensation for satellite enterprises will spread responsibility across the Semco map. With income and security at risk – and with information readily available – people try hard to stay aware of everyone else's performance.

To give an idea of how all of this works in practice, let's take a look of one of those turnkey cookie factories. The Big Cracker Company of Chicago wants a plant that will turn out a thousand tons a month of, say, butterscotch macaroons. To begin with, an independent agent will tell us of the project in return for a finder's fee. We will probably put in an initial customer interface in the hands of a satellite company – four men who used to be on our payroll and now work for themselves. They'll go through the specifications with the customer, then they'll share that information widely, announce a meeting (to which anyone can come and no one is summoned), and chair the discussion (which will cover several unexpected proposals from unanticipated participants like the guy from refrigeration with a special point of view about handling butter and coconut). Someone, a group of employees or satellites, will take on the job of costing the project, and with this estimate in hand, a Semco counsellor and biscuit-division co-ordinators will then set a margin and deliver the quote to Big Cracker.

(A couple of times, we have even communicated this margin to the customer, because we thought it would justify, for example, a 12% net margin than to play the disingenuous game of claiming pencil-thin profits and no room for compromise. Our chief argument has been our profit sharing program, since it seems so clear to us that people will work harder for more money and that a generous margin will therefore buy the customer much extra care and effort. But I'm afraid we've had only limited success with this approach.)

This margin-setting discussion often produces serious disagreements. In one case, we battled out the margin in a long, heated debate, and then the sales manager lowered it dramatically when he sat down with the customer.

By Semco rules, that kind of last minute capitulation is perfectly legitimate. Battle or no battle, he was the customer, not we. Whoever holds the spear is completely in charge of bringing down the mammoth. Let's say Big Cracker accepts our bid and the order comes in, 600 pages long. Let's say we choose a co-ordinator for the project from the outside company, and lets call him Bob. Bob will go through the contract and decide how he wants to divide it up. He may get help from engineering. He will certainly get help from all the meetings he holds to make decisions, which he will chair and where he will lobby for the people he wants to do each job. Next, the biscuit division's purchasing department will negotiate contracts with the dozens of suppliers chosen. In 1991, we did about 70% of such contracts in-house. Today, that's down to 35% or 40%.

When Bob has put together a completion schedule and time chart, everyone will go to work – each contractor, employee, and satellite responsible to no single authority but answerable to everyone. At most companies, when something goes wrong the real responsibility falls between the cracks. At Semco, the fact that Bob is not an employee makes everyone react much faster when there looks like trouble.

And Lack of Control

Semco needs to maintain in-house just a limited number of functions – top management, applications engineering, some R&D, and some high-tech, capital-intensive skills that we do exceptionally well. We don't care how everything else gets done, whether by contractors or subcontractors, satellites or nonsatellites, former employees or total strangers or by the very people who do the same thing for our competition. None of that matters.

When we started, people warned me that all sorts of information about our company would get into the wrong hands, that we had to protect ourselves. I heard the same argument when we started distributing profit-and-loss statements to our employees. But it's a waste of time to worry about leaks.

First of all, we no longer know whose the wrong hands are. The competition used to be a company a mile away that made the same products that we did, but now the competition comes from companies we've never even heard of in Taiwan and Finland. Second, I've never seen a company overtake another because it had its 10K or even the specifications for a valve. Third, we want to be a moving target. We don't care about yesterday's information or last year's oil pump, which in any case the competition can buy, take apart, and study to his heart's content.

Finally, we don't think people give out information anyway. I know, I've tried on numerous occasions to get a copy of, let's say, a pamphlet some company passed out to 1,000 employees, and nobody can lay their hands on one. The Chinese printed hundreds of millions of copies of Chairman Mao's *Little Red Book*, and still they're as rare as hen's teeth.

People also warned me about the loss of central goal setting and control. I admit that the lack of control is often hard to live with. But, let's not compare Semco's circumstances with some ideal world where managers actually get to decide what people will do and when and how they'll do it. We have limited control over the day-to-day behavior of the people who make most of our components, but so do companies that do all their work in-house. At least none of our satellite people work nine to five and leave their problems at the plant when they go home at night – which means leaving them to management. We have motivation and responsibility working on our side. Our satellite workers are in business for themselves, so they'll work all night to complete an order to specification and in time. And if the order is late or fails to meet our quality standards, then we're free to give the next order to someone else. We can forget the witch-hunt and all the grief that goes into firing people or not promoting them.

As for planning and the control it presupposes, I think good planning is always situational. Thinking about the future is a useful, necessary exercise, but translating such conjecture into 'Strategic Planning' is worse than useless. It's an actual barrier to survival. Strategic planning leads us to *make* things happen that fly full in the face of reality and opportunity.

For example, Semco is today in the environmental consulting business, which I could not have imagined five years ago. Our gadfly NTI group was looking at one customer's need for an environmentally active pump – a pump that would shred and process the material it moved – and saw that the company could reengineer its productions line to do away with the pump altogether. Had we said 'We're in the pump business, not the environmental business,' we might never have pursued the problem. As it was, we addressed the company's overall need, jettisoned the pump, and when it was all over, we'd also acquired a small environmental consulting firm to flesh out our own limited expertise. More recently, we've also entered into a joint venture with one of the world's leading environmental groups. Today, the division represents about 14% to 15% of our total business and is growing at a rate of 30% to 40% a year.

The lesson this story teaches me is about the negative value of structure. Structure creates hierarchy, and hierarchy creates constraint. We have not utterly abandoned all control, but the old pyramidal hierarchy is simply unable to make leaps of insight, technology, and innovation. Within their own industries, pyramidal hierarchies can generate incremental change.

Take dishwashers, one of Semco's businesses. Dishwashers are expensive to operate and messy to use, but over the last 50 years, dishwashers have changed hardly at all. What the customer wants is machines that washes dishes silently, cheaply and without any mess at all, which probably means without water. I've recently seen indications that such a thing may be possible, but the idea could never come from a pyramid of Semco dishwashing executives. It was one of our satellites that brought us the idea. In fact, about two-thirds of our new products come from satellite companies.

What goes for planning goes equally for culture, vision, and responsibility. We find that fragmentation is strength in all these areas. Semco has no corporate credo, for example, and no mission statement. An articulation of company values or vision is just a photograph of the company as it is, or wants to be, at one given moment. Snapshots of this kind seem to hold some companies together, but they are terribly static devices. No one can impose corporate consciousness from above. It moves and shifts with every day and every worker. Like planning, vision at its best is dynamic and dispersed.

At Semco, so is responsibility. We have little control, even less organization, and no conventional discipline at all. People come and go whenever they like; many set their own compensation; divisions and units perpetuate themselves on however they can; satellite companies work on our machines, in our factories for us and others in a great confusion of activity; the system tying it all together is painfully loose – and this is *manufacturing*, much of it assembly-line manufacturing.

When I describe Semco to other manufacturers, they laugh. 'What do you make,' they ask me 'beads?' And I say, 'no, among other things, we make rocket-fuel propellant mixers for satellites.' And they say, 'That's not possible.' And I say, 'Nevertheless …'

The point is simple but perhaps not obvious. Semco has abandoned a great many traditional business practices. Instead, we use minimal hierarchies, ad hoc structures, self-control, and the discipline of our own community marketplace of jobs and responsibilities to achieve high quality, on time performance. Does it make me feel that I have given up power and governance? You bet it does. But do I have more sleepless nights than the manufacturer who runs his business with an iron hand and whose employees leave their troubles in his lap every night? I think I probably sleep better. I know I sleep as well.

We delivered our last cookie factory with all its 16,000 components right on time. One of our competitors, a company with tight controls and hierarchies, delivered a similar factory to the same client a year and two months late.

Note

1   In 1990 and again in 1992, Ricardo Semler was elected business leader of the year by a poll of 52,000 Brazilian executives.

Development

Creativity develops over time. Henry explores how openness, autonomy and support feature in creative endeavour, development and well-being. Argyris shows how psychological defenses can inhibit managers' personal learning and defeat their organizational change efforts. Krackhardt and Hansen illustrate the importance of informal networks and the values of mapping links.

Creative work is more likely to emerge where people are pursuing work they value. In organizations an open culture may help make this more likely. The wise are noted for their capacity to see the bigger picture and take action that is right for the parties involved. A capacity for empathy together with a detachment from a need for a particular outcome can help. Studies show those exhibiting well-being are often absorbed in what they are doing and feel part of a supportive social network. Giving people as much control as possible over how they set about their work makes this more likely. In this chapter Henry explores the development of qualities like openness, autonomy, relativistic thinking, flexibility, the capacity for absorption and social embeddedness that appear to underpin creative work, healthy development and well-being.

Chris Argyris is well-known for his articulation of the practical effects of the shadow side of organizations. He differentiates between theories in action and theories in use and explains how defensive routines prevent learning. Here, he discusses some of the inherent contradictions typically found in organizational change programs designed to bring about empowerment. Recognizing that empowerment necessarily entails a commitment that comes about through participation, Argyris explains how organizational change efforts are often sabotaged through a design that accords with top managers 'preferred strategy and process.' This specification can comfort top management with the control it appears to afford them, but leaves little scope for staff to identify with or feel ownership of the change process.

Networks are generally critical to the emergence of creative endeavour. Here Krackhardt and Hansen focus on naturally occuring networks of work colleagues and advocate explicitly mapping the interconnections between them. They show how managers can map the informal communications channels between people and how this can help determine the appropriate manager for different jobs. Related mapping procedures can be used to show the interconnections between ideas, approaches and actions in other areas. Mapping is a very useful way of getting to grips with complex interrelationships and, like a picture, a visual map can be worth a thousand words.

13

Creativity, Development and Well-being

Jane Henry

People generally want to be happy, fulfilled and useful. This chapter explores aspects of what it is to be a successful and mature human being, specifically what it is to be creative, developed and to have a sense of well-being. It considers what helps sustain these states of being, notes some implications for management and organizational practise and discusses commonalities across positive states of creativity, development and well-being.

Supporting Creativity

Research has found that creative people in a wide variety of fields including science, business and the arts tend to share certain characteristics, notably they are experienced in the area they are being creative in, are intrinsically motivated, pursuing work in an area of interest to them and they exhibit some flexibility of thought as to how they achieve their goal (e.g Amabile, 1975).

*Experienc*e in the field gives people a more sophisticated understanding of the area and this leaves them better placed to recognize key questions, ones worth devoting their time too. Creative ideas often require considerable persistence to take forward and people are more prepared to go the extra mile in the face of difficulties in areas they care about. Creative people are also known to spend more time at the front end deciding which angle to take before pressing forward with a particular solution.

Given the importance of intrinsic *motivation*, experience and flexibility, the question arises as to how a manager can best elicit and support the creativity of their staff. Two things seem particularly important: an open culture and as much freedom as possible as to how to set about work tasks.

We know that children and mosts adults are more likely to explore new possibilities when they feel safe. Encouraging *openness* at work makes it more likely a greater number of employees will feel able to make suggestions for improvement and challenge existing practice without fear of being snapped at, ridiculed or punished in some way. Managers can help here by walking the talk and encouraging and receiving suggestions for improvement with good grace. Some organizations formalize this through the use of suggestion schemes.

The organizational culture can also have a big impact on whether people can pursue areas of intrinsic interest to them that are also potentially creative for their organization. It helps to allow staff *freedom* as to how they organize their work and achieve their goals. The trend towards pushing decisions down and empowering staff helps in this respect whereas increasing scrutiny of all aspects of work can inhibit creativity at work. There are a number of different ways of allowing staff to pursue projects of intrinsic interest to them. Organizations such as 3M and Google allow some staff a proportion of their time to work on projects of their own choosing. 3M has offered scientists 15% of their time for such projects. They also offer genesis grants to help develop ideas generated in this free-time. Google requires staff to attract colleagues to devote some of their free work-time to that project to demonstrate support for its viability. Flatter structures and simplified reporting procedures tend to give new ideas a better chance of getting off the ground as they are less likely to become bogged down in the red tape of a long committee-bound reporting structure.

In most spheres creativity is less common in an inward looking organization than one that is more outward oriented and it is the latter that are better placed to capitalize on new opportunities in the surrounding environment. Encouraging staff to network outside the organization can help here.

In addition creativity is generally more likely where groups contain a mix of *diverse* perspectives and skills. Managers can help by mixing people with different personalities, roles and expertise. The now commonplace use of multidisciplinary teams helps. Integrating processes and procedures across departments also helps mix the perspectives that are brought to bear on an issue. A job rotation scheme exposing staff to the different viewpoints in different departments may also help keep minds more open.

Creativity Training

Research shows that one characteristic common in creative people is a capacity to tolerate ambiguity. Lay theories *associate* creativity with new ideas and generally assume that these ideas come about through a mental flexibility that allows people to apply thinking from one domain to another. For example, applying the idea of x-rays to food to get the microwave. Given this view it is no surprise that creative thinking is associated with thinking out of the box and creativity training is often focused round techniques designed to produce lots of ideas.

In organizations this often takes the form of training people in various creativity techniques. Four well-known ways of generating ideas creatively are: listing ideas, lateral thinking, analytical thinking and intuitive thinking.

Brainstorming asks individuals to volunteer as many ideas as they can think of, brainwriting asks people to start by noting their ideas privately before they are grouped together. *Lateral thinking* introduces a new element such as a random word or an analogy, to interrupt the current train of thought. Then asks people to generate associations to that new item and force fit the new ideas back to the issue under consideration to generate new approaches. *Analytical* techniques comprise a systemic consideration of possible approaches, for example considering the attributes of a bicycle in turn and deciding how each might be improved or drawing up a matrix, for example of materials and functions and seeing if one can generate a new product in each cell. For example using a metal connector to join two bicycles to make a tandem.

All these approaches work by generating a mass of ideas on the assumption that within this mass there will be some quality ideas that had not previously been identified.

There are many other ways of coming up with ideas including more intuitive approaches. The latter generally attempt to change the participant's state of mind, for example through a relaxation procedure, followed by a visualization or drawing, with a view to unearthing a quality idea, the wise idea straight off.

Creativity techniques are often more powerful when embedded within a *creative problem-solving* process. This employs various techniques within a staged process that allows time to consider different aspects of the issue under consideration, including what is the most important issue to address, what angle to take on it, various possible ways forward and a consideration of the acceptability of different possible courses of action. One distinguishing characteristic of creative problem-solving is the inclusion of a divergent phase where 'anything goes', preceding the convergent phrase where decisions are made. In contrast, in normal rational thinking, ideas are examined for their logical consistency every step of the way.

In addition to encouraging silly ideas and banning criticism in the divergent phases creative problem solving typically comprises several other key processes. Often a number of the techniques entail *non-verbal* processes. These might include a picture of what people would like to happen or a map of the components in a complicated problem. The work generated is also *displayed publicly*. This generally makes it much easier for participants to follow each other's thinking and keep track of all the possible ways forward than if they were merely discussing the issue.

Although ostensibly framed as a cognitive process, creativity training of the kind described, normally embodies *principles* in line with those discussed earlier in that it encourages openness, engineers diverse perspectives and entails flexibility. Various devices are used to encourage everybody to participate: such as a round robin where everybody gets a chance to volunteer their thoughts in turn so no person can dominate, the fact that all ideas are accepted and silly ideas are welcomed and in brainstorming criticism of the ideas put forward is banned. These rules make participation less threatening. Creative thinking is often done in small groups so different individuals can provide contrasting perspectives on the issue at hand. The sheer range of ideas considered also helps widen the diversity of perspectives considered. The fun aspect of some of the techniques can help promote a relaxed state of attention that appears to make it easier for creative ideas to emerge.

Creativity training can encourage participants to work on issues of particular interest to them including issues they have been stuck on. With such topics the process often challenges the 'client's' deeply held assumptions, but in a way that is more acceptable to many than more obviously psychological and psychotherapeutic processes.

Creativity training may include work on differences in cognitive *style*. For example participants may be asked to complete a personality inventory such as MBTI, NEO or KAI (e.g. Furnham, 2006). Creative thinking is a powerful way of pointing up differences in cognitive style as people get repeated opportunities to see how their colleagues think about and tackle problems differently from themselves. For example, that the

KAI adaptors really do attend to more of the detail than the innovators, and it is those scoring high on openness (NEO), who are more likely to query if the group is addressing the right question. The intuitive perceivers (MBTI) really do look at the bigger picture and the sensing, thinking, judging types map out a more detailed and orderly response (e.g. Hirsch and Kummerow, 1994). Undertaking a process of this kind points up the different ways people think.

Over a period of time engagement in creative thinking processes can help people appreciate differences between different ways of working and develop greater respect for different ways of addressing problems as tracking the genesis of accepted ideas shows they often start from unexpected quarters. At its best the process breeds tolerance. After a course of creative problem solving the greatest lasting change can be one of *attitude*. Along with a greater openness to the value of other people's contribution there can be a shift to a more open and relaxed way of attending to problems and challenges, a less anxious and driven approach and more playful, relaxed and open state to problem exploration and resolution. In some cases there is also a greater commitment to act on things that are perceived as important and/or an acceptance and understanding of why they are not likely to do so.

In a sense one could say creativity training offers a way to teach the rudiments of *wisdom*. Baltes and his colleagues who have been studying wisdom for many years view wise people as those who have developed expertise in the fundamental pragmatics of life (Baltes and Smith, 1990). Another characteristic of wise people is that they have a relativistic perspective on life, they are very good at seeing the other person's point of view and the systemic considerations affecting people's thoughts and behaviour. Creativity training at its best can help engender this kind of understanding.

Individual Development

Researchers studying adult development note that the capacity to think relativistically is noticeably lacking in early development. Young children are characterized by self-centred and egocentric behaviour (familiar to any parent of a two year old) where the child wants their own way over others. At intermediate stages of development people become more aware of others and more identified with and interested in belonging to a group which leads to a concern with seeking approval from others, especially the group they identify with. This kind of behaviour is seen in teenagers and gang members. At this stage people will conform to the social rules of their group to gain approval. At the later post-conventional stage of development individuals internalize principles that are important to them and act autonomously on the basis of their conscience. They learn to appreciate that others have different principles and practices and develop a more pluralistic perspective on life. There is a shift to a wider identification and a concern with the welfare of an increasing number of people at the more mature levels of development.

Table 13.1 synthesises ideas from developmental theorists attracted to staged conceptions of ontogenesis (individual development) such as Piaget (1929), Kolhberg (1969), Loevinger (1976), Maslow (1962), Kegan (1982), Miller and Cook-Greuter (1999) and Torbert (2004).

Table 13.1 *Stages of development*

Stage	Identification/ to Concern	Moral Development (Kohlberg)	Management Goal (Torbert)	Strategy
Preconventional				Power
1 Impulsive	Me survive	obedient punish	impulsive	coerce
2 Egocentric	safe	hedonism	opportunist: I win, control, short-timescale	manipulate
Conventional	Us			Conformity
3 Interpersonal	belong	approval	diplomat: on time, doing what supposed to do, routine, 1–2 month purview	bargain
4 Institutional	conform	law order	expert : efficient, problem-solver, cognitive mastery, 6m–1yr achiever: systems aware, juggles priorities for greater good, 1–3yrs	rules, norms, laws
Postconventional				Autonomy
5 Interindividual	All pluralism	social contract	individualist: meaning, multiple action logics	commitment, internalized principles
6 Intuitive	communion, respect	ethics	strategist: shared decision making alchemist: present-centered, apprehends	synergy inclusive, authentic, networking

Source: Henry, 2006.

One characteristic of most stage theories of development is that immaturity appears to be characterized by an egocentric identification with self and concern with one's one own small world and short time-scales. Intermediate stages of development are characterized by identification with an in-group and a concern with conformity to rules. Maturity is characterized by a wider identification, a more relativistic viewpoint that takes account of others perspective, the bigger picture and a longer time-scale, notions of good behaviour are internalized and there is a recognition of others rights to their differing conceptions.

It can be argued that management strategies go through a parallel series of developments. Torbert (2004) suggests seven different ways of managing and leading reflecting different types of concern which can be related to the development phases shown in Table 13.1. The *management* equivalent of the first pre-conventional stage entails a pre-occupation with *power* and attempts to control others and make them do what you want by manipulation and coercion, popularized in the traditional picture of the ruthless manager and fat cat leader. On this reckoning the more immature and egocentric management style focuses on controlling situations from the manager's point of view with the goal of winning being to get the others to do things your way.

In the conventional stage management is more about *conforming* to accepted rules for advantage. Initially this may involve bargaining with people for a reward. In larger groupings rules, norms and laws are established, and order is then maintained through conformity to these procedures, stereotypically pictured in the idea of the rule-bound bureaucrat. At this intermediate stage of development approval and conformity are central to activity and so Torbert's Diplomat is concerned with doing things as expected and doing routine things on time. His Experts focus on technical mastery of an area in order to solve problems in that area efficiently.

It has been suggested that more mature ways of managing recognize that there are many different ways of making sense of and tackling tasks, and that with this pluralist appreciation comes the introduction of principles, rights and a social contract reflecting common understandings of decent ways to behave. Managers may also give up a lot of the need for day-to-day control over others, adopting a more distributed style of leadership. Torbert's Achievers juggle varying goals within a system with a view to taking timely action. His Individualists appreciate that there are different ways of tackling situations, and different ways of making sense of a situation. The Strategists make a point of involving others in their decisions. Alchemists maintain a detached focus on the present so that they are better placed to apprehend the right action.

Of course many factors impinge upon management style, including personality, context, situation and expectation and most individuals employ a number of different styles according to circumstances, nervertheless on this reading, the more inclusive and participative styles can be considered more developed than the less inclusive and participative.

Mature Communication

In addition to there being more mature ways of acting and managing in a wise fashion, various commentators assert that there are more and less mature ways of communicating. Partly mature communication is seen less as a matter of I win and more win-win but it is also about being more open, direct and respectful. Kegan and Lahey (2001) suggest mature communication entails moving from a focus on complaint to one of commitment, from blame to personal responsibility, from praise to ongoing regard, from rules to public agreement, from hiding behind vague comments, blaming others or making points long after the event to being direct, specific and timely.

The developed person it seems takes time to understand others, adopts a more open form of communication, communicating in ways that is more likely to appeal to the recipient. They appreciate that new ideas and relationships need nurturing. They are also more open and better able to raise and deal with issues that can cause conflict in themselves and with others and to accept paradox and ambiguity.

Groups, organizations and countries all have cultures that incline them to make more or less use of different defenses. Generally the more immature reaction is to blame others for your problems and the more mature one is to think what you can do about the situation for the greater good.

There also appear to be more and less mature ways of dealing with difficult situations. When people find themselves in situations that make them uncomfortable they normally resort of one or more of the psychological *defenses* that we all use. These can be grouped into four levels shown below:

Pathological – denial, distortion, delusion

Immature – fantasy, projection, hypochondria, passive aggression, acting out

Neurotic – intellectualization, repression, displacement, reaction formation, dissociation

Mature – sublimation, altruism, anticipation, humour

Children and those with severe mental problems often use the pathological defenses to allow them to experience reality more as they would wish it to be, not as it is. (Faced with a fire for example, young children often hide rather than try to escape, as if pretending nothing is happening.) Immature defences are common in adolescents with their fantasy crushes on pop-stars and some pupils undue concern that they are not looking quite as perfect as they feel they should. They are also seen in adults who are not well grounded. Many adults use neurotic defenses. In the short-term, repression, a displacement activity and dissociation can be helpful but long-term their use can be less advisable as problems are avoided rather than dealt with.

Argyris (1994) has long argued that immature defensive behaviour is rife in organizations and that many managers routinely avoid difficult issues rather than deal with the ensuing conflict raising these issues is likely to entail. Over time this kind of attitude can build to denial or suppression of the existence of a problem. For example when NASA famously ignored rather than dealt adequately with problems with their space programme heat protection system, which led to the Challenger disaster.

In contrast healthy adults tend to make more use of the so-called mature defenses which enable them to manage conflicting emotions and sometimes transform a potentially negative or conflictual situation into something positive, to view a difficulty as an opportunity for learning, or a boring meeting as a chance to help others, for example. Those making more use of the *mature defenses* tend to report higher job satisfaction, take less days off sick, have better health and lower divorce rates than those who make more use of the more immature defenses (Vallaint, 1993).

Well-being

It is much easier to be more open and less defensive when you are enjoying life and feeling good about yourself. Happiness also has a direct impact on our capacity for creativity. When people feel happier they seem to broaden the associations the brain is able to make so it is easier to generate new ideas. In contrast, people in sad states seem to search in narrower areas and are thus less likely to come up with creative ideas (Fredrikson, 2002) (though Kaufmann (2003) presents evidence suggesting the relationship between mood and creativity is not so simple).

However there are wide individual and country differences in the levels of well-being and happiness people report. Extroverts for example typically report higher levels of well-being than introverts. Many people who have studied satisfaction and well-being reckon about *half* the reported level of satisfaction with life can be accounted for by innate disposition. These individual differences tend to be relatively *stable* over the life-course. So stable in fact that most lottery winners return close to their baseline level of happiness with a year of winning and the majority of people in serious accidents also return close to their baseline level of happiness after a period of acclimatization. There are however some things we can do to improve our sense of well-being. For example, one way to help develop a more optimistic attitude is by taking time to count your blessings rather than spending too much time concentrating on failures. Exercise also helps.

Comparing various happiness or life satisfaction ratings across countries reveals many interesting and relatively stable differences. On the whole countries where there is less trust between people show lower satisfaction ratings. (Unfortunately trust between people has been diminishing in the UK and US since the 1950s though it has been increasing in continental Europe.) For example few people in the former communist countries rate themselves as very happy compared to elsewhere. A relative lack of stability and control are assumed to be factors contributing to their low rating. Of the richer countries, Scandinavians rate their happiness particularly highly. The degree of inequality between the rich and poor in Scandinavia is among the least in the world. It has been suggested that this makes citizens feel respected and therefore fundamentally more content.

One might imagine that increased *income* would improve well-being and satisfaction with life but this only appears to be true up to a certain basic level of security, currently about $20,000 per annum. GDP has more than doubled over the last half century in countries like the UK and US and yet the proportion of people rating themselves as very happy remains roughly constant at around a third (Myers, 2000). Above a basic level of comfort, satisfaction and happiness show very little relationship with income.

It seems it is other factors that have a greater effect on well-being. The most critical factor for most people's happiness is not income but their *relationships*. People are more likely to report themselves as happy when they are in *relationship* with others, especially significant others, (i.e. someone or several people they are very close to, such as a partner, children, close family and friends). More married people generally report themselves as happier than the single, widowed and divorced. People with social support also tend to recover quicker from illness and live longer than their more isolated compatriots.

Satisfaction at Work

For most people *work* is an important component of their well-being. It affords them an identity, structures a lot of their time, usually offers social relations and support and often a sense of belonging and meaning (Jahoda, 1982). On the whole people in work rate themselves happier than the unemployed (with the exception of the early retired with sufficient funds to follow their chosen interests) (Haworth, 1997).

Individuals at all levels of work report satisfaction at work, most take pride in doing their job well, though on average Delle Fave (2001) reports *flow*, a state of satisfied absorption in activities, is more commonly reported by professionals, craft workers and farmers than people in white collar jobs.

Well-being is generally enhanced where people have some *control* over the activities they are undertaking. So offering people flexible working hours and allowing them as much freedom as possible as to how they set about work tasks, is likely to make than happier than predetermining how they do things. Warr's (1999) account of individual and situational determinants of well-being found that variables such as control and challenge had differing effects on work satisfaction according to the *degree* to which they are present. For example some control over and challenge in a job is perceived as rewarding and enhances satisfaction at work, but too much challenge (beyond a person's's capabilities) is inclined to make them feel pressured and anxious and to report less work satisfaction. Equally a job that is not challenging enough and affords little opportunity for self-expression is often experienced as unsatisfying.

Given that management rhetoric currently supports notions of increased participation, empowered working and decentralized decision making, conditions that afford workers more control of their working lives, one might expect satisfaction at work to be increasing. However worryingly exactly the opposite is the case, surveys of *satisfaction* at work have show a decline in the US and UK in recent years (e.g. White, 2001). One interpretation of this finding is that heavy workloads, coupled with increasing scrutiny of performance and less opportunity for security, promotion and control over work life has led to increased stress and hence less satisfaction. (As regards workload, a comparison of current time-use with time distribution 50 years back suggests that the major difference is that people do less chores and watch more TV!)

There are a number of things people can do to help improve their own and their colleague's well-being. Getting *actively involved* in the world seems to help, especially in areas that are of intrinsic interest to you (Csikszentmihalyi, 1996). People tend to report themselves as less happy and absorbed when undertaking passive activities such as watching TV or listening to staff talk in a meeting they did not wish to attend than when participating more actively, for example making something, playing sport, gardening, or playing with children.

More generally an attitude of *appreciation* towards people and life can help enhance a sense of well-being. This applies as much in work as elsewhere and colleagues usually appreciate being recognised for any job they did well. All of us have to do some things that may appear less than enticing and you might think that would mean all of us have some times when we are not happy. However enjoyment is very much affected by the attitude the individual brings to bear to the job. An *attitude* that looks to help or make a difference in others lives can help us enjoy activities that are less directly related to our own goals. Most jobs present opportunities to meet many different people and all of us can aim to say or do something to lift some of the people we come across, if only with a smile of recognition.

Policy

At present most countries set *policy* with a view to maximising GDP with economic considerations as the key drivers for policy. Given that above a certain minimum level of comfort social factors seem to be more important than income in determining people's well-being some economists have begun to question whether governments should devote so much of their energy and *policy* to increasing wealth. This has led some economists to shift their attention from hard to soft measures of well-being.

Bhutan, partly influenced by its Buddhist spiritual tradition, already considers its citizen's social and psychological welfare as well as their economic well-being when setting policy. For example they banned plastic bags on the grounds that the environmental and aesthetic drawbacks outweighed the possible advantage of convenience. They also banned the advertising of sugary drinks such as Coca-Cola, on the grounds that the country offered healthier indigenous equivalents.

Some Western economists have begun to articulate what a switch in policy to granting well-being more prominence would entail. The New Economics Foundation (NEF), a UK-based think tank has advocated that the UK adopt policies that take account of social rather than solely economic well-being. For example recognising the tendency to overestimate the amount of happiness work and income brings us, they recommend curtailing working excessively long hours, e.g the UK accepting a maximum working week of 48 hours, and working towards reducing this to a 35-hour week. They also advocate taking productivity gains in time not pay, to increase the time available to spend with family and friends, an area generally more critical to well-being. NEF also suggest banning advertising to the under 8's and policing adverts aimed at the 8–16 year-olds in an attempt to diminish the hold materialistic concerns seem to have on society.

Given that environmental considerations may force us to change lifestyles to some degree, (taking fewer cheap flights for example to reduce carbon emissions to help stabilise global warming) the idea of emphasising social rather than pecuniary aspects of well-being seems timely.

If we look at creativity, development and well-being we see certain parallel themes. Creative people are self-starters who are intrinsically motived, mature people operate autonomously according to internalized values, those exhibiting well-being find meaning and pleasure by engaging actively with life. The more developed among us appreciate different viewpoints, creative people accept ambiguity, and part of well-being seems to entail an attitude of appreciation. Creative mature human beings who exhibit well-being are more likely to be open, have a positive attitude, be involved in things that interest them and live happily with a considerable degree of ambiguity.

One of the main ways we can support this kind of behaviour is to allow people as much control as possible over the way they live their lives and organize their work. Also to allow them to maintain and work through their social network. In organizations this probably requires an open climate, flexible ways of working, transparent communication and a culture than recognizes contributions so people feel valued.

Traditional ways of managing treat employees somewhat like children, in that they are told what to do, often how to do it and their efforts are scrutinized in detail, a strategy that promotes passivity. In contrast happy and fulfilled people undertaking creative work are more likely to be acting like adults – working in areas they have an interest in, where they have some control over the way they do their work, often with others from a social network that they may have built up gradually over many years. Allowing staff to self-organize as much as possible could improve their quality of life as well as enhance creativity at work and draw out mature behaviour.

References

Amabile, T. (1975) *The Social Psychology of Creativity*. New York: Springer-Verlag.

Argyris, C. (1994) Communication that blocks learning. *Harvard Business Review*, July/August, 77–85.

Baltes, P.B. and Smith, J. (1990) Towards a psychology of wisdom and its ontogenesis. In R.J. Sternberg, *Wisdom: Its nature, origins and development*. Cambridge: Cambridge University Press.

Csikszentmihalyi, M. (1996) *Creativity: Flow and the Psychology of Discovery and Invention*. New York: HarperCollins.

Delle Fave, A. (2001) Flow and optimal experience. Presentation to ESRC Work and Well-being seminar, Dec 18th. Manchester Metropolitan University.

Fredrikson, B.L. (2002) Positive emotions. In C.R. Snyder and S. L. Lopez, *Handbook of Positive Psychology*. Oxford: Oxford University Press.

Furham, A. (2006) *Personality and Intelligence at Work*. London: Psychology Press.

Haworth, J. (1997) *Work, Leisure and Well-being*. London: Routledge.

Henry, J. (2006) *Creativity, development and change*. Paper presented to Chartered Management Institute National Convention, Leeds, October.

Hirsch, S.K. and Kummerow, J.M. (1994) *Introduction to Type in Organizations*, Oxford: Oxford Psychologist Press.

Jahoda, M. (1982) *Employment and Unemployment: A social psychological analysis*. Cambridge: Cambridge University Press.

Kaufmann, G. R. (2003) Expanding the mood-creativity question. *Creativity Research Journal*, 15, 2 and 3, 131–5.

Kegan, R. (1982) *The Evolving Self*. Cambridge, MA: Harvard University Press.

Kegan, R. and Lahey, L. (2001) *How the Way we Talk can Change the Way we Work*. San Francisco: Josey–Bass.

Kohlberg, L. (1969) Stage and Sequence, the cognitive-developmental approach to Socialization. In D.A. Goslin, *Handbook of Socialisation Theory and Research*. Chicago: Rand McNally.

Loevinger, J. (1976) *Ego Development*. San Francisco: Josey-Bass.

Maslow, A.H. (1962) *Towards a Psychology of Being*. Princeton, NJ: Van Nostrand.

Miller, M. and Cook-Greuter, S. (1999) *Creativity, Spirituality, and Transcendence: Paths to Integrity and Wisdom in the Mature Self*. New York: Ablex.

Myers, D. (2000) The funds, friends and faith of happy people. *American Psychologist,* Jan, 55, 1, 56–67.

Piaget, J. (1929) *The Child's Conception of the World*. New York: Harcourt Brace.

Taylor, R. (2002) *The Future of Work-Life Balance*. London: ESRC.

Torbet, B. and Associates (2004) *Action Inquiry, The secret of timely and transforming leadership*. San Francisco: Berret-Koehler.

Vallaint, G. (1993) *The Wisdom of the Ego*. London: Harvard University Press.

White, M. (2001) The changing face of employment: Conditions for active well-being in working life, Presentation to ESRC Work and Well-being Seminar, December 18th. Manchester Metropolitan University.

Warr, P. (1999) Well-being and the Workplace. In D. Kahneman, E. Deiner, and N. Schwartz (Eds) *Well-being: The Foundations of Hedonic Psychology*. New York: Russell. (pp. 392–412).

14

Empowerment: The Emperor's New Clothes

Chris Argyris

Change Programs Increase Inner Contradictions

Major change programs are rife with inner contradictions. By this, I mean that even when these programs and policies are implemented correctly, they do not – and cannot – foster the behavior they are meant to inspire. If the inner contradictions are brought to the surface and addressed, they can be dealt with successfully; that is, they will not inhibit the kind of personal commitment that management says it wants. But if the contradictions remain buried and unacknowledged, as they usually do, they become a destructive force. Not only do they stifle the development of empowerment, they also sap the organization's efficiency by breeding frustration and mistrust.

To illustrate, consider the advice that currently represents best practice for implementing and promoting organizational change. That advice breaks the process down into four basic steps:

- Define a *vision*
- Define a competitive *strategy* consistent with the vision
- Define organizational *work processes* that, when executed, will implement the strategy
- Define individual *job requirements* so that employees can carry out the processes effectively

The underlying pattern of these instructions is consistent with what change researchers and practitioners have learned about effective implementation over the years. Start with a clear framework – a vision – and progressively make it operational so that it will come alive. So that no one will have any doubts about how to align the four parts of the process, management is advised to speak with one voice. This process makes sense. It is rational.

Yet the process is so riddled with inner contradictions that change programs that follow it will only end up creating confusion, particularly at the implementation stage.

Source: C. Argyris (1998) *Harvard Business Review*, May, 98–105.

Table 14.1   *How commitment differs*

External Commitment	Internal Commitment
Tasks are defined by others	Individuals define tasks
The behaviour required to perform tasks is defined by others	Individuals define the behaviour required
Performance goals are defined by management	Management and individuals jointly define performance goals that are challenging for the individual
The importance of the goal is defined by others	Individuals define the importance of the goal

Given that all the steps have been so precisely described through a set of instructions, the advice actually encourages more external than internal commitment (see Table 14.1). Clearly, when employees' actions are defined almost exclusively from the outside (as they are in most change programs), the resulting behavior cannot be empowering and liberating. One immediate consequence is that employees react to the change program by quietly distancing themselves from it. Thus the change program is successful in terms of improving performance because it helps reduce mistakes, as in the case of TQM, or because it helps employees embrace best practices. But at the same time, it undermines internal commitment. In short, the advice for implementing change simply does not provide the new source of energy that many executives want.

But the real danger is that change programs end up poisoning the entire corporation with long-lasting mixed messages. Internally committed employees interpret these messages as 'do your own thing – the way we tell you'. They reluctantly toe the line. Employees who prefer external commitment will also pick up the mixed messages; however, these people will be relieved because they feel protected from having to take any personal responsibility. In this way, the very working habits that executives do not want to see continued in their organizations are strengthened and reinforced. The result is invariably more inner contradictions and more inefficiency and cynicism, all of which get in the way of real change.

CEOs Undermine Empowerment

CEOs work against empowerment both consciously and unconsciously. Surprisingly – at least to outsiders – executives do not always seem to want what they say they need. Consider a few typical remarks that I came across during my research. These remarks – excerpted from a roundtable discussion of executives from world-class companies – indicate very clearly the ambivalence of CEOs toward internal commitment and empowerment. The first CEO noted that with 'well-defined processes where the variances are small and the operating limits are well defined', you no longer need the old command-and-control approach. Workers are now empowered, 'provided they respect the process', he said. The second CEO agreed that these 'processes are liberating', while the third observed that many employees have a tough time understanding what it means for processes to be 'reliable, respectable, and in control'.

Let us stop a moment and ask ourselves how there can be empowerment when there is neither guesswork nor challenges – when the job requirements are predetermined and the processes are controlled. For employees operating in such a world, the environment is not empowering; it is foolproof. This is not a milieu in which individuals can aspire to self-governance. On the contrary, as long as they buy in and follow the dictates of the processes, the employees in the companies just described will only become more externally motivated.

The enthusiastic use of champions in virtually all contemporary change programs sense a similar mixed message from CEOs to employees. Top management is well aware of the dangers of piecemeal implementation and eventual fade-out in major change programs. They strive to overcome those problems by anointing champions. The champions pursue performance objectives with tenacity, managing by decree. They have generous resources available to ensure compliance, and they monitor employees' progress frequently. Altogether, these behaviors reinforce the top–down control features of the external commitment model. The single voice of fervent champions leads employees to feel that management is in control, and it drives out the sense of internal responsibility and personal empowerment. How can employees feel empowered if someone is always 'selling' them or controlling them from the top down? Indeed, such champions would not be necessary if employees were internally committed.

The result of all these interventions is disarray. Managers and the change programs they use undermine the empowerment they so desperately want to achieve. Why does this occur? Could it be that today's top-level managers don't truly want empowered employees? In truth, they are probably unsure. At the same time, employees do not hold executives to task for their behavior. Employees have their own mixed feelings about empowerment.

Employees Have Their Doubts

External commitment is a psychological survival mechanism for many employees – it is a form of adaptive behavior that allows individuals to get by in most work environments. How that survival mechanism works is illustrated quite dramatically today in the former East Germany.

When the Berlin Wall came down, a routine way of life for East German workers came to an end. Most workers had learned to survive by complying. For 40 years, most plants were run in accordance with the dictates of central planners. If many East Germans had pushed for greater control over their destinies, their lives might have been endangered. As a result, East German workers over the years learned to define performance as doing the minimum of what was required of them.

After the fall of communism, I participated in many discussions with West German executives who were surprised and baffled by the lack of initiative and aspiration displayed by the East Germans. What those executives failed to understand is how bewildering – indeed, how threatening – it can be for people to take internal commitment seriously, especially those who have lived their entire lives by the rules of external commitment. As I listened to the West German executives who wanted to make East German employees more internally committed, I thought of several cases in the United States and elsewhere where similar problems exist. Again and again in my experience, prolonged external commitment made internal commitment extremely unlikely, because a sense of empowerment is not innate. It is something that must be learned, developed, and honed.

The question, then, is how do you produce internal commitment? One thing for sure is that the incentive programs executives have used – for instance, higher compensation, better career paths, 'employee of the month' recognition awards – simply do not work. On the contrary, in all my years as a change consultant, I have repeatedly witnessed how offering employees the 'right' rewards creates dependency rather than empowerment. Inevitably, the power of such methods wears off with use, and all that has been created is more external commitment.

Consider one company with substantial financial woes. In that case, the CEO decided at considerable personal sacrifice to raise his employees' salaries. But his own research later showed that the employees merely considered their raises to be in keeping with their equity in the labor market. Internal commitment had not increased. Employees continued to do only what was asked of them as long as the rewards were increased. They followed the rules, but they did not take any initiative. They did not take risks, nor did they show the sense of personal responsibility that management sought. The CEO was surprised, but I thought that these results were entirely predictable for two reasons. First, pay, like other popular incentive schemes, often advances external commitment. Second, and more fundamental, many employees do not embrace the idea of empowerment with any more gusto than management does. For a lot of people, empowerment is just too much work. Like the workers in East Germany, almost all employees have learned to survive by depending on external commitment.

When it comes to empowerment, executives and employees are engaged in shadowboxing. Management says it wants employees who participate more; employees say they want to be more involved. But it is difficult to know who means what. Is it just a charade? Employees push for greater autonomy; management says the right thing but tries to keep control through information systems, processes, and tools. Employees see vestiges of the old command-and-control model as confirming their worse suspicions – that superiors want unchallenged power. Management just wants to see better numbers. Thus the battle between autonomy and control rages on, and meanwhile, as companies make the transition into the next century, the potential for real empowerment is squandered.

Change Professionals Inhibit Empowerment

During the past decade, I have had the opportunity to work with more than 300 change experts in different organizations. Such individuals differ in their practices and their effectiveness, of course, but more striking than the differences are the patterns that recur.

Caught in the middle of the battle between autonomy and control, the change professional has a tough assignment. The role of the change professional, whether internal or external, is ostensibly to facilitate organizational change and continuous learning. In their own way, however, the vast majority of change professionals actually inhibit empowerment in organizations.

To understand how that occurs, consider what happens as Tom, a change agent, tries to work with Jack, a line manager. (Both are composite figures typical of those I encountered in my research.) Jack is told by his boss to work with Tom, who is there to 'help' Jack empower his organization. The change program begins with a series of meetings and discussions. Tom talks passionately about openness, honesty, and trust as the foundations of empowerment. Many employees leave these meetings feeling hopeful about the direction that the company is taking toward more open communication. A month into the program, however, Tom observes that Jack has fallen back into his old style of management. He decides that he had better confront Jack:

Tom's unspoken thoughts:		What Tom and Jack say:	
Tom:	*Things aren't going well*	Tom:	So how's everything going?
		Jack:	Things are going pretty well. There's a lot of pressure from above, but we're meeting the numbers.
Tom:	*Oh great. All Jack cares about is the numbers. Empowerment isn't even on his agenda.*	Tom:	Great. Super. But I was also wondering how well we're doing at getting people more committed to their jobs. How empowered do you think people feel?
		Jack:	Well, I think we're doing okay. If there are problems, people come to me and we work it out. Sure, some people are never satisfied. But that's just a few people, and we can handle them.
Tom:	*Just what I feared. Jack's not 'walking the talk'. He just doesn't get it at all.*	Tom:	Look, Jack, if you solve all their problems, how are we going to empower our employees?
Tom:	*This is hopeless! There's got to be an easier way to make a living. I'll never get through to him. I wish I could tell Jack what I think, but I don't want to put him on the defensive. I've got to stay cool.*	Jack:	Well, to be honest with you, Tom, the signal I'm getting from above is that my job is to produce the numbers without, you know, upsetting people. To be fair, I think I'm doing that.

What's happening here? The change program that began with great enthusiasm is clearly in deep trouble. It's a pattern I've observed over and over again. After the initial excitement passes, reality inevitably settles in. Put aside the nice rhetoric of empowerment, employees *will* have problems. They *will* ask their managers for help, and their managers *will* tell them what to do. That is how most work gets done and how organizations meet their numbers. And in many cases, there's absolutely nothing wrong with this, except that it goes against the theory of empowerment.

What does Tom do when he observes Jack telling his employees what to do? Instead of figuring out whether Jack is doing the right thing in this situation, change experts like Tom will almost always be dismayed, because the managers aren't walking the talk of empowerment. Rarely have I seen a change professional help a manager deal effectively with being caught between a rock and a hard place. Even more uncommon is a change agent who offers practical advice to the manager about what to do.

Not only is Tom unwilling to acknowledge the real problem Jack is having, but he papers over his own thoughts. He tries to act as if he still believes the program can be successful when, in fact, he has given up hope. Tom himself is guilty of not walking the talk of openness, honesty, and trust.

In my experience, line managers are far more willing to acknowledge the inner contradictions of change programs – at least, in private. They will admit to distancing themselves from the soft stuff – two-way participation, internal commitment, and discontinuous thinking – to focus instead on the numbers. Managers like Jack often conclude – rightly, I'm afraid – that the change agent does not know how to help them. So Jack listens politely as Tom warns him about the dangers of backsliding and exhorts him to be more persistent. And then Jack goes on about his business.

In the end, everyone is frustrated. In theory, empowerment should make it easier for organizations to meet their numbers. But when change programs are imposed without recognizing the limitations of empowerment and when managers and employees are not helped to deal effectively and openly with them, the organization ends up worse off than it was to begin with. Empowerment too often enters the realm of political correctness, which means that no one can say what he or she is thinking: this is just nonsense. In this scenario, if you challenge the change agent, you become an enemy of change.

So instead of feeling more empowered, people throughout the organization feel more trapped and less able to talk openly about what's really going on. Is it any wonder that change programs don't succeed and that they actually undermine the credibility of top management?

Informal Networks:
The Company Behind the Chart

David Krackhardt and Jeffrey R. Hanson

The Steps of Network Analysis

Much research has already established the influence of central figures in informal networks. Our studies of public and private companies showed that understanding these networks could increase the influence of managers outside the inner circle. If they learned who wielded power in networks and how various coalitions functioned, they could work with the informal organization to solve problems and improve performance.

Mapping advice networks, our research showed, can uncover the source of political conflicts and failure to achieve strategic objectives. Because these networks show the most influential players in the day-to-day operations of a company, they are useful to examine when a company is considering routine changes. Trust networks often reveal the causes of non-routine problems such as poor performance by temporary teams. Companies should examine trust networks when implementing a major change or experiencing a crisis. The communication network can help identify gaps in information flow, the inefficient use of resources, and the failure to generate new ideas. They should be examined when productivity is low.

Managers can analyze informal networks in three steps. Step one is conducting a network survey using employee questionnaires. The survey is designed to solicit responses about who talks to whom about work, who trusts whom, and who advises whom on technical matters. It is important to pretest the survey on a small group of employees to see if any questions are ambiguous or meet with resistance. In some companies, for example, employees are comfortable answering questions about friendship; in others, they deem such questions too personal and intrusive. The following are among the questions often asked.

Source: D. Krackhardt and J.R. Hanson (1993) *Harvard Business Review*, 104–11.

- Whom do you talk to every day?
- Whom do you go to for help or advice at least once a week?
- With one day of training, whose job could you step into?
- Whom would you recruit to support a proposal of yours that could be unpopular?
- Whom would you trust to keep in confidence your concerns about a work-related issue?

Some companies also find it useful to conduct surveys to determine managers' *impressions* of informal networks so that these can be compared with the actual networks revealed by the employee questionnaires. In such surveys, questions are posed like this:

- Whom do you think Steve goes to for work-related advice?
- Whom would Susan trust to keep her confidence about work-related concerns?

The key to eliciting honest answers from employees is to earn their trust. They must be assured that managers will not use their answers against them or the employees mentioned in their responses and that their immediate colleagues will not have access to the information. In general, respondents are comfortable if upper-level managers not mentioned in the surveys see the results.

After the questionnaires are completed, the second step is cross-checking the answers. Some employees, worried about offending their colleagues, say they talk to *everyone* in the department on a daily basis. If Judy Smith says she regularly talks to Bill Johnson about work, make sure that Johnson says he talks to Smith. Managers should discount any answers not confirmed by both parties. The final map should not be based on the impressions of one employee but on the consensus of the group.

The third step is processing the information using one of the several commercially available computer programs that generate detailed network maps (drawing maps is a laborious process that tends to result in curved lines that are difficult to read). Maps in hand, a skilled manager can devise a strategy that plays on the strengths of the informal organization, as David Leers, the founder and CEO of a California-based computer company, found out.

Whom Do You Trust?

David Leers thought he knew his employees well. In 15 years, the company had trained a cadre of loyal professionals who had built a strong regional reputation for delivering customized office information systems (see Figure 15.1). The field design group, responsible for designing and installing the systems, generated the largest block of revenues. For years it had been the linchpin of the operation, led by the company's technical superstars, with whom Leers kept in close contact.

But Leers feared that the company was losing its competitive edge by short-changing its other divisions, such as software applications and integrated communications

Leers (CEO)

Software Applications	Field Design	Integrated Communications Technologies	Data Control Systems
O'Hara (SVP)	Calder (SVP)	Lang (SVP)	Stern (SVP)
– Bair	– Harris	– Muller	– Huttle
– Stewart	– Benson	– Jules	– Atkins
– Ruiz	– Fleming	– Baker	– Kibler
	– Church	– Daven	
	– Martin	– Thomas	
	– Lee	– Zanado	
	– Wilson		
	– Swinney		
	– Carlson		
	– Hoberman		
	– Fiola		

Figure 15.1   *The formal chart shows who's on top*

technologies. When members of field design saw Leers start pumping more money into these divisions, they worried about losing their privileged position. Key employees started voicing dissatisfaction about their compensation, and Leers knew he had the makings of a morale problem that could result in defections.

To persuade employees to support a new direction for the company, Leers decided to involve them in the planning process. He formed a strategic task force composed of members of all divisions and led by a member of design to signal his continuing commitment to the group. He wanted a leader who had credibility with his peers and was a proven performer. Eight-year company veteran Tom Harris seemed obvious for the job.

Leers was optimistic after the first meeting. Members generated good discussion about key competitive dilemmas. A month later, however, he found that the group had made little progress. Within two months, the group was completely deadlocked by members championing their own agendas. Although a highly effective manager, Leers lacked the necessary distance to identify the source of his problem.

An analysis of the company's trust and advice networks helped him get a clearer picture of the dynamics at work in the task force. The trust map turned out to be most revealing. Task force leader Tom Harris held a central position in the advice network – meaning that many employees relied on him for technical advice (see Figure 15.2). But he had only *one* trust link with a colleague (see Figure 15.3). Leers concluded that Harris's weak position in the trust network was a main reason for the task force's inability to produce results.

In his job, Harris was able to leverage his position in the advice network to get work done quickly. As a task force leader, however, his technical expertise was less important that his ability to moderate conflicting views, focus the group's thinking, and win the commitment of task force members to mutually agreed-upon strategies. Because he was a loner who took more interest in computer games than in colleagues' opinions, task force members didn't trust him to take their ideas seriously or look out for their interests. So they focused instead on defending their turf.

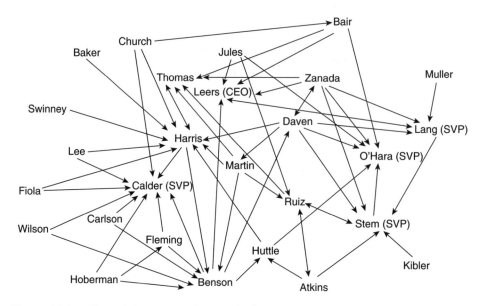

Figure 15.2 *The advice network reveals the experts*

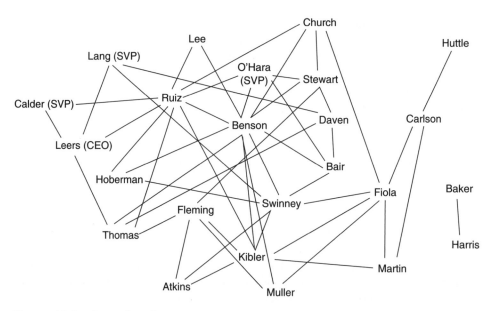

Figure 15.3 *But when it comes to trust ...*

With this critical piece of information, the CEO crafted a solution. He did not want to undermine the original rationale of the task force by declaring it a failure. Nor did he want to embarrass a valued employee by summarily removing him as task force head. Any response, he concluded, had to run with the natural grain of the informal organization. He decided to redesign the team to reflect the inherent strengths of the trust network.

Referring to the map, Leers looked for someone in the trust network who could share responsibilities with Harris. He chose Bill Benson, a warm, amiable person who occupied a central position in the network and with whom Harris had already established a solid working relationship. He publicly justified his decision to name two task force heads as necessary, given the time pressures and scope of the problem.

Within three weeks, Leers could see changes in the group's dynamics. Because task force members trusted Benson to act in the best interest of the entire group, people talked more openly and let go of their fixed positions. During the next two months, the task force made significant progress in proposing a strategic direction for the company. And in the process of working together, the task force helped integrate the company's divisions.

A further look at the company's advice and the trust networks uncovered another serious problem, this time with the head of field design, Jim Calder.

The CEO had appointed Calder manager because his colleagues respected him as the most technically accomplished person in the division. Leers thought Calder would have the professional credibility to lead a diverse group of very specialized design consultants. This is a common practice in professional service organizations: make your best producer the manager. Calder, however, turned out to be a very marginal figure in the trust network. His managerial ability and skills were sorely lacking, which proved to be a deficit that outweighed the positive effects derived from his technical expertise. He regularly told people they were stupid and paid little attention to their professional concerns.

Leers knew that Calder was no diplomat, but he had no idea to what extent the performance morale of the group was suffering as a result of Calder's tyrannical management style. In fact, a map based on Leers's initial perceptions of the trust network put Calder in a central position (see Figure 15.4). Leers took for granted that Calder had good personal relationships with the people on his team. His assumption was not unusual. Frequently, senior managers presume that formal work ties will yield good relationship ties over time, and they assume that if *they* trust someone, others will too.

The map of Calder's perceptions was also surprising (see Figure 15.5). He saw almost no trust links in his group at all. Calder was oblivious to *any* of the trust dependencies emerging around him – a worrisome characteristic for a manager.

The information in these maps helped Leers formulate a solution. Again, he concluded that he needed to change the formal organization to reflect the structure of the informal network. Rather than promoting or demoting Calder, Leers cross-promoted him to an elite 'special situation team', reporting directly to the CEO. His job involved working with highly sophisticated clients on specialized problems. The position took better advantage of Calder's technical skills and turned out to be good for him socially as well. Calder, Leers learned, hated dealing with formal management responsibilities and the pressure of running a large group.

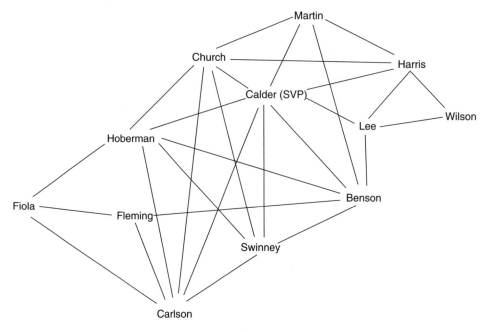

Figure 15.4 *How the CEO views the trust network*

Fleming ———————————— Hoberman

Figure 15.5 *The trust network according to Calder*

Leers was now free to promote John Fleming, a tactful, even-tempered employee, to the head of field design. A central player in the trust network, Fleming was also influential in the advice network. The field group's performance improved significantly over the next quarter, and the company was able to create a highly profitable revenue stream through the activities of Calder's new team.

Experienced network managers who can use maps to identify, leverage and revamp informal networks will become increasingly valuable as companies continue to flatten and rely on teams. As organizations abandon hierarchical structures, managers will have to rely less on overseeing employees 'below' them and more on managing people across functions and disciplines. Understanding relationships will be the key to managerial success.

F

Perception

The policy we follow is determined by our perceptions. The three papers here show how framing issues differently leads to very different understandings and courses of action. Shiva asserts that fragmented Western thinking has led to the dominance of unsustainable Western patterns of cultivation and the neglect of traditional local knowledge that offers sustainable alternatives. Lovins et al. argue that a change in business values that takes greater cogniscence of how nature operates can help businesses operate both sustainably and profitably. Pascale illustrates how applying ideas from the science of complexity in business leads to a very different way of handling strategy.

Vandana Shiva is an Indian environmentalist and BBC Reith lecturer. She explains how Western patterns of thought lead to particular ways of being in the world which make it natural for the West to export its approaches and assume that this knowledge is appropriate in other settings, aptly summarised in her title 'Monocultures of the Mind'. Shiva argues that the fragmented nature of Western thought leads them to ignore holistic aspects of problems in a way which would be unthinkable in traditional society, and that imposing Western accounting and agricultural systems discounts important local knowledge to the detriment of the local inhabitants and their environment.

Hunter and Amory Lovins and Paul Hawken argue for the merits of what they term Natural Capitalism. They champion the potential for industry to mimic nature through systems of closed-loop manufacturing, and to make money in the process. Their diagnosis is that our current habits of thought and accounting lead us to make non-optimum decisions, a problem for which they advocate a switch to whole systems thinking, for example basing purchasing decisions on the life cycle cost, not purchase price. Also improved incentives, for example a system that compensates you for what you save rather than what you spend. One telling example they offer is the idea of a redefinition of business purpose around value rather than output, (such as selling illumination rather than light bulbs) which they argue is both environmentally and business friendly. They quote elevator and chemical companies who have begun to lease their products rather than sell them; with this the business incentives shift towards manufacturing fewer longer lasting products rather than cheaper and more wasteful ones, an environmentally desirable goal.

Pascale discusses the merit of ideas from the science of complexity for management and illustrates how the underlying principles can be applied in organizations, strategic thinking and change management. This way of viewing change seems to offer a valuable way of understanding and facilitating emergence.

16

Monocultures of the Mind

Vandana Shiva

The 'Disappeared' Knowledge Systems

The disappearance of local knowledge through its interaction with the dominant Western knowledge takes place at many levels, through many steps. First, local knowledge is made to disappear by simply not seeing it, by negating its very existence. The Western systems of knowledge have generally been viewed as universal. However, the dominant system is also a local system, with its social basis in a particular culture, class and gender. It is the globalized version of a very local and parochial tradition.

Emerging from a dominating and colonizing culture, modern knowledge systems are themselves colonizing. They are associated with a set of values based on power which emerged with the rise of commercial capitalism. Power is also built into the perspective which views the dominant system not as a globalized local tradition, but as a universal tradition, inherently superior to local systems. When local knowledge does appear in the field of globalizing visions, it is made to disappear by denying it the status of a systematic knowledge, and assigning it the adjectives 'primitive' and 'unscientific'. Correspondingly, the Western system is assumed to be uniquely 'scientific' and universal. Scientists, in accordance with an abstract scientific method, were viewed as putting forward statements corresponding to the realities of a directly observable world. The theoretical concepts in their discourse were in principle seen as reducible to directly verifiable observational claims. New trends in the philosophy and sociology of science challenged the positivist assumptions, but did not challenge the assumed superiority of Western systems.

However, the historical experience of non-Western culture suggests that it is the Western systems knowledge which are blind to alternatives. The 'scientific' label assigns a kind a sacredness or social immunity to the Western system. By elevating itself *above* society and other knowledge systems and by simultaneously excluding other knowledge systems from the domain of reliable and systematic knowledge, the dominant system creates its exclusive monopoly. Paradoxically, it is the knowledge

Source: V. Shiva (1993) Edited extract from *Monocultures of the Mind*. London: Zed Books

systems which are considered most open, that are, in reality, closed to scrutiny and evaluation. Modern Western science is not to be evaluated, it is merely to be accepted.

The Cracks of Fragmentation

The dominant system also makes alternatives disappear by erasing and destroying the reality which they attempt to represent. The fragmented linearity of the dominant knowledge disrupts the integrations between systems. Local knowledge slips through the cracks of fragmentation. Dominant scientific knowledge breeds a monoculture of the mind by making space for local alternatives to disappear, very much like monocultures of introduced plant varieties leading to the displacement and destruction of local diversity. Dominant knowledge also destroys the very *conditions* for alternatives to exist, very much like the introduction of monocultures destroying the very conditions for diverse species to exist.

As a metaphor, the monoculture of the mind is best illustrated in the knowledge and practise of forestry and agriculture. 'Scientific' forestry and 'scientific' agriculture, split the plant artificially into separate, non-overlapping domains, on the basis of separate commodity markets to which they supply raw materials and resources. In local knowledge systems, the plant world is not artificially separated between a forest supplying commercial wood and agricultural land supplying food commodities. The forest and the field are in ecological continuum, and activities in the forest contribute to the food needs of the local community, while agriculture itself is modelled on the ecology of the tropical forest. Some forest dwellers gather food directly from the forest, while many communities practise agriculture outside the forest, but depend on the fertility of the forest for the fertility of agricultural land.

In the 'scientific' system which splits forestry from agriculture and reduces forestry to timber and wood supply, food is no longer a category related to forestry. The cognitive space that relates forestry to food production, either directly, or through fertility links, is therefore erased with the split. Knowledge systems which have emerged from the food giving capacities of the forest are therefore eclipsed and finally destroyed (see Fig. 16.1.)

Most local knowledge systems have been based on the life support capacities of tropical forests, not on their commercial timber value. These systems fall in the blind spot of a forestry perspective that is based exclusively on the commercial exploitation of forests. Food systems based on the forest, are therefore non-existent in the field of vision of a reductionist forestry and a reductionist agriculture even though they have been and still are the sustenance base for many communities of the world. Famine has never been a problem in Bastar as tribes have always been able to draw half of their food from the innumerable edible forest products.

In non-tribal areas, too, forests provide food and livelihood through critical inputs to agriculture, through soil and water conservation, and through inputs of fodder and organic fertiliser. Indigenous silvicultural knowledge is passed on from generation to generation, through participation in the processes of forest renewal and of drawing sustenance from the forest ecosystems.

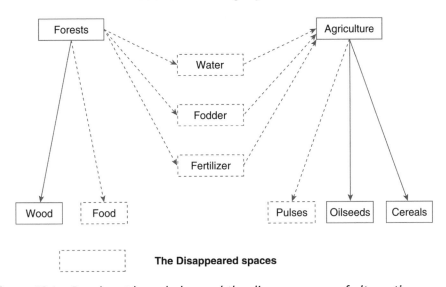

Figure 16.1 *Dominant knowledge and the disappearance of alternatives*

In countries like India, the forest has been the source of fertility renewal of agriculture. The forest as a source of fodder and fertilizer has been a significant part of the agricultural ecosystem. In the Himalaya, the oak forests have been central to sustainability of agriculture. Estimates show that over 50% of the total fodder supply for peasant communities in the Himalaya comes from forest sources, with forest trees supplying 20%. Forests also make an important contribution to hill farming in the use of plant biomass as bedding for animals. Forests are the principal source of fallen dry leaf-litter, and lopped green foliage of trees and herbaceous species which are used for animal bedding and composting. Forest biomass, when mixed with animal dung, forms the principal source of soil nutrients for hill agriculture. As the input declines, agricultural yields also go down.

The diverse knowledge systems which have evolved with the diverse uses of the forest for food and agriculture were eclipsed with the introduction of 'scientific' forestry, which treated the forest only as a source of industrial and commercial timber. The linkages between forests and agriculture, were broken and the function of the forest as a source of food was no longer perceived.

When the West colonized Asia, it colonized her forests. It brought with it the ideas of nature and culture as derived from the model of the industrial factory. The forest was no longer viewed as having a value itself, in all its diversity. Its value was reduced to the value of commercially exploitable industrial timber. Having depleted their forests at home, European countries started the destruction of Asia's forests. England searched in the colonies for timber for its navy because the oak forests in England were depleted.

'Scientific forestry' was the false universalization of a local tradition of forestry which emerged from the narrow commercial interest which viewed the forest only in terms of commercially valuable wood. It first reduced the value of diversity of life in the forest to the value of a few commercially valuable species, and further reduced the value of these species to the value of their dead product – wood. The reductionism of the scientific forestry paradigm created by commercial industrial interests violates the integrity of the forests and the integrity of forest cultures who need the forest in its diversity to satisfy their needs for food, fibre and shelter.

The existing principles of scientific forest management leads to the destruction of the tropical forest ecosystem because it is based on the objective of modelling the diversity of the living forest on the uniformity of the assembly line. The system of 'scientific management', as it has been practised over a century is thus a system of tropical deforestation, which transforms the forest from a renewable to a non-renewable resource. Tropical timber exploitation thus becomes like mining, and tropical forests become a timber mine.

The tropical forests, when modelled on the factory and used as a timber mine, becomes a non-renewable resource. Tropical peoples also become a dispensable and historical waste. In place of cultural and biological pluralism, the factory produces non-sustainable monocultures in nature and society. There is no place for the small, no value for the insignificant. Organic diversity gives way to fragmented atomism and uniformity. The diversity must be weeded out, and the uniform monocultures – of plants and people – must now be externally managed because they are no longer self-regulated and self-governed. Those that do not fit into the uniformity must be declared unfit. Symbiosis must give way to competition, domination and dispensability. There is no survival possible for the forest of its people when they become feedstock for industry. The survival of the tropical forest depends on the survival of human societies modelled on the principles of the forest. These lessons for survival do not come from text of 'scientific forestry'. They lie hidden in the lives and beliefs of the forest peoples of the world.

There are in Asia today two paradigms of forestry – one life enhancing, the other life destroying. The life-enhancing paradigm emerges from the forest and forest communities – the life destroying from the market. The life-enhancing paradigm creates a sustainable, renewable forest system, supporting and renewing food and water systems. *The maintenance of conditions for renewability is the primary management objective of the former.* The maximizing of profits through commercial extraction is the primary management objective of the latter. Since maximizing profits is consequent upon destruction of conditions of renewability, the two paradigms are cognitively and ecologically incommensurate. Today, in the forests of Asia the two paradigms are struggling against each other. This struggle is very clear in the two slogans on the utility of the Himalayan forests, one emanating from the ecological concepts of Garhwali women, the other from the sectoral concepts of those associated with trade in forest products. When Chipko became an ecological movement in 1977, the spirit of local science was captured in the slogan:

What do forests bear?

Soil, water and pure air.

This was the response to the commonly accepted slogan of the dominant science:

What do the forests bear?

Profit on resin and timber.

The Chipko movement was transformed qualitatively from being based merely on conflicts over resources to involving conflicts over scientific perceptions and philosophical approaches to nature. The slogan has become the scientific and philosophical message of the movement, and has laid the foundations of an alternative forestry science, oriented to the public interest and ecological in nature.

The Destruction of Diversity as 'Weeds'

The destruction of biological diversity is intrinsic to the very manner in which the reductionist forestry paradigm conceives of the forest. The forest is defined as 'normal' according to the objective of managing the forest for maximizing production of marketable timber. Since the natural tropical forest is characterized by richness in diversity, including the diversity of non-marketable, non-industrial species, the 'scientific forestry' paradigm declares the natural forest as 'abnormal'. In Sclich's words, forest management implies that 'the abnormal conditions are to be removed'.

The natural forest, in its diversity, is thus seen as 'chaos'. The man-made forest is 'order'. 'Scientific' management of forests therefore has a clear anti-nature bias, and a bias for industrial and commercial objectives, for which the natural forest must be sacrificed. Diversity thus gives way to uniformity of even-aged, single species stands, and this uniformity is the ideal of the normal forestry towards which all silvicultural systems aim. The destruction and dispensability of diversity is intrinsic to forest management guided by the objective of maximizing commercial wood production, which sees non-commercial parts and relationships of a forest ecosystem as valueless – as weeds to be destroyed. Nature's wealth characterized by diversity is destroyed to create commercial wealth characterized by uniformity.

In biological terms, tropical forests are the most productive biological systems on our planet. However, in the reductionist commercial forestry, the overall productivity is not important, nor are the functions of tropical forests in the survival of tropical peoples.

The industrial materials standpoint is the capitalist reductionist forestry which splits the living diversity and democracy of the forest into commercially valuable dead wood and destroys the rest as 'weeds' and 'waste'. This 'waste' however is the wealth of biomass that maintains nature's water and nutrient cycles and satisfies needs of food, fuel, fodder, fertilizer, fibre and medicine of agricultural communities.

Just as 'scientific' forestry excludes the food producing functions of the forest, and destroys the forest diversity as 'weeds', 'scientific' agriculture too destroys species which are useful as food, even though they may not be useful on the market.

The Green Revolution has displaced not just as seed varieties but entire crops in the Third World. What have usually been called 'marginal crops' or 'coarse grains' are nature's most productive crops in terms of nutrition. That is why women in Garhwal continue to cultivate mandua and women in Karnataka cultivate ragi inspite of all attempts by state policy to shift to cash crops and commercial foodgrains, to which all financial incentives of agricultural 'development' are tied. What the Green Revolution has declared 'inferior' grains are actually superior in nutritive content to the so-called 'superior' grains, rice and wheat.

Not being commercially useful, people's crops are treated as 'weeds' and destroyed with poisons. The most extreme example of this destruction is that of bathua, an important green leafy vegetable, with a very high nutritive value and rich in Vitamin A, which grows as an associate of wheat. However, with intensive chemical fertilizer use bathua becomes a major competitor of wheat and has been declared a 'weed' that is killed with herbicides. Forty thousand children in India go blind each year from lack of Vitamin A, and herbicides contribute to this tragedy by destroying the freely available sources of Vitamin A. Thousands of rural women who make their living by basket and mat-making, with wild reeds and grasses, are also losing their livelihoods because the increased use of herbicide is killing the reeds and grasses. The introduction of herbicide-resistant crops will increase herbicide use and thus increase the damage to economically and ecologically useful plant species. Herbicide resistance also excludes the possibility of rotational and mixed-cropping, which are essential for a sustainable and ecologically balance agriculture, since the other crops would be destroyed by the herbicide. US estimates now show a loss of US $4 billion per annum due to loss as a result of herbicide spraying. The destruction in India will be far greater because of higher plant diversity, and the prevalence of diverse occupations based on plants and biomass.

Strategies for genetic engineering resistance which are destroying useful species of plants can also end up creating superweeds. There is an intimate relationship between weeds and crops, especially in the tropics where weedy and cultivated varieties have genetically interacted over the centuries and hybridize freely to produce new varieties. Genes for herbicides tolerance, that genetic engineers are striving to introduce into crop plants, may be transferred to neighbouring weeds as a result of naturally occurring gene transfer.

Scarcities of locally useful plant varieties have been created because the dominant knowledge system discounts the value of local knowledge and declares locally useful plants to be 'weeds'. Diversity is thus destroyed in plant communities and forest and peasant communities, because in commercial logic it is not 'useful'. When what is useful and what is not is determined one-sidedly, all other systems of determining value are displaced.

'Miracle Trees' and 'Miracle Seeds'

The one-dimensional perspective of dominant knowledge is rooted in the intimate links of modern science with the market. As multidimensional integrations between agriculture and forestry at the local level are broken, new integrations between non-local markets and local resources are established. Since economic power is concentrated in these remote centres of exploitation, knowledge develops according to the linear logic of maximising flow at the local level. The integrated forest and farm gives way to the separate spheres of forestry and agriculture. The diverse forest and agricultural ecosystems are reduced to 'preferred' species by selective annihilation of species diversity which is not 'useful' from the market perspective. Finally, the 'preferred' species themselves have to be engineered and introduced on the basis of 'preferred' traits. The natural, native diversity is displaced by introduced monocultures of trees and crops.

In forestry, as the paper and pulp industry rose in prominence, pulp species became the 'preferred' species by the dominant knowledge system. Natural forest were clear-felled and replaced by monocultures of the exotic Eucalyptus species which were good for pulping. However, 'scientific' forestry did not project its practise as a particular response to the particular interest of the pulp industry. It projected its choice as based on a universal and objective criteria of 'fast growth' and 'high yields'. In the 1980s, when the concern about deforestation and its impact on local communities and ecological stability created the imperative for afforestation programmes, the eucalyptus was proposed world-wide as a 'miracle' tree. However, local communities everywhere seemed to think otherwise.

The main thrust of conservation struggles like Chipko is that forests and trees are life-support systems, and should be protected and regenerated for their biospheric functions. The monoculture mind on the other hand sees the natural forest and trees as 'weeds' and converts even afforestation into deforestation and desertification. From life-support systems, trees are converted into green gold – all planting is motivated by the slogan, 'Money grows on trees'. Whether it is schemes like social forestry or waste-land development, afforestation programmes are conceived at the international level by 'experts' whose philosophy of tree planting falls within the reductionist paradigm of producing wood for the market, not biomass for maintaining ecological cycles or satisfying local needs of food, fodder and fertilizer. All official programmes of afforestation, based on heavy funding and centralized decision making, act in two ways against the local knowledge systems – they destroy the forest as a diverse and self-producing system, and destroy it as commons, shared by a diversity of social groups with even the smallest having rights, access and entitlements.

'Social' Forestry and the 'Miracle' Tree

Social forestry projects are a good example of single species, single commodity production plantations, based on reductionist models which divorce forestry from agriculture and water management, and seeds from markets.

A case study of World Bank-sponsored social forestry in Kolar district of Karnataka (Shiva 1981) is an illustration of reductionism and maldevelopment in forestry being extended to farmland. Decentred agro-forestry, based on multiple species and private and common tree-stands, has been India's age-old strategy for maintaining farm productivity in arid and semi-arid zones. The honge, tamarind, jackfruit and mango, the jola, gobli, kagli and bamboo traditionally provided food and fodder, fertilizer and pesticide, fuel and small timber. The invisible, decentred agro-forestry model was significant because the humblest of species and the smallest of people could participate in it, and with space for the small, everyone was involved in protecting and planting.

The reductionist mind took over tree planting with 'social forestry'. Plans were made in national and international capitals by people who could not know the purpose of the honge and the neem, and saw them as weeds. The experts decided that indigenous knowledge was worthless and 'unscientific', and proceeded to destroy the diversity of indigenous species by replacing them with row after row of eucalyptus seedlings in polythene bags, in government nurseries. Nature's locally available seeds were laid waste; people's locally available knowledge and energies were laid waste. With imported seeds and expertise came the import of loans and debt and the export of wood, soils and people. Trees, as a living resource, maintaining the life of the soil and water and of local people, were replaced by trees whose dead wood went straight to a pulp factory hundreds of miles away. The smallest farm became a supplier of raw material to industry and ceased to supply food to local people. Local work, linking the trees to the crops, disappeared and was replaced by the work of brokers and middle-men who brought the eucalyptus trees on behalf of industry. Industrialists, foresters and bureaucrats loved the eucalyptus because it grows straight and is excellent pulp-wood, unlike the honge which shelters the soil with its profuse branches and dense canopy and whose real worth is as a living tree on a farm.

The honge could be nature's idea of the perfect tree for arid Karnataka. It has rapid growth of precisely those parts of the tree, the leaves and small branches, which go back to the earth, enriching and protecting it, conserving its moisture and fertility. The eucalyptus on the other hand, when perceived ecologically, is unproductive, even negative, because this perception assesses the 'growth' and 'productivity' of trees in relation to soil fertility and in relation to human needs for food and food production. The eucalyptus has destroyed the water cycle in arid regions due to its high water demand and its failure to produce humus, which is nature's mechanism for conserving water.

Most indigenous species have a much higher biological productivity than the eucalyptus, when one considers water yields and water conservation. The non-woody biomass of trees has never been assessed by forest measurements, yet it is this very biomass that functions in conserving water and building soils.

Eucalyptus

The most powerful argument in favour of the expansion of Eucalyptus is that it is faster growing than all indigenous alternatives. Even where biotic and climatic factors are conducive to good growth, Eucalyptus cannot compete with a number of indigenous fast growing species.

The points that emerge are:

i)   In terms of yields measured as mean annual increment (MAI) Eucalyptus is a slow producer of woody biomass even under very good soil conditions and water availability.

ii) When the site is of poor quality such as eroded soils or barren land, Eucalyptus yields are insignificant.

iii) The growth rate of Eucalyptus under the best conditions is not uniform for different age groups. It falls very drastically after 5 or 6 years.

The Eucalyptus, quite clearly, will not fill the gap in the demand of woody biomass more effectively then other faster growing species which are also better adapted to the Indian conditions.

The assessment of yields in social forestry must include the diverse types of biomass which provides inputs to the agro-ecosystem. When the objective for tree planting is the production of fodder or green fertilizer, it is relevant to measure crown biomass productivity. India, with its rich genetic diversity in plants and animals, is richly endowed with various types of fodder trees which have annual yields of crown biomass that is much higher than the total biomass produced by Eucalyptus plantations.

An important biomass output of trees that is never assessed by foresters who look for timber and wood is the yield of seeds and fruits. Fruit trees such as jack, jaman, mango, tamarind etc. have been important components of indigenous forms of social forestry as practised over centuries in India. Tamarind trees yield fruits for over two centuries. Other trees, such as, neem, pongamia and sal provide annual harvest of seeds which yield valuable non-edible oils. In contrast, the biomass of the Eucalyptus is useful only after the tree is felled.

Figures 16.2 and 16.3 describe the comparative biomass contribution of indigenous trees and Eucalyptus. Afforestation strategies based dominantly on Eucalyptus are not therefore, the most effective mechanism for tiding over the serious biomass crisis facing the country. The benefits of Eucalyptus have often been unduly exaggerated through the myth of its fast growth and high yields. The myth has become pervasive because of the unscientific and unjustified advertisement of the species. It has also been aided by the linear growth of Eucalyptus in one dimension while most indigenous trees have broad crowns that grow in three dimensions.

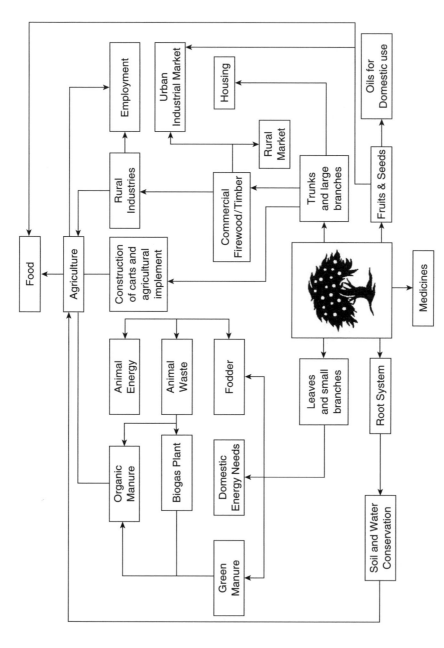

Figure 16.2   *The contribution of traditional tree species to the rural life-support system*

Source: Shiva et al, 1981

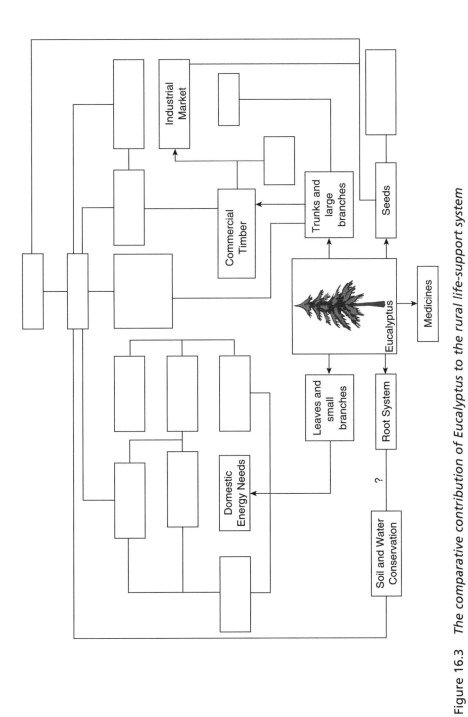

Figure 16.3   *The comparative contribution of Eucalyptus to the rural life-support system*

Source: Shiva et al, 1981

The Green Revolution and 'Miracle' Seeds

In agriculture, too, the monoculture mind creates the monoculture crop. The miracle of the new seeds has most often been communicated through the term 'high-yielding varieties' (HYV). The HYV category is a central category of the Green Revolution paradigm. Unlike what the term suggests, there is no neutral or objective measure of 'yield' on the basis of which the cropping systems based on miracle seeds, can be established to be higher yielding than the cropping systems they replace.

Cropping systems, in general, involve an interaction between soil, water and plant genetic resources. In indigenous agriculture, for example, cropping systems include a symbiotic relationship between soil, water, farm animals and plants. Green Revolution agriculture replaces this integration at the level of the farm with the integration of inputs such as seeds and chemicals. The seed/chemical package sets up its own inter-actions with soils and water systems, which are, however, not taken into account on the assessment of yields.

Modern plant breeding concepts like HYVs reduce farming systems to individual crops and part crops. Crop components of one system are then measured with crop components of another. Since the Green Revolution strategy is aimed at increasing the output of a single component of a farm, at the cost of decreasing other components and increasing external inputs, such a partial comparison is by definition biased to make the new varieties 'high yielding' although at the systems level, they may not be.

Traditional farming systems are based on mixed rotational cropping systems of cereals, pulses, oilseeds with diverse varieties of each crop, while the Green Revolution package is based on genetically uniform monocultures. No realistic assessments are ever made of the yield of the diverse crop outputs in the mixed and rotational systems. Usually the yield of a single crop like wheat or maize is singled out and compared to yields of new varieties. Even if the yields of all the crops were included, it is difficult to convert a measure of pulse into an equivalent measure of wheat, for example, because in the diet and in the ecosystem, they have distinctive functions.

The protein value of pulses and the calorie value of cereals are both essential for a balanced diet, but in different ways and one cannot replace the other. Similarly, the nitrogen fixing capacity of pulses is an invisible ecological contribution to the yield of associated cereals. The complex and diverse cropping systems based on indigenous vari-eties are therefore not easy to compare to the simplified monocultures of HYV seeds. Such a comparison has to involve entire systems and cannot be reduced to a compari-son of a fragment of the farm system. In traditional-farming systems, production has also involved maintaining the conditions of productivity. The measurement of yields and productivity in the Green Revolution paradigm is divorced from seeing how the processes of increasing output affect the processes that sustain the condition for agri-cultural production. While these reductionist categories of yield and productivity allow a higher destruction that affects future yields, they also exclude the higher perception of how the two systems differ dramatically in terms of inputs (Figure 16.4).

The indigenous cropping systems are based only on internal organic inputs. Seeds come from the farm, soil fertility comes from the farm and pest control is built into the

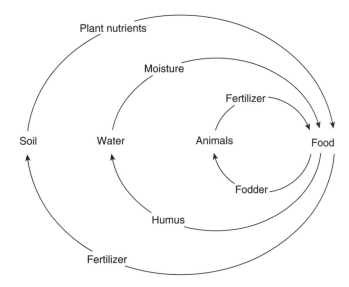

Figure 16.4 *Internal input farming system*

Source: Shiva, 1989

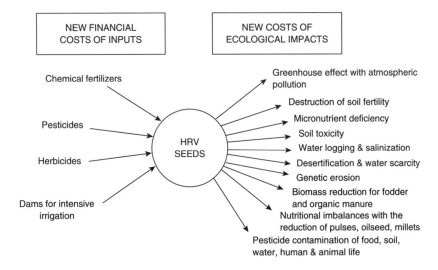

Figure 16.5 *External input farming system*

Source: Shiva, 1989

crop mixtures. In the Green Revolution package, yields are intimately tied to purchased inputs of seeds, chemical fertilizers, pesticides, petroleum and to intensive and accurate irrigation. High yields are not intrinsic to the seeds, but are a function of the availability of required inputs, which in turn have ecologically destructive impacts (Figure 16.5).

The distinguishing feature of the seeds is that they are highly responsive to certain key inputs such as fertilizers and irrigation. Palmer therefore suggested the term 'high-responsive-varieties' (HRVs) in place of 'high yielding varieties' (Lappe and Collins 1982). In the absence of additional inputs of fertilizers and irrigation, the new seeds perform worse than the indigenous varieties. With the additional inputs, the gain in output is insignificant compared to the increase in inputs. The measurement of output is also biased by restricting it to the marketable part of crops.

The Green Revolution package was built on the displacement of genetic diversity at two levels. Firstly, mixtures and rotation of diverse crops like wheat, maize, millets, pulses, and oil seeds were replaced by monocultures of wheat and rice. Secondly, the introduced wheat and rice varieties reproduced over large-scale as monocultures came from a very narrow genetic base, compared to the high genetic variability in the population of traditional wheat or rice plants. When 'HYV' seeds replace native cropping systems diversity is lost and irreplaceable.

The destruction of diversity and the creation of uniformity simultaneously involves the destruction of stability and the creation of vulnerability. Local knowledge on the other hand, focuses on multiple-use of diversity. Rice is not just grain, it provides straw for thatching and mat-making, fodder for livestock, bran for fishponds, husk for fuel. Local varieties of crops are selected to satisfy these multiple uses. The so-called HYV varieties increase grain production, by decreasing all other outputs, increasing external inputs, and introducing ecologically destructive impacts.

There is, moreover, a cultural bias, which favours the modern system, a bias which becomes evident in the naming of plant varieties. The indigenous varieties, evolved through both natural and human selection produced and used by Third World farmers worldwide, are called 'primitive cultivar'. Those varieties created by modern plant breeders in international agricultural research centres of transnational seed corporations are called 'advanced' or 'elite'.

The Non-sustainability of Monocultures

The crucial characteristic of monocultures is that they do not merely displace alternatives they destroy their own basis. They are neither tolerant of other systems, nor are they able to reproduce themselves sustainably. The uniformity of the 'normal' forest that 'scientific' forestry attempts to create becomes a prescription for non-sustainability.

Since the biological productivity of the forest is ecologically based on its diversity, the destruction of local knowledge, and with it plant diversity, leads to a degradation of the forest and an undermining of its sustainability. The increase in productivity from the commercial point of view destroys productivity from the perspective of local communities. The uniformity of the managed forest is meant to generate 'sustained yields'. However, uniformity destroys the conditions of renewability of forest ecosystems, and is ecologically non-sustainable.

In the commercial forestry paradigm 'sustainability' is a matter of supply to the market, not the production of an eco-system in its biological diversity or hydrological and climatic stability. Sustained yield management is aimed at producing 'the best financial results, or the greatest volume', or the 'most suitable class of produce'.

Uniformity in the forest is the demand of centralized markets and centralized industry. However, uniformity acts against nature's processes. The transformation of mixed natural forests into uniform mononcultures allows the direct entry of tropical sun and rain, baking the forest soils dry in the heat, washing the soils off in the rain. Less humid conditions are the reason for rapid retrogression of forest regions. The fires of Kalimantan are largely related to the aridization caused by the conversion of rainforests into plantations of Eucalyptus and Acacias. Floods and drought are created where the tropical forest has earlier cushioned the discharge of water.

This paradigm which destroys the diversity of the forest community either by clear felling or selective felling simultaneously destroys the very *conditions* for the renewal of the forest community. While species diversity is what makes the tropical forest biologically rich, and sustainable, this same diversity leads to allow density of individual species. The reductionist paradigm thus converts a biologically rich system into an impoverished resource and hence a non-renewable one.

In the dominant system, financial survival strategies determine the concept of 'sustained yield', which are in total violation of the principles of sustaining biological productivity. Sustained yields based on continuously reducing exploitable diameter classes leads to biological suicide, and a total destruction of forests.

Where the local knowledge is not totally extinct, communities resist the ecological destruction of introduced monocultures. 'Greening' with Eucalyptus works against nature and its cycles, and it is being resisted by communities who depend on the stability of nature's cycles to provide sustenance in the form of food and water. The Eucalyptus guzzles nutrients and water and, in the specific conditions of low rainfall zones, gives nothing back but terpenes to the soil. These inhibit the growth of other plants and are toxic to soil organisms which are responsible for building soil fertility and improving soil structure. The Eucalyptus certainly increased cash and commodity flows, but it resulted in a disastrous interruption of organic matter and water flows within the local ecosystem. Its proponents failed to calculate the costs in terms of the destruction of life in the soil, the depletion of water resources and the scarcity of food and fodder that Eucalyptus cultivation creates. Nor did they, while trying to shorten rotations for harvesting, see that tamarind, jackfruit and honge have very short rotations of one year in which the biomass harvested is far higher than that of Eucalyptus, which they nevertheless declared a 'miracle' tree. People everywhere have resisted the expansion of Eucalyptus because of its destruction of water, soil and food systems.

The destruction of diversity in agriculture has also been a source of non-sustainability. The 'miracle' varieties displaced the traditionally grown crops and through the erosion of diversity, the new seeds became a mechanism for introducing and fostering pests. Indigenous varieties, or land races are resistant to locally occurring pests and diseases. Even if certain diseases occur, some of the strains may be susceptible, while others will have the resistance to survive. Crop rotations also help in pest control. Since many pests are specific in particular plants, planting crops in different seasons and different years causes large reductions in pest population. On the other hand, planting the same crop over large areas year after year encourages pest build-ups. Cropping systems based on diversity thus have a built-in protection.

Having destroyed nature's mechanisms for controlling pests through the destruction of diversity, the only miracle that seems to have been achieved with the breeding strategy of the Green Revolution is the creation of new pests and diseases, and with them the ever increasing demand for pesticides. Yet the new costs of new pests and poisonous pesticides were never counted as part of the 'miracle' of the new seeds that modern plant breeders had given the world in the name of increasing 'food security'.

The 'miracle seeds' of the Green Revolution were meant to free the Indian farmer from constraints imposed by nature. Instead, large-scale monocultures of exotic varieties generated a new ecological vulnerability by reducing genetic diversity and destabilising soil and water systems. The Green Revolution led to a shift from earlier rotations of cereals, oilseeds, and pulses to a paddy-wheat rotation with intensive inputs of irrigation and chemicals. The paddy-wheat rotation has created an ecological backlash with serious problems of waterlogging in canal-irrigated regions and groundwater mining in tubewell irrigated regions. Further, the high yielding varieties have led to large-scale micronutrient deficiencies in soils, particularly iron in paddy cultivation and manganese in wheat.

These problems were built into the ecology of the HYV's even through they were not anticipated. The high water demands of these seeds necessitated high water inputs, and hence the hazards of desertification through water logging in some regions and desertification and aridization in others. The high nutrient demands caused micronutrient deficiencies on the one hand, but were also unsustainable because increased applications of chemical fertilizers were needed to maintain yields, thus increasing costs without increasing returns. The demand of the HYV seeds for intensive and uniform inputs of water and chemicals also made large-scale monocultures an imperative, and monocultures being highly vulnerable to pests and diseases, a new cost was created for pesticide applications. The ecological instability inherent in HYV seeds was thus translated into economic non-viability. The miracle seeds were not such a miracle after all.

Sustainable agriculture is based on the recycling of soil nutrients. This involves returning to the soil, part of the nutrients that come from the soil either directly as organic fertiliser or indirectly through the manure from farm animals. Maintenance of the nutrient cycle, and through it the fertility of the soil, is based on this inviolable law of return, which is a timeless, essential element of sustainable agriculture.

The Green Revolution paradigm substituted the nutrient cycle with linear flows of purchased inputs of chemical fertilizers from factories and marketed outputs of agricultural commodities.

The Green Revolution created the perception that soil fertility is produced in chemical factories, and agricultural yields are measured only through marketed commodities. Nitrogen fixing crops like pulses were therefore displaced. Millets which have high yields from the perspective of returning organic matter to the soil, were rejected as 'marginal' crops. Biological products not sold on the market but used as internal inputs for maintaining soil fertility were totally ignored in the cost–benefit equations of the Green Revolution miracle. They did not appear in the list of inputs because they were not purchased, and they did not appear as outputs because they were not sold.

Table 16.1   *Comparison of local and dominant knowledge systems*

Local System	Dominant System
Forestry and agriculture integrated	Forestry separate from agriculture
Integrated systems have multidimensional outputs. Forests produce wood, food, fodder, water etc. Agriculture produces diversity of food crops	Each separate system made one dimensional Forests produce only commercial wood. Agriculture produces only commercial crops with industrial inputs
Productivity in local system is a multidimensional measure, which has a conservation aspect	Productivity is a one-dimensional measure which is unrelated to conservation
Increasing productivity in these knowledge systems involves increasing the multidimensional outputs, and strengthening the integration	Increasing productivity in these knowledge systems involves increasing one-dimensional output by breaking up integrations and displacing diverse outputs
Productivity based on conservation of diversity	Productivity based on creation of moncultures and destruction of diversity
Sustainable system	Non-sustainable system

Yet what is 'unproductive' and 'waste' in the commercial context of the Green Revolution is now emerging as productive in the ecological context and as the only route to sustainable agriculture. By treating essential organic inputs that maintain the integrity of nature as 'waste', the Green Revolution strategy ensured that fertile and productive soils are actually laid waste. The 'land augmenting' technology has proved to be a land-degrading and land-destroying technology. With the greenhouse effect and global warming, a new dimension has been added to the ecologically destructive effect of chemical fertilisers. Nitrogen based fertilizers release nitrous oxide to the atmosphere which is one of the greenhouse gases causing global warming. Chemical farming has thus contributed to the erosion of food security through the pollution of land, water and the atmosphere (Shiva 1989).

Democratizing Knowledge

Modern silviculture as an exclusivist knowledge system, which focuses exclusively on industrial wood production, displaces local knowledge systems which view the forest in the perspective of food production, fodder production and water production. The exclusive focus on industrial wood destroys the food, fodder and water production capacities of the forest. It disrupts links between forestry agriculture, and in attempting to increase commercial/industrial wood, it creates a monoculture of tree species. The Eucalyptus has become a symbol of this monoculture. (See Table 16.1.)

Modern agriculture focuses exclusively on agricultural commodity production. It displaces local knowledge systems which view agriculture as the production of diverse food crops with internal inputs, and replaces it with monocultures of introduced varieties needing external industrial inputs. The exclusive focus on external inputs and commercial outputs, destroys diverse food crops such as pulses, oilseeds and millets, disrupts the local ecological cycles; and in attempting to increase single crop output, it creates monocultures of crop varieties. The HYV becomes a symbol of monoculture.

The crises of the dominant knowledge systems has many facets:

1. Since dominant knowledge is deeply wedded to economism, it is unrelated to human needs. Ninety percent of such production of knowledge could be stopped without any risk to human deprivation. On the contrary, since a large part of such knowledge is a source of hazards, and threats to human life (Bhopal, Chernobyl, Sandoz).
2. The political implications of the dominant knowledge system are inconsistent with equality and justice. It is disrupting of cohesion within local communities and polarises society into those with access and those without it, both in respect to the knowledge systems and the power system.
3. Being inherently fragmenting and having built in obsolescence, dominant knowledge creates an alienation of wisdom from knowledge and dispenses with the former.
4. It is inherently colonizing.
5. It breaks away from concrete contexts, disqualifying as inadequate the local and concrete knowledge.
6. It closes access and participation to a plurality of actors.
7. It leaves out a plurality of paths to knowing nature and the universe. It is a monoculture of the mind.

Modern Western knowledge is a particular cultural system with a particular relationship to power. It has, however, been projected as above and beyond culture and politics. Its relationship with the project of economic development has been invisible; and therefore it has become a more effective legitimizer for the homogenization of the world and the erosion of its ecological and cultural richness. The tyranny and hierarchy privileges that are part of the development paradigm is rooted and from which it derives its rationalization and legitimization. The power by which the dominant knowledge system has subjugated all others makes it exclusive and undemocratic.

Democratizing of knowledge becomes a central precondition for human liberation because the contemporary knowledge system excludes the humane by its very structure. Such a process of democratization would involve a redefining of knowledge such that the local and diverse become legitimate as knowledge, and they are viewed as indispensable knowledge because concreteness is the reality, and globalization and universalization are abstractions which have violated the concrete and hence the real. Such a shift from the globalizing to the local knowledge is important to the project of human freedom because it frees knowledge from the dependency on established regimes of thought, making it simultaneously more autonomous and more authentic. Democratization based on such an 'insurrection of subjugated knowledge' is both a desirable and necessary component of the larger processes of democratization because the earlier paradigm is in crisis and inspite of its power to manipulate, is unable to protect both nature and human survival.

References and further reading

Chin, S.C. (1989) *The Sustainability of Shifting Cultivation*. Penang: World Rainforest Movement.

Horton, R. (1967) African Traditional Thought and Western Science. *Africa 37*: 2.

Lappe, F.M. and Collins, J. (1982) *World Hunger: 10 Myths*. Institute for Food Developments Policy.

Richaria, R.H. (1986) Paper presented at Seminar on Crisis in Modern Science, Penang.

Shiva, V. (1981) *Ecology and the Politics of Survival*. New Delhi: Sage.

Shiva, V. (1989a) *Staying Alive*. London: Zed Books. p. 59.

Shiva, V. (1989) *The Violence of the Green Revolution*. Dehra Dun: *Research Foundation of Science and Ecology*.

Shiva, V., Bandyopadhyay, J. and Sharatchandra, H.C. (1981) *The Social Ecological and Economic Impact of Social Forestry in Kolar*. Bangalore: IIM.

Troup, R.S. (1916) *Silviulture Systems*. Oxford: Oxford University Press.

17

A Road Map for Natural Capitalism

Amory B Lovins, L. Hunter Lovins and Paul Hawken

Business strategies built around the radically more productive use of natural resources can solve many environmental problems at a profit.

The earth's ability to sustain life, and therefore economic activity, is threatened by the way we extract, process, transport, and dispose of a vast flow of resources – some 220 billion tons a year, or more than 20 times the average American's body weight every day. With dangerously narrow focus, our industries look only at the exploitable resources of the earth's ecosystems – its oceans, forests, and plains – and not at the larger services that those systems provide for free. Resources and ecosystem services both come from the earth – even from the same biological systems – but they're two different things. Forests, for instance, not only produce the resource of wood fiber but also provide such ecosystem services as water storage, habitat, and regulation of the atmosphere and climate. Yet companies that earn income from harvesting the wood fiber resource often do so in ways that damage the forest's ability to carry out its other vital tasks.

Unfortunately, the cost of destroying ecosystem services becomes apparent only when the services start to break down. In China's Yangtze basin in 1998, for example, deforestation triggered flooding that killed 3,700 people, dislocated 223 million, and inundated 60 million acres of cropland. That $30 billion disaster forced a logging moratorium and a $12 billion crash program of reforestation.

The reason companies (and governments) are so prodigal with ecosystem services is that the value of those services doesn't appear on the business balance sheet. But that's a staggering omission. The economy, after all, is embedded in the environment. Recent calculations published in the journal *Nature* conservatively estimate the value of all the earth's ecosystem services to be at least £33 trillion a year. That's close to the gross world product, and it implies a capitalized book value on the order of half a quadrillion dollars. What's more, for most of these services, there is no known substitute at any price, and we can't live without them.

Source: A. Lovins, L.H. Lovins, P. Hawken (1999) *Harvard Business Review*, May, 145–58.

This article puts forward a new approach not only for protecting the biosphere but also improving profits and competitiveness. Some very simple changes to the way we run our businesses, built on advanced techniques for making resources more productive, can yield startling benefits both for today's shareholders and for future generations.

This approach is called *natural capitalism* because it's what capitalism might become if its largest category of capital – the 'natural capital' of ecosystems services – were properly valued. The journey to natural capitalism involves four major shifts in business practices, all virtually interlinked:

- *Dramatically increase the productivity of natural resources.* Reducing the wasteful and destructive flow of resources from depletion to pollution represents a major business opportunity. Through fundamental changes in both production design and technology, farsighted companies are developing ways to make natural resources – energy, minerals, water, forests – stretch 5, 10, even 100 times further than they do today. These major resource savings often yield higher profits than small resource savings do – or even saving no resource at all would – and not only pay for themselves over time bit in many cases reduce the initial capital investments.
- *Shift to biologically inspired production models.* Natural capitalism seeks not merely to reduce waste but to eliminate the very concept of waste. In closed-loop production systems, modeled on nature's designs; every output either is returned harmlessly to the ecosystem as a nutrient, like compost, or becomes an input for manufacturing another product. Such systems can often be designed to eliminate the use of toxic materials, which can hamper nature's ability to reprocess the materials.
- *Move to a solutions-based business model.* The business model of traditional manufacturing rests on the sale of goods. In the new model, value is instead delivered as a flow of services – providing illumination, for example, rather than selling lightbulbs. This model entails a new perception of value, a move from the acquisition of goods as a measure of affluence to one where well being is measured by the continuous satisfaction of changing expectations for quality, utility, and performance. The new relationship aligns the interests of providers and customers in ways that reward them for implementing the first two innovations and closed-loop manufacturing.
- *Reinvest in natural capital.* Ultimately, business must restore, sustain, and expand the planet's ecosystems so that they can produce their vital services and biological resources even more abundantly. Pressures to do so are mounting, as human needs expand, the costs endangered by deteriorating ecosystems rise, and the environmental awareness of consumers increases. Fortunately, these pressures all create business value.

Natural capitalism is not motivated by a current scarcity of natural resources. Indeed, although many biological resources, like fish, are becoming scarce, most mined resources, such as copper and oil, seem ever more abundant. Indices of average commodity prices are at 28-year lows; thanks partly to powerful extractive technologies, which are often subsidized and whose damage to natural capital remains unaccounted for. Yet even despite these artificially low prices, using resources manifold more productively can now be so profitable that pioneering companies – large and small – have already embarked on the journey toward natural capitalism.

Still the question arises – if large resource savings are available and profitable, why haven't they all been captured already? The answer is simple: scores of common practices in both the private and public sectors systematically reward companies for wasting natural resources and penalize them for boosting resource productivity. For example, most companies expense their consumption of raw materials through the income statement but pass the resource-saving investment through the balance sheet. That distortion makes it more tax efficient to waste fuel than to invest in improving fuel efficiency. In short, even though the road seems clear, the compass that companies use to direct their journey is broken. Later we'll look in more detail at some of the obstacles to resource productivity of the important business opportunities they reveal. But first, let's map the route toward the natural capitalism.

Dramatically Increase the Productivity of Natural Resources

In the first stage of a company's journey toward natural capitalism, it strives to wring out the waste of energy, water, materials, and other resources throughout its productions systems and other operations. There are two main ways companies can do this at a profit. First, they can adopt a fresh approach to design that considers industrial systems as a whole rather than part by part. Second, companies can replace old industrial technologies with new ones, particularly with those based on natural processes and materials.

Implementing Whole-system Design

Inventor Edwin Land once remarked that "people who seem to have had a new idea have often simply stopped having an old idea." This is particularly true when designing for resource savings. The old idea is one of diminishing returns – the greater the resource saving the higher the cost. But that old idea is giving way to the new idea that bigger savings can cost less – that saving a large fraction of resources can actually cost less than saving a small fraction of resources. This is the concept of expanding returns, and it governs much of the revolutionary thinking behind the whole-system design. Lean manufacturing is an example of whole-system thinking that has helped many companies dramatically reduce such forms of waste as lead times, defect rates, and inventory. Applying whole-system thinking to the productivity of natural resources can achieve even more.

Consider Interface Corporation, a leading maker of materials for commercial interiors. In its new Shanghai carpet factory, a liquid had to be circulated through a standard pumping loop similar to those used in nearly all industries. A top European company designed the system to use pumps requiring a total of 95 horsepower. But before construction began, Interface's engineer, Jan Schilham, realized that two embarrassingly simple design changes would cut that power requirement to only 7 horsepower – a 92% reduction. His redesigned system cost less to build, involved no new technology, and worked better in all respects.

What two design changes achieved this 12-fold saving in pumping power? First, Schilham chose fatter-than-usual pipes, which create much less friction than thin pipes do and therefore need far less pumping energy. The original designer had chosen thin pipes because, according to the textbook method, the extra cost of fatter ones wouldn't be justified by the pumping energy that they would save. This standard design trade-off optimizes the pipes by themselves but 'pessimizes' the larger system. Schilham optimized the *whole* system by counting not only the higher capital cost of the fatter pipes but also the *lower* capital cost of the smaller pumping equipment that would be needed. The pumps, motors, motor controls, and electrical components could all be much smaller because there'd be less friction to overcome. Capital cost would fall far more for the smaller equipment than it would rise for the fatter pipe. Choosing big pipes and small pumps – rather than small pipes and big pumps – would therefore make the whole system cost less to build, even before counting its future energy savings.

Schilam's second innovation was to reduce the friction even more by making the pipes short and straight rather than long and crooked. He did this by laying out the pipes first, *then* positioning the various tanks, boilers, and other equipment that they connected. Designers normally locate the production equipment in arbitrary positions and then have a pipe fitter connect everything. Awkward placement forces the pipes to make numerous bends that greatly increase friction. The pipe fitters don't mind: they're paid by the hour, they profit from the extra pipes and fittings, and they don't pay for the oversized pumps or inflated electric bills. In addition to reducing those four kinds of costs, Schilham's short, straight pipes were easier to insulate, saving an extra 70% kilowatts of heat loss and repaying the insulation's cost in three months.

This small example has big implications for two reasons. First, pumping is the largest application of motors, and motors use three-quarters of all industrial electricity. Second, the lessons are very widely relevant. Interface's pumping loop shows how simple changes in design mentality can yield huge resource savings and returns on investment. This isn't rocket science, often it's just a rediscovery of good Victorian-engineering principles that have been lost because of specialization.

Whole-system thinking can help managers find small changes that lead to big savings that are cheap, free, or even better than free (because they make the whole system cheaper to build). They can do this because often the right investment in one part of the system can produce multiple benefits throughout the system. For example, companies would gain 18 distinct economic benefits – of which direct energy savings is the only one – if they switched from ordinary motors to premium-efficiency motors or from ordinary lighting to ballasts that automatically dim the lamps to match available daylight. If everyone in America integrated these and other selected technologies into all existing motor and lighting systems in an optimal way, the nation's $220-billion-a-year electric bill would be cut in half. The after-tax return on investing in these changes would in most cases exceed 100% per year.

The profits from saving electricity could be increased even further if companies also incorporated the best off-the-shelf improvements into their building structure and their office, heating, cooling, and other equipment. Overall, such changes could cut national electricity consumption by at least 75% and produce returns of around 100% a year on investments made. More important, because workers would be more comfortable, better able to see, and less fatigued by noise, their productivity and the quality of their output would rise. Eight recent case studies of people working in well-designed, energy efficient buildings measured labor productivity gains of 6% to 16%. Since a typical office pays about 100 times as much for people as it does for energy, this increased productivity in people is worth about 6 to 16 times as much as eliminating the entire energy bill.

Energy-saving, productivity-enhancing improvements can often be achieved at even lower cost by piggybacking them onto the periodic renovations that all buildings and factories need. A recent proposal for reallocating the normal 20-year renovation budget for a standard 200,000-square-foot glass-clad office tower near Chicago, Illinois shows the potential of whole-system design. The proposal suggested replacing the aging glazing system with a new kind of window that lets in nearly six times more daylight than the old sun-blocking glass units. The new windows would reduce the flow of heat and noise four times better than traditional windows do. So even though the glass costs slightly more, the overall cost of the renovation would be reduced because the windows would let in cool, glare-free daylight that, when combined with more efficient lighting and office equipment, would reduce the need for air-conditioning by 75%. Installing a fourfold more efficient, but fourfold smaller, air conditioning system would cost $200,000 less than giving the old system its normal 20-year renovation. The $200,000 saved would, in turn, pay for the extra cost of the new windows and other improvements. This whole-system approach to renovation would not only save 75% of the building's total energy use, it would also greatly improve the building's comfort and marketability. Yet it would cost essentially the same as the normal renovation. There are about 100,000 twenty-year-old glass office towers in the United States that are ripe for such improvement.

Major gains in resource productivity require that the right steps be taken in the right order. Small changes made at the downstream end of a process often create far larger savings further upstream. In almost any industry that uses a pumping system, for example, saving one unit of liquid flow or friction in an exit pipe saves about ten units of fuel, cost, and pollution at the power station.

Of course, the original reduction in flow itself can bring direct benefits, which are often the reason changes are made in the first place. In the 1980s, while California's industry grew 30%, for example, its water use was cut by 30%, largely to avoid increased wastewater fees. But the resulting reduction in pumping energy (and the roughly tenfold larger saving in power-plant fuel and pollution) delivered bonus savings that were at the time largely unanticipated.

To see how downstream cuts in resource consumption can create huge savings upstream, consider how reducing the use of wood fiber disproportionately reduces the pressure to cut down forests. In round numbers, half of all harvested wood fiber is used for such structural products as lumber; the other half is used for paper and cardboard. In both cases, the biggest leverage comes from reducing the amount of the retail product used. If it takes, for example, three pounds of harvested trees to produce one pound of product, then saving one pound of all product will save three pounds of trees – plus all the environmental damage avoided by not having to cut them down in the first place.

The easiest savings come from not using paper that's unwanted or unneeded. In an experiment at its Swiss headquarters, for example, Dow Europe cut office paper flow by about 30% in six weeks simply by discouraging unneeded information. For instance, mailing lists were eliminated and senders of memos got back receipts indicating whether each recipient had wanted the information. Taking those and other small steps, Dow was also able to increase labor productivity by a similar proportion because people could focus on what they really needed to read. Similarly, Danish hearing-aid maker Oticon saved upwards of 30% of its paper as a by-product of redesigning its business processes to produce better decisions faster. Setting the default on office printers and copiers to double-sided mode reduced AT&T's paper costs by about 15%. Recently developed copiers and printers can even strip off old toner and ink, permitting each sheet to be reused about ten times.

Further savings can come from using thinner but stronger and more opaque paper, and from designing packaging more thoughtfully. In a 30-month effort at reducing such waste, Johnson & Johnson saved 2,750 tons of packaging, 1,600 tons of paper, $2.8 million, and at least 330 acres of forest annually. The downstream savings in paper use are multiplied by the savings further upstream, as less need for paper products (or less need for fiber to make each product) translates into less raw paper, less raw paper means less pulp, and less pulp requires fewer trees to be harvested from the forest. Recycling paper and substituting alternative fibers such as wheat straw will save even more.

Comparable savings can be achieved for the wood fiber used in structural products. Pacific Gas and Electric, for example, sponsored an innovative design developed by Davis Energy Group that used engineered wood products to reduce the amount of wood needed in a stud wall for a typical tract house by more than 70%. These walls were stronger, cheaper, more stable, and insulated twice as well. Using them enabled the designers to eliminate heating and cooling equipment in a climate where temperatures range from freezing to 113° F. Eliminating the equipment made the whole house much less expensive both to build and to run while still maintaining high levels of comfort. Taken together, these and many other savings in the paper and construction industries could make our use of wood fiber so much more productive that, in principle, the entire world's present wood fiber needs could probably be met by an intensive tree farm about the size of Iowa.

Adopting Innovative Technologies

Implementing whole-system design goes hand in hand with introducing alternative, environmentally friendly technologies. Many of these are already available and profitable but not widely known. Some, like the 'designer catalysts' that are transforming the chemical industry, are already runaway successes. Others are still making their way to market, delayed by cultural rather than by economic or technical barriers.

The automobile industry is particularly ripe for technological change. After a century of development, motorcar technology is showing signs of age. Only 1% of the energy consumed by today's cars is actually used to move the driver: only 15% to 20% of the power generated by burning gasoline reaches the wheels (the rest is lost in the engine and drive-train) and 95% of the resulting propulsion moves the car, not the driver. The industry's infrastructure is hugely expensive and inefficient. Its convergent products compete for narrow niches in saturated core markets at commodity-like prices. Auto making is capital intensive, and product cycles are long. It is profitable in good years but subject to large losses in bad years. Like the typewriter industry just before the advent of personal computers, it is vulnerable to displacement by something completely different.

The Hypercar

Enter the Hypercar. Since 1993, when Rocky Mountain Institute places this automotive concept in the public domain, several dozen current and potential auto manufacturers have committed billions of dollars to its development and commercialization. The Hypercar integrates the best existing technologies to reduce the consumption of fuel as much as 85% and the amount of materials used up to 90% by introducing four main innovations.

First, making the vehicle out of advance polymer composites, chiefly carbon fiber, reduces its weight by two-thirds while maintaining crashworthiness. Second, aerodynamic design and better tires reduce air resistance by as much as 70% and rolling resistance by up to 80%. Together, these innovations save about two-thirds of the fuel. Third, 30% to 50% of the remaining fuel is saved by using a 'hybrid-electric' drive. In such a system, the wheels are turned by electric motors whose power is made onboard by a small engine or turbine, or even more efficiently by a fuel cell. The fuel cell generates electricity directly by chemically combining stored hydrogen with oxygen, producing pure hot water as its only by-product. Interactions between the small, clean, efficient power source and the ultralight, low-drag auto body then further reduces the weight, cost, and complexity of both. Fourth, much of the traditional hardware – from transmissions and differentials to gauges and certain parts of the suspension – can be replaced by electronics controlled with highly integrated, customizable, and upgradable software.

These technologies make it feasible to manufacture pollution-free, high-performance cars, sport utilities, pickup trucks, and vans that get 80 to 200 miles per gallon (or its energy equivalent in other fuels). These improvements will not require any compromise in quality or utility. Fuel savings will not come from making vehicles small, sluggish, unsafe, or unaffordable, nor will they depend on government fuel taxes, mandates, or subsidies. Rather, Hypercars will succeed for the same reason that people buy compact discs instead of phonograph records: the CD is a superior product that redefines marker expectations. From the manufacturers' perspective, Hypercars will cut cycle times, capital needs, body part counts, and assembly effort and space by as much as tenfold. Early adopters will have a huge competitive advantage – which is why dozens of corporations, including most automakers, are now racing to bring Hypercar-like products to market.[1]

In the long term, the Hypercar will transform industries other than automobiles. It will displace about an eighth of the steel market directly and most of the rest eventually, as carbon fiber becomes far cheaper. Hypercars and their cousins could ultimately save as much oil as OPEC now sells. Indeed, oil may well become uncompetitive as a fuel long before it becomes scarce and costly. Similar challenges face the coal and electricity industries because the development of the Hypercar is likely to accelerate greatly the commercialization of inexpensive hydrogen fuels. These fuel cells will help shift power production from centralized coalfired and nuclear power stations to networks of decentralized, small-scale generators. In fact, fuel-cell-powered Hypercars could themselves be part of these networks. They'd be, in effect, 20-kilowatt power plants on wheels. Given that cars are left parked – that is, unused – more than 95% of the time, these Hypercars could be plugged into the grid and could then sell back enough electricity to repay as much as half the predicted cost of leasing them. A national Hypercar fleet could ultimately have five to ten times the generating capacity of the national electric grid.

As radical as it sounds, the Hypercar is not an isolated case. Similar ideas are emerging in such industries as chemicals, semiconductors, general manufacturing, transportation, water and wastewater treatment, agriculture, forestry, energy, real estate, and urban design. For example, the amount of carbon dioxide released for each microchip manufactured can be reduced almost 100-fold through improvements that are now profitable or soon will be.

Some of the most striking developments come from emulating nature's techniques. In her book, *Biomimicry*, Janine Benyus points out that spiders convert digested crickets and flies into silk that's as strong as Kelvar without the need for boiling sulfuric acid and high-temperature extruders. Using no furnaces, abalone can convert seawater into an inner shell twice as tough as our best ceramics. Trees turn sunlight, water, soil, and air into cellulose, a sugar stronger than nylon but one-fourth as dense. They then bind it into wood, a natural composite with a higher bending strength than concrete, aluminum alloy, or steel. We may never become as skillful as spiders, abalone, or trees, but smart designers are already realizing that nature's environmentally benign chemistry offers attractive alternatives to industrial brute force.

Whether through better design or through new technologies, reducing waste represents a vast business opportunity. The U.S. economy is not even 10% as energy efficient as the laws of physics allow. Just the energy thrown off as waste heat by U.S. power stations equals the total energy use of Japan. Materials efficiency is even worse: only about 1% of all materials mobilized to serve America is actually made into products and still in use six months after sale. In every sector, there are opportunities for reducing the amount of resources that go into a production process, the steps required to run that process, and the amount of pollution generated and by-products discarded at the end. These all represent avoidable costs and hence profits to be won.

Redesign Production According to Biological Models

In the second stage on the journey to natural capitalism, companies use closed-loop manufacturing to create new products and processes that can totally prevent waste. This plus more efficient production processes could cut companies' long-term materials requirements by more than 90% in most sectors.

The central principle of closed-loop manufacturing, as architect Paul Bierman-Lytle of the engineering firm CH2M Hill puts it, is 'waste equals food'. Every output of manufacturing should be either composted into natural nutrients or remanufactured into technical nutrients – that is, it should be returned to the ecosystem or recycled for further production. Closed-loop production systems are designed to eliminate any materials that incur disposal costs, especially toxic ones, because the alternative – isolating them to prevent harm to natural systems – tends to be costly and risky. Indeed, meeting EPA and OSHA standards by eliminating harmful materials often makes a manufacturing process cost less than the hazardous process it replaced. Motorola, for example, formerly used chlorofluorocarbons for cleaning printed circuit boards after soldering. When CFCs were outlawed because they destroy stratospheric ozone, Motorola at first explored such alternatives as orange-peel terpenes. But it turned out to be even cheaper – and to produce a better product – to redesign the whole soldering process so that it needed no cleaning operations or cleaning materials at all.

Closed-loop manufacturing is more than just a theory. The U.S. remanufacturing industry in 1996 reported revenues of $53 billion – more than consumer-durables manufacturing (appliances, furniture, audio, video, farm, and garden equipment). Xerox, whose bottom line has swelled by $700 million from remanufacturing, expects to save another $1 billion just by manufacturing its new, entirely reusable or recyclable line of 'green' photocopiers. What's more, policy makers in some countries are already taking steps to encourage industry to think along these lines. German law, for example, makes many manufacturers responsible for their products forever, and Japan is following suit.

Combining closed-loop manufacturing with resource efficiency is especially powerful. Dupont, for example, now makes much of its polyester film ever stronger and thinner so it uses less material and costs less to make. Yet because the film performs better, customers are willing to pay more for it. As DuPont chairman Jack Krol noted in 1997, 'Our ability to continually improve the inherent properties [of our films] enables this process [of developing more productive materials, at lower cost, and higher profits] to go on indefinitely.'

Interface is leading the way to this next frontier of industrial ecology. While its competitors are 'down cycling' nylon-and-PVC-based carpet into less valuable carpet backing, Interface has invented a new floor covering material called Solenium, which can be completely remanufactured into identical new product. This fundamental innovation emerged from a clean-sheet redesign. Executives at Interface didn't ask how they could sell more carpet of the familiar kind; they asked how they could create a dream product that would best meet their customers' needs while protecting and nourishing natural capital.

Solenium lasts four times longer and uses 40% less material than ordinary carpets – an 86% reduction in materials intensity. What's more, Solenium is free of chlorine and other toxic materials, is virtually stainproof, doesn't grow mildew, can easily be cleaned with water, and offers aesthetic advantages over traditional carpets. It's so superior in every respect that Interface doesn't market it as an environmental product – just a better one.

Solenium is only one part of Interface's drive to eliminate every form of waste. Chairman Ray C. Anderson defines waste as 'any measurable input that does not produce customer value', and he considers all inputs to be waste until shown otherwise. Between 1994 and 1998, this zero-waste approach led to a systematic treasure hunt that helped to keep resource inputs constant while revenues rose by $200 million. Indeed, $67 million of the revenue increase can be directly attributed to the company's 60% reduction in landfill waste.

Subsequently, president Charlie Eitel expanded the definition of waste to include all fossil fuel inputs, and now many customers are eager to buy products from the company's recently opened solar-powered carpet factory. Interface's green strategy has not only won plaudits from environmentalists, it has also proved a remarkably successful business strategy. Between 1993 and 1998, revenue has more than doubled, profits have more than tripled, and the number of employees has increased by 73%.

Change the Business Model

In addition to its drive to eliminate waste, Interface has made a fundamental shift in its business model – the third stage on the journey toward natural capitalism. The company has realized that clients want to walk on and look at carpets – but not necessarily to own them. Traditionally, broadloom carpets in office buildings are replaced every decade because some portions look worn out. When that happens, companies suffer the disruption of shutting down their offices and removing their furniture. Billions of pounds of carpets are removed each year and sent to landfills, where they will last up to 20,000 years. To escape this unproductive and wasteful cycle, Interface is transforming itself from a company that sells and fits carpets into one that provides floor-covering services.

Under its Evergreen Lease, Interface no longer sells carpets but rather leases a floor-covering service for a monthly fee, accepting responsibility for keeping the carpet fresh and clean. Monthly inspections detect and replace worn carpet tiles. Since at most 20% of an area typically shows at least 80% of the wear, replacing only the worn parts reduces the consumption of carpeting material by about 80%. It also minimizes the disruption that customers experience – worn tiles are seldom found under furniture. Finally, for the customer, leasing carpets can provide a tax advantage by turning a capital expenditure into a tax-deductible expense. The result: the customer gets cheaper and better services that cost the supplier far less to produce. Indeed, the energy saved from not producing a whole new carpet is in itself enough to produce all the carpeting that the new business model requires. Taken together, the 5-fold savings in carpeting material that Interface achieves through the Evergreen Lease and the 7-fold materials savings achieved through the use of Solenium deliver a stunning 35-fold reduction in the flow of materials needed to sustain a superior floor-covering service. Remanufacturing, and even making carpet initially from renewable materials, can reduce the extraction of virgin resources essentially to the company's goal of zero.

Interface's shift to a service-leasing business reflects a fundamental change from the basic model of most manufacturing companies, which still look on their businesses as machines for producing selling products. The more products sold, the better – at least for the company, if not always for the customer or the earth. But any model that wastes natural resources also wastes money. Ultimately, that model will be unable to compete with a service model that emphasizes solving problems and building long-term relationships with customers rather than making and selling products. The shift to what James Womack of the Lean Enterprise Institute calls a 'solutions economy' will almost always improve customer value *and* providers' bottom lines because it aligns both parties' interests, offering rewards for doing more and better with less.

Interface is not alone. Elevator giant Schindler, for example, prefers leasing vertical transportation services to selling elevators because leasing lets it capture the savings from its elevators' lower energy and maintenance costs. Dow Chemical and Safety Kleen prefer leasing dissolving services to selling solvents because they can reuse the same solvent scores of times, reducing costs. United Technologies' Carrier division, the world's largest manufacturer of air-conditioners, is shifting its mission from selling air conditioners to leasing comfort. Making its air conditioners more durable and efficient may compromise future equipment sales, but it provides what customers want and will pay for – better comfort at lower cost. But Carrier is going even further. It's starting to team up with other companies to make buildings more efficient so that they need less air-conditioning, or even none at all, to yield the same level of comfort. Carrier will get paid to provide the agreed-upon level of comfort, however, that's delivered. Higher profits will come from providing better solutions rather than from selling more equipment. Since comfort with little or no air-conditioning (via better building designs) works better and costs less than comfort with copious air-conditioning, Carrier is smart to capture this opportunity itself before its competitors do. As they say at 3M: 'We'd rather eat our *own* lunch, thank you.'

The shift to a service business model promises benefits not just to participating businesses but to the entire economy as well. Womack points out that by helping customers reduce their need for capital goods such as carpets or elevators, and by rewarding suppliers for extending and maximizing asset values rather than for churning them, adoption of the service model will reduce the volatility in the turnover of capital goods that lies at the heart of the business cycle. That would significantly reduce the overall volatility of the world's economy. At present, the producers of capital goods face feast or famine because the buying decisions of households and corporations are extremely sensitive to fluctuating income. But in a continuous-flow-of services economy, those swings would be greatly reduced, bringing a welcome stability to businesses. Excess capacity – another form of waste and source of risk – need no longer be retained for meeting peak demand. The result of adopting the new model would be an economy in which we grow and get richer by using less and become stronger by being leaner and more stable.

Reinvest in Natural Capital

The foundation of textbook capitalism is the prudent reinvestment of earnings in productive capital. Natural capitalists who have dramatically raised their resource productivity, closed their loops, and shifted to a solutions-based business model have one key task remaining. They must reinvest in restoring, sustaining, and expanding the most important form of capital – their own natural habitat and biological resource base.

This was not always so important. Until recently, business could ignore damage to the ecosystem because it didn't affect production and didn't increase costs. But that situation is changing. In 1998 alone, violent weather displaced 300 million people and caused upwards of $90 billion worth of damage, representing more weather-related destruction than was reported through the entire decade of the 1980s. The increase in damage is strongly linked to deforestation and climate change, factors that accelerate the frequency and severity of natural disasters and are the consequences of inefficient industrialization. If the flow of services from industrial systems is to be sustained or increased in the future for a growing population, the vital flow of services from living systems will have to be maintained or increased as well. Without reinvestment in natural capital, shortages of ecosystem services are likely to become the limiting factor to prosperity in the next century. When a manufacturer realizes that a supplier of key components is overextended and running behind on deliveries, it takes immediate action lest its own production lines come to a halt. The ecosystem is a supplier of key components for the life of the planet, and it is now falling behind on its orders.

Failure to protect and reinvest in natural capital can also hit a company's revenues indirectly. Many companies are discovering that public perceptions of environmental responsibility, or its lack thereof, affect sales. MacMillan Bloedel, targeted by environmental activists as an emblematic clear-cutter and chlorine user, lost 5% of its sales almost overnight when dropped as a U.K. supplier by Scott Paper and Kimberly-Clark. Numerous case studies show that companies leading the way in implementing changes that help protect the environment tend to gain disproportionate advantage, while companies perceived as irresponsible lose their franchise, their legitimacy, and their shirts. Even businesses that claim to be committed to the concept of sustainable development but whose strategy is seen as mistaken, like Monsanto, are encountering stiffening public resistance to their products. Not surprisingly, University of Oregon business professor Michael Russo, along with many other analysts has found that a strong environmental rating is 'a consistent predictor of profitability'.

The pioneering corporations that have made reinvestments in natural capital are starting to see some interesting paybacks. The independent power producer AES, for example, has long pursued a policy of planting trees to offset the carbon emissions of its power plants. The ethical stance, once thought quixotic, now looks like a smart investment because a dozen brokers are now starting to create markets in carbon reduction. Similarly, certification by the Forest Stewardship Council of certain sustainably grown and harvested products has given Collins Pine the extra profit margins that enabled its U.S. manufacturing operations to survive brutal competition. Taking an even longer view, Swiss Re and other European reinsurers are seeking to cut their storm-damage losses by pressing for international public policy to protect the climate and by investing in climate-safe technologies that also promise good profits. Yet most companies still do not realize that a vibrant ecological web underpins their survival and their business success. Enriching natural capital is not just a public good – it is vital to every company's longevity.

It turns out that changing industrial processes so that they actually replenish and magnify the stock of natural capital can prove especially profitable because the nature does the production; people need just to step back and let life flourish. Industries that directly harvest living resources, such as forestry, farming, and fishing, offer the most suggestive examples. Here are three:

- Allan Savory of the Center for Holistic Management in Albuquerque, New Mexico, has redesigned cattle ranching to raise the carrying capacity of rangelands, which have often been degraded not by overgrazing but by undergrazing and grazing the wrong way. Savory's solution is to keep the cattle moving from place to place, grazing intensively but briefly at each site, so that they mimic the dense but constantly moving herds of native grazing animals that co-evolved with grasslands. Thousands of ranchers are estimated to be applying this approach, improving both their range and their profits. This 'management-intensive rotational grazing' method, long standard in New Zealand, yields such clearly superior returns that over 15% of Wisconsin's dairy farms have adopted it in the past few years.

- The California Rice Industry Association has discovered that letting nature's diversity flourish can be more profitable than forcing it to produce a single product. By flooding 150,000 to 200,000 acres of Sacramento valley rice fields – about 30% of California's rice-growing area – after harvest, farmers are able to create seasonal wetlands, replenish groundwater, improve fertility, and yield other valuable benefits. In addition, the farmers bale and sell the rice and straw, whose high silica content – formerly an air-pollution hazard when the straw was burned – adds insect resistance and hence value as a construction material when it's resold instead.
- John Todd of Living Technologies in Burlington, Vermont, has used biological Living Machines – linked tanks of bacteria, algae, plants, and other organisms – to turn sewage into clean water. That not only yields cleaner water at a reduced cost, with no toxicity or odor, but it also produces commercially valuable flowers and makes the plant compatible with its residential neighborhood. A similar plant at the Ethel M Chocolates factory in Las Vegas, Nevada, not only handles difficult industrial wastes effectively but is showcased in its public tours.

Although such practices are still evolving, the broad lessons they teach are clear. In almost all climates, soils, and societies, working with nature is more productive than working against it. Reinvesting in nature allows farmers, fishermen, and forest managers to match or exceed the high yields and profits sustained by traditional input-intensive, chemically driven practices. Although much of mainstream business is still headed the other way, the profitability of sustainable, nature-emulating practices is already being proven. In the future, many industries that don't now consider themselves dependent on a biological resource base will become more so as they shift their raw materials and production processes more to biological ones. There is evidence that many business leaders are starting to think this way. The consulting firm Arthur D. Little surveyed a group of North American and European business leaders and found that 83% of them already believe that they can derive 'real business value [from implementing a] sustainable-development approach to strategy and operations'.

A Broken Compass?

If the road ahead is clear, why are so many companies straying or falling by the way-side? We believe the reason is that the instruments companies use to set their targets, measure their performance, and hand out rewards are faulty. In other words, the markets are full of distortions and perverse incentives. Of the more than 60 specific forms of misdirection that we have identified,[2] the most obvious involve the ways companies allocate capital and the way governments set policy and impose taxes. Merely correcting these defective practices would uncover huge opportunities for profit.

Consider how many companies make purchasing decisions. Decisions to buy small items are typically based on their initial cost rather than their full lifecycle cost, a practice that could add up to major wastage. Distribution transformers that supply electricity to buildings and factories, for example, are a minor item at just $320 apiece, and most companies try to save a quick buck by buying the lowest price models. Yet nearly all the nation's electricity must flow through transformers, and using cheaper but less efficient models wastes $1 billion a year. Such examples are legion. Equipping standard new office-lighting circuits with fatter wire that reduces electrical resistance could generate after-tax returns of 193% a year. Instead, wire as thin as the National Electrical Code permits is usually selected because it costs less up-front. But the code is meant only to prevent fires from overheated wiring, not to save money. Ironically, an electrician who chooses fatter wire – thereby reducing long-term electricity bills – doesn't get the job. After paying for the extra copper, he's no longer the low bidder.

Some companies do consider more than just the initial price in their purchasing decisions but still don't go far enough. Most of them use a crude payback estimate rather than more accurate metrics like discounted cash flow. A few years ago, the median simple payback these companies were demanding from energy efficiency was 1.9 years. That's equivalent to requiring an after-tax return of around 71% per year – about six times the marginal cost of capital.

Most companies also miss major opportunities by treating their facilities costs as an overhead to be minimized, typically by laying off engineers, rather than as profit center to be optimized – by using those engineers to save resources. Deficient measurement and accounting practices also prevent companies from allocating costs – and waste – with any accuracy. For example, only a few semiconductor plants worldwide regularly and accurately measure how much energy they're using to produce a unit of chilled water or clean air for their clean-room production facilities, That makes it hard for them to improve efficiency. In fact, in an effort to save time, semiconductor makers frequently build new plants as exact copies of previous ones – a design method nick-named 'infectious repetitis'.

Many executives pay too little attention to saving resources because they are often a small percentage of total costs (energy costs run to about 2% in most industries). But those resource savings drop straight to the bottom line and so represent a far greater percentage of profits. Many executives also think they already 'did' efficiency in the 1970s, when the oil shock forced them to rethink old habits. They're forgetting that with today's far better technologies, it's profitable to start all over again. Malden Mills, the Massachusetts maker of such products as Polartec, was already using 'efficient' metal-halide lamps in the mid 1990s. But a recent warehouse retrofit reduced the energy used for lighting by another 93%, improved visibility, and paid for itself in 18 months.

The way people are rewarded often creates perverse incentives. Architects and engineers, for example, are traditionally compensated for what they spend, not for what they save. Even the striking economics of the retrofit design for the Chicago office tower described earlier wasn't incentive enough to actually implement it. The property was controlled by a leasing agent who earned a commission every time she leased space, so she didn't want to wait the few extra months needed to refit the building. Her decision to reject the efficiency-quadrupling renovation proved costly for both her and her client. The building was so uncomfortable and expensive to occupy that it didn't lease, so ultimately the owner had to unload it at a firesale price. Moreover, the new owner will for the next 20 years be deprived of the opportunity to save capital cost.

If corporate practices obscure the benefits of natural capitalism, government policy positively undermines it. In nearly every country on the planet, tax laws penalize what we want more of – jobs and income – while subsidizing what we want less of – resource depletion and pollution. In every state but Oregon, regulated utilities are rewarded for selling more energy, water, and other resources, and penalized for selling less, even if increased production would cost more then improved customer efficiency. In most of America's arid western states, use-it-or-lose-it water laws encourage inefficient water consumption. Additionally, in many towns, inefficient use of land is enforced though outdated regulations, such as guidelines for ultrawide suburban streets recommended by 1950s civil-defense planners to accommodate the heavy equipment needed to clear up rubble after a nuclear attack.

The costs of these perverse incentives are staggering: $300 billion in annual energy wasted in the United States, and £1 trillion already misallocated to unnecessary air-conditioning equipment and the power supplies to run it (about 40% of the nation's peak electric load). Across the entire economy, unneeded expenditures to subsidize, encourage, and try to remedy inefficiency and damage that should not have occurred in the first place probably account for most, if not all, of the GDP growth of the past two decades. Indeed, according to former World Bank economist Herman Daly and his colleague John Cobb (along with many other analysts), Americans are hardly better off than they were in 1980. But if the U.S. government and private industry could redirect the dollars currently earmarked for remedial costs toward reinvestment in natural and human capital, they could bring about a genuine improvement in the nation's welfare. Companies, too, are finding that wasting resources also means wasting money and people, These intertwined forms of waste have equally intertwined solutions. Firing the unproductive tons, gallons, and kilowatt-hours often makes it possible to keep the people, who will have more and better work to do.

Recognizing the Scarcity Shift

In the end, the real trouble with our economic compass is that it points in exactly the wrong direction. Most businesses are behaving as if people were scarce and nature still abundant – the conditions that helped to fuel the first Industrial Revolution. At that time, people were relatively scarce compared with the present-day population. The repaid mechanization of the textile industries caused explosive economic growth that created labor shortages in the factory and the field. The Industrial Revolution, responding to those shortages and mechanizing one industry after another, made people a hundred times more productive than they had ever been.

The logic of economizing on the scarcest resource, because it limits progress, remains correct. But the pattern of scarcity is shifting: now people aren't scarce but nature is. This shows up first in industries that depend directly on ecological health. Here, production is increasingly constrained by fish rather than by boats and nets, by forests rather than by chain saws, by fertile topsoil rather than by plows. Moreover, unlike the traditional factors of industrial production – capital and labor – the biological limiting factors cannot be substituted for one other. In the industrial system, we can easily exchange machine for labor. But no technology or amount of money can substitute for a stable climate and a productive biosphere. Even proper pricing can't replace the priceless.

Natural capitalism addresses those problems reintegrating ecological with economic goals. Because it is both necessary and profitable, it will subsume traditional industrialism just as industrialism previously subsumed agrarianism. The companies that first make the changes we have described will have a competitive edge. Those that don't make the effort won't be a problem because ultimately they won't be around. In making the choice, as Henry Ford said, 'Whether you believe you can, or whether you believe you can't you're absolutely right'.

Notes

1 Non-proprietary details are posted at http://www.hypercar.com.
2 Summarized in the report 'Climate: making sense *and* making money' at http://www.rmi.org/catalog/climate.htm.

18

Surfing the Edge of Chaos

Richard T. Pascale

Treating organizations as complex adaptive systems provides powerful insights into the nature of strategic work.

Every decade or two during the past one hundred years, a point of inflection has occurred in management thinking. These breakthroughs are akin to the S-curves of technology that characterize the life cycle of many industrial and consumer products: Introduction → Acceleration → Acceptance → Maturity. Each big idea catches hold slowly. Yet, within a relatively short time, the new approach becomes so widely accepted that it is difficult even for oldtimers to reconstruct how the world looked before.

The decade following World War II gave birth to the 'strategic era'. While the tenets of military strategy had been evolving for centuries, the link to commercial enterprise was tenuous. Before the late 1940s, most companies adhered to the tenet 'make a little, sell a little, make a little more'. After the war, faculty at the Harvard Business School (soon joined by swelling ranks of consultants) began to take the discipline of strategy seriously. By the late 1970s, the array of strategic concepts (SWOT analysis, the five forces framework, experience curves, strategic portfolios, the concept of competitive advantage) had become standard ordnance in the management arsenal. Today, a mere twenty years later, a grasp of these concepts is presumed as a threshold of management literacy. They have become so familiar that it is hard to imagine a world without them.

It is useful to step back and reflect on the scientific underpinnings to this legacy. Eric Beinhocker writes:

> The early micro-economists copied the mathematics of mid-nineteenth century physics equation by equation. ['Atoms'] became the individual, 'force' became the economists' notion of 'marginal utility' (or demand), 'kinetic energy' became total expenditure. All of this was synthesized into a coherent theory by Alfred Marshall – known as the theory of industrial organization.[1]

Source: R. Pascale (1999) *Sloan Management Review, 40*(3), 83–94.

Marshall's work and its underpinnings in nineteenth century physics exert a huge influence on strategic thinking to this day. From our concept of strategy to our efforts at organizational renewal, the deep logic is based on assumptions of deterministic cause and effect (i.e., a billiard ball model of how competitors will respond to a strategic challenge or how employees will behave under a new incentive scheme). And all of this, consistent with Newton's initial conceptions, is assumed to take place in a world where time, space (i.e., a particular industry structure or definition of a market), and dynamic equilibrium are accepted as reasonable underpinnings for the formulation of executive action. That's where the trouble begins. Marshall's equilibrium model offered appropriate approximations for the dominant sectors of agriculture and manufacturing of his era and are still useful in many situations. But these constructs run into difficulty in the far from equilibrium conditions found in today's service, technology, or communications-intensive businesses. When new entrants such as Nokia, Amazon.com, Dell Computer, or CNN invade a market, they succeed despite what traditional strategic thinkers would write off as a long shot.

During the 1980s and 1990s, *performance improvement* (e.g., total quality management, kaizen, just-in-time, reengineering) succeeded the strategic era. It, too, has followed the S-curve trajectory. Now, as it trails off, an uneasiness is stirring, a feeling that 'something more' is required. In particular, disquiet has arisen over the rapidly rising fatality rates of major companies. Organizations cannot win by cost reduction alone and cannot invent appropriate strategic responses fast enough to stay abreast of nimble rivals. Many are exhausted by the pace of change, and their harried attempts to execute new initiatives fall short of expectations.

The next point of inflection is about to unfold. To succeed, the next big idea must address the biggest challenge facing corporations today – namely, to dramatically improve the hit rate of strategic initiatives and attain the level of renewal necessary for successful execution. As in the previous eras, we can expect that the next big idea will at first seem strange and inaccessible.

Here's the good news. For well over a decade, the hard sciences have made enormous strides in understanding and describing how the living world works. Scientists use the term 'complex adaptive systems' ('complexity' for short) to label these theories. To be sure, the new theories do not explain everything. But the work has identified principles that apply to many living things – amoebae and ant colonies, beehives and bond traders, ecologies and economies, you and me.

For an entity to qualify as a complex adaptive system, it must meet four tests. First, it must be comprised of many agents acting in parallel. It is not hierarchically controlled. Second, it continuously shuffles these building blocks and generates multiple levels of organization and structure. Third, it is subject to the second law of thermodynamics, exhibiting entropy and winding down over time unless replenished with energy. In this sense, complex adaptive systems are vulnerable to death. Fourth, a distinguishing characteristic, all complex adaptive systems exhibit a capacity for pattern recognition and employ this to anticipate the future and learn to recognize the anticipation of seasonal change.

Many systems are complex but not adaptive (i.e., they meet some of the above conditions, but not all). If sand is gradually piled on a table, it will slide off in patterns. If a wave in a stream is disturbed, it will repair itself once the obstruction is removed. But neither of these complex systems anticipates and learns. Only living systems cope with their environment with a predictive model that anticipates and pro-acts. Thus, when the worldwide community of strep bacteria mutates to circumvent the threat of the latest antibiotic (as it does rather reliably within three years), it is reaffirming its membership in the club of complexity.

Work on complexity originated during the mid-1980s at New Mexico's Santa Fe Institute. A group of distinguished scientists with backgrounds in particle physics, microbiology, archaeology, astrophysics, paleontology, zoology, botany, and economics were drawn together by similar questions.[2] A series of symposia, underwritten by the Carnegie Foundation, revealed that all the assembled disciplines shared, at their core, building blocks composed of many agents. These might be molecules, neurons, a species, customers, members of a social system, or networks of corporations. Further, these fundamental systems were continually organizing and reorganizing themselves, all flourishing in a boundary between rigidity and randomness and all occasionally forming larger structures through the clash of natural accommodation and competition. Molecules form cells; neurons cluster into neural *networks* (or brains); species form ecosystems; individuals form tribes or societies; consumers and corporations form economies. These self-organizing structures give rise to emergent behavior (an example of which is the process whereby prebiotic chemicals combined to form the extraordinary diversity of life on earth). Complexity science informs us about organization, stability, and change in social and natural systems. 'Unlike the earlier advances in hard science,' writes economist Alex Trosiglio, 'complexity deals with a world that is far from equilibrium, and is creative and evolving in ways that we cannot hope to predict. It points to fundamental limits to our ability to understand, control, and manage the world, and the need for us to accept unpredictability and change'.[3]

The science of complexity has yielded four bedrock principles relevant to the new strategic work:

1. Complex adaptive systems are at *risk when in equilibrium*. Equilibrium is a precursor to death.[4]
2. Complex adaptive systems exhibit the capacity of *self-organization* and emergent complexity.[5] Self-organization arises from intelligence in the remote clusters (or 'nodes') within a network. Emergent complexity is generated by the propensity of simple structures to generate novel patterns, infinite variety, and often, a sum that is greater than the parts. (Again, the escalating complexity of life on earth is an example.)
3. Complex adaptive systems tend to move toward the edge of chaos when provoked by a complex task.[6] *Bounded instability is more conducive to evolution* than either stable equilibrium or explosive instability. (For example, fire has been found to be a critical factor in regenerating healthy forests and prairies.) One

important corollary to this principle is that a complex adaptive system, once having reached a temporary 'peak' in its fitness landscape (e.g., a company during a golden era), must then 'go down to go up' (i.e., moving from one peak to a still higher peak requires it to traverse the valleys of the fitness landscape). In cybernetic terms, *the organism must be pulled by competitive pressures far enough out of its usual arrangements before it can create substantially different forms and arrive at a more evolved basin of attraction.*

4. One cannot direct a living system, only disturb it.[7] Complex adaptive systems are characterized by weak cause-and-effect linkages. Phase transitions occur in the realm where one relatively small and isolated variation can produce huge effects. Alternatively, large changes may have little effect. (This phenomenon is common in the information industry. Massive efforts to promote a superior operating system may come to naught, whereas a series of serendipitous events may establish an inferior operating system – such as MS-DOS – as the industry standard.)

Is complexity just interesting science, or does it represent something of great importance in thinking about strategic work? As these illustrations suggest, treating organizations as complex adaptive systems provides useful insight into the nature of strategic work. In the following pages, I will (1) briefly describe how the four bedrock principles of complexity occur in nature, and (2) demonstrate how they can be applied in a managerial context. In particular, I use the efforts underway at Royal Dutch/Shell to describe an extensive and pragmatic test of these ideas.

The successes at Shell and other companies described here might be achieved with a more traditional mind-set (in much the same way as Newton's laws can be used to explain the mechanics of matter on earth with sufficient accuracy so as to not require the General Theory of Relativity). But the contribution of scientific insight is much more than descriptions of increasing accuracy. Deep theories reveal previously unsuspected aspects of reality that we don't see (the curvature of space-time in the case of relativity theory) and thereby alter the fabric of reality. This is the context for an article on complexity science and strategy. Complexity makes the strategic challenge more understandable and the task of strategic renewal more accessible. In short, this is not a polemic against the traditional strategic approach, but an argument for broadening it.

Stable Equilibrium Equals Death

An obscure but important law of cybernetics, the law of requisite variety, states: For any system to survive, it must cultivate variety in its internal controls. If it fails to do so internally, it will fail to cope with variety successfully when it comes from an external source.[8] Here, in the mundane prose of a cybernetic axiom, is the rationale for bounded instability.

A perverse example of this axiom in action was driven home by the devastating fires that wiped out 25 percent of Yellowstone National Park in 1992. For decades, the

National Park Service had imposed equilibrium on the forest by extinguishing fires whenever they appeared. Gradually, the forest floor became littered with a thick layer of debris. When a lightening strike and ill-timed winds created a conflagration that could not be contained, this carpet of dry material burned longer and hotter than normal. By suppressing natural fires for close to 100 years, the park service had prevented the forest floor from being cleansed in a natural rhythm. Now a century's accumulation of deadfall generated extreme temperatures. The fire incinerated large trees and the living components of top soil that would otherwise have survived. This is the price of enforced equilibrium.

The seductive pull of equilibrium poses a constant danger to successful established companies. Jim Cannavino, a former IBM senior executive, provides an anecdote that speaks to the hazards of resisting change. In 1993, Cannavino was asked by IBM's new CEO, Lou Gerstner, to take a hard look at the strategic planning process. Why had IBM so badly missed the mark? Cannavino dutifully examined the work product – library shelves filled with blue binders containing twenty years of forecasts, trends, and strategic analysis. 'It all could be distilled down to one sentence', he recounts. '"We saw it coming" – PC open architecture, networking intelligence in microprocessors, higher margins in software and services than hardware; it was all there. So I looked at the operating plans. How did they reflect the shifts the strategists had projected? These blue volumes (three times as voluminous as the strategic plans) could also be summarized in one sentence: "Nothing changed". And the final dose of arsenic to this diet of cyanide was the year-end financial reconciliation process. When we rolled up the sector submissions into totals for the corporation, the growth opportunities never quite covered the erosion of market share. This shortfall, of course, was the tip of an iceberg that would one day upend our strategy and our primary product – the IBM 360 mainframe. But facing these fundamental trends would have precipitated a great deal of turmoil and instability. Instead, year after year, a few of our most senior leaders went behind closed doors and raised prices.'[9]

While equilibrium endangers living systems, it often wears the disguise of an attribute. Equilibrium is concealed inside strong values or a coherent, close-knit social system, or within a company's well-synchronized operating system (often referred to as 'organizational fit'). Vision, values, and organizational fit are double-edged swords.

Species are inherently drawn toward the seeming oasis of stability and equilibrium – and the further they drift toward this destination, the less likely they are to adapt successfully when change is necessary. So why don't all species drift into the thrall of equilibrium and die off? Two forces thwart equilibrium and promote instability: (1) the threat of death, and (2) the promise of sex.

The Darwinian process, called 'selection pressures' by natural scientists, imposes harsh consequences on species entrapped in equilibrium. Most species, when challenged to adapt too far from their origins, are unable to do so and gradually disappear. But from the vantage point of the larger ecological community, selection pressures enforce an ecological upgrade, insofar as mutations that survive offer a better fit with the new environment. Natural selection exerts itself most aggressively during periods of radical change. Few readers will have difficulty identifying these forces at work in industry today. There are no safe havens. From toothpaste to camcorders, pharmaceuticals to office supplies, bookstores to booster rockets for space payloads, soap to software, it's a Darwinian jungle out there, and it's not getting easier.

As a rule, a species becomes more vulnerable as it becomes more genetically homogeneous. Nature hedges against this condition through the reproductive process. Of the several means of reproduction that have evolved on the planet, sex is best. It is decisively superior to parthenogenesis (the process by which most plants, worms, and a few mammals conceive offspring through self-induced combination of identical genetic material).

Sexual reproduction maximizes diversity. Chromosome combinations are randomly matched in variant pairings, thereby generating more permutations and variety in offspring. Oxford's evolutionary theorist, William Hamilton, explains why this benefits a species. Enemies (i.e., harmful diseases and parasites) find it harder to adapt to the diverse attributes of a population generated by sexual reproduction than to the comparative uniformity of one produced by parthenogenesis.[10]

How does this relate to organizations? In organizations, people are the chromosomes, the genetic material that can create variety. When management thinker Gary Hamel was asked if he thought IBM had a chance of leading the next stage of the information revolution, he replied: 'I'd need to know how many of IBM's top 100 executives had grown up on the west coast of America where the future of the computer industry is being created and how many were under forty years of age. If a quarter or a third of the senior group were both under forty and possessed a west coast perspective, IBM has a chance.'[11]

Here's the rub: The 'exchanges of DNA' attempted within social systems are not nearly as reliable as those driven by the mechanics of reproductive chemistry. True, organizations can hire from the outside, bring seniors into frequent contact with iconoclasts from the ranks, or confront engineers and designers with disgruntled customers. But the enemy of these methods is, of course, the existing social order, which, like the body's immune defense system, seeks to neutralize, isolate, or destroy foreign invaders. 'Antibodies' in the form of social norms, corporate values, and orthodox beliefs nullify the advantages of diversity. An executive team may include divergent interests, only to engage in stereotyped listening (e.g., 'There goes Techie again') or freeze iconoclasts out of important informal discussions. If authentic diversity is sought, all executives, in particular the seniors, must be more seeker than guru.

Disturbing Equilibrium at Shell

In 1996, Steve Miller, age fifty-one, became a member of Shell's committee of managing directors – the five senior leaders who develop objectives and long-term plans for Royal Dutch/Shell.[12] The group found itself captive to its hundred-year-old history. The numbing effects of tradition – a staggering $130 billion in annual revenues, 105,000 predominantly long-tenured employees, and global operations – left Shell vulnerable. While profits continued to flow, fissures were forming beneath the surface.

Miller was appointed group managing director of Shell's worldwide oil products business (known as 'Downstream'), which accounts for $40 billion of revenues within the Shell Group. During the previous two years, the company had been engaged in a program to 'transform' the organization. Yet the regimen of massive reorganization, traumatic downsizing, and senior management workshops accomplished little. Shell's earnings, while solid, were disappointing to financial analysts who expected more from the industry's largest competitor. Employees registered widespread resignation and cynicism. And the operating units at the 'coal face' (Shell's term for its front-line activities within the 130 countries where Downstream does business) saw little more than business as usual.

For Steve Miller, Shell's impenetrable culture was worrisome. The Downstream business accounted for 37 percent of Shell's assets. Among the businesses in the Shell Group's portfolio, Downstream faced the gravest competitive threats. From 1992 to 1995, a full 50 percent of Shell's retail revenues in France fell victim to the onslaught of the European hypermarkets; a similar pattern was emerging in the United Kingdom. Elsewhere in the world, new competitors, global customers, and more savvy national oil companies were demanding a radically different approach to the marketplace. Having observed Shell's previous transformation efforts, Miller was convinced that it was essential to reach around the resistant bureaucracy and involve the front lines of the organization, a formidable task given the sheer size of the operation. In addition to Downstream's 61,000 full-time employees, Shell's 47,000 filling stations employed hundreds of thousands, mostly part-time attendants and catered to more than 10 million customers every day. In the language of complexity, Miller believed it necessary to tap the emergent properties of Shell's enormous distribution system and shift the locus of strategic initiative to the front lines. He saw this system as a fertile organism that needed encouragement to, in his words, 'send green shoots forth'.

In an effort to gain the organization's attention (i.e., disturb equilibrium), beginning in mid-1996, Miller reallocated more than 50 percent of his calendar to work directly with front-line personnel. Miller states:

> Our Downstream business transformation program had bogged down largely because of the impasse between headquarters and the operating companies, Shell's term for its highly independent country operations. The balance of power between headquarters and field, honed during a period of relative equilibrium, had ground to a stalemate. But the forces for continuing in the old way were enormous and extended throughout the organization. We were overseeing the most decentralized operation in the world, with country chief executives that had, since the 1950s, enjoyed enormous autonomy. This had been part of our success formula. Yet we were encountering a set of daunting competitive threats that transcended national boundaries. Global customers – like British Airways or Daimler Benz – wanted to deal with one Shell contact, not with a different Shell representative in every country in which they operate. We had huge overcapacity in refining, but each country CEO (motivated to maximize his own P&L) resisted the consolidation of refining

capacity. These problems begged for a new strategic approach in which the task at the top was to provide the framework and then unleash the regional and local levels to find a path that was best for their market and the corporation as a whole.

Shell had tried to rationalize its assets through a well-engineered strategic response: directives were issued by the top and driven through the organization. But country heads successfully thwarted consolidation under the banner of host-country objections to the threatened closing of their dedicated refining capacity. Miller continues: 'We were equally unsuccessful at igniting a more imaginative approach toward the marketplace. It was like the old game of telephone that we used to play when we were kids: you'd whisper a message to the person next to you, and it goes around the circle. By the time you get to the last person, it bears almost no resemblance to the message you started with. Apply that to the 61,000 people in the Downstream business across the globe, and I knew our strategic aspirations could never penetrate through to the marketplace. The linkages between directives given and actions taken are too problematic.' What made sense to Miller was to fundamentally alter the conversation and unleash the emergent possibilities. Midway through the process, Miller became acquainted with core principles of living systems and adopted them as a framework to provide his organization with a context for renewal.

Miller's reports in the operating companies were saying, 'Centralization will only bog us down.' 'They were partly right', he acknowledges. 'These are big companies. Some earn several hundreds of millions a year in net income. But the alternative wasn't centralization – it was a radical change in the responsiveness of the Downstream business to the dynamics of the marketplace – from top to bottom such that we could come together in appropriate groups, solve problems, and operate in a manner which transcended the old headquarters versus field schism. What initially seemed like a huge conflict has gradually melted away, I believe, because we stopped treating the Downstream business like a machine to be driven and began to regard it as a living system that needed to evolve.'

Miller's solution was to cut through the organization's layers and barriers, put senior management in direct contact with the people at the grassroots level, foster strategic initiatives, create a new sense of urgency, and overwhelm the old order. The first wave of initiatives spawned other initiatives. In Malaysia, for example, Miller's pilot efforts with four initiative teams (called 'action labs') have proliferated to forty. 'It worked', he states, 'because the people at the coal face usually know what's going on. They see the competitive threats and our inadequate response every day. Once you give them the context, they can do a better job of spotting opportunities and stepping up to decisions. In less than two years, we've seen astonishing progress in our retail business in some twenty-five countries. This represents around 85 percent of our retail sales volume, and we have now begun to use this approach in our service organizations and lubricant business. Results? By the end of 1997, Shell's operations in France had regained initiative and achieved double-digit growth and double-digit return on capital. Market share was increasing after years of decline.' Austria went from a probable exit candidate to a highly profitable operation. Overall, Shell gained in brand-share preference throughout Europe and ranked first in share among other major oil companies. By the close of 1998, approximately 10,000 Downstream employees have been involved in this effort with audited results (directly attributed to the program) exceeding a $300 million contribution to Shell's bottom line.

Self-organization and Emergent Complexity

Santa Fe Institute's Stuart Kauffman is a geneticist. His lifetime fascination has been with the ordered process by which a fertilized egg unfolds into a newborn infant and later into an adult. Earlier Nobel Prize-winning work on genetic circuits had shown that every cell contains a number of 'regulatory' genes that act as switches to turn one another on and off. Modern computers use sequential instructions, whereas the genetic system exercises most of its instructions simultaneously. For decades, scientists have sought to discover the governing mechanism that causes this simultaneous, non-linear system to settle down and replicate a species.[13]

Kauffman built a simple simulation of a genetic system. His array of 100 light bulbs looked like a Las Vegas marquee. Since regulatory genes cause the cells (like bulbs) to turn on or off, Kauffman arranged for his bulbs to do just that, each independently of the other. His hypothesis was that no governing mechanism existed; rather, random and independent behavior would settle into patterns – a view that was far from self-evident. The possible combinations in Kauffman's arrangement of blinking lights was two (i.e., on and off), multiplied by itself 100 times (i.e., almost one million, trillion, trillion possibilities!).

When Kauffman switched the system on, the result was astonishing. Instead of patterns of infinite variety, the system always settled down within a few minutes to a few more or less orderly states. The implications of Kauffman's work are far-reaching. Theorists had been searching for the sequence of primordial events that could have produced the first DNA – the building block of life. Kauffman asked instead, 'What if life was not just standing around and waiting until DNA happened? What if all those amino acids and sugars and gasses and solar energy were each just doing their thing like the billboard of lights?' If the conditions in primordial soup were right, it wouldn't take a miracle (like a million decks of cards falling from a balcony and all coming up aces) for DNA to randomly turn up. Rather, the compounds in the soup could have formed a coherent, self-reinforcing web of reactions and these, in turn, generated the more complex patterns of DNA.[14]

Emergent complexity is driven by a few simple patterns that combine to generate infinite variety. For example, simulations have shown that a three-pronged "crow's foot" pattern, if combined in various ways, perfectly replicates the foliage patterns of every fern on earth. Similar phenomena hold true in business. John Kao, a specialist in creativity, has observed how one simple creative breakthrough can evoke a cascade of increasing complexity.[15] 'Simple' inventions such as the wheel, printing press, or transistor lead to 'complex' offshoots such as automobiles, cellular phones, electronic publishing, and computing.

The phenomenon of emergence arises from the way simple patterns combine. Mathematics has coined the term 'fractals' to describe a set of simple equations that combine to form endless diversity.[16] Fractal mathematics has given us valuable insight into how nature creates the shapes we observe. Mountains, rivers, coastline vegetation, lungs, and circulatory systems are fractal, replicating a dominant pattern at several smaller levels of scale. Fractals, in effect, act like genetic algorithms enabling a species to efficiently replicate essential functions.

One consequence of emerging complexity is that you cannot see the end from the beginning. While many can readily acknowledge nature's propensity to self-organize and generate more complex levels, it is less comforting to put oneself at the mercy of this process with the foreknowledge that we cannot predict the shape that the future will take. Emerging complexity creates not one future but many.

Self-organization and Emergence at Shell

Building on (1) the principles of complexity, (2) the fracta-like properties of a business model developed by Columbia University's Larry Seldon,[17] and (3) a second fracta-like process, the action labs, Steve Miller and his colleagues at Shell tapped into the intelligence in the trenches and channeled it into a tailored marketplace response.[18]

Miller states: 'We needed a vehicle to give us an energy transfusion and remind us that we could play at a far more competitive level. The properties of self-organization and emergence make intuitive sense to me. The question was how to release them. Seldon's model gave us a sharp-edged tool to identify customer needs and markets and to develop our value proposition. This, in effect, gave our troops the "ammunition" to shoot with – analytical distinctions to make the business case. Shell has always been a wholesaler. Yet the forecourt of every service station is an artery for commerce that any retailer would envy. Our task was to tap the potential of that real estate, and we needed both the insight and the initiatives of our front-line troops to pull it off. For a company as large as Shell, leadership can't drive these answers down from the top. We needed to tap into ideas that were out there in the ranks – latent but ready to bear fruit if given encouragement.'

At first glance, Shell's methods look pedestrian. Miller began bringing six- to eight-person teams from a half-dozen operating companies from around the world into 'retailing boot camps'. The first five-day workshop introduced tools for identifying and exploiting market opportunities. It also included a dose of the leadership skills necessary to enroll others back home. Participants returned ready to apply the tools to achieve breakthroughs such as doubling net income in filling stations on the major north-south highways of Malaysia or tripling market share of bottled gas in South Africa. As part of the discipline of the model, every intention (e.g., 'to lower fuel delivery costs') was translated into 'key business activities' (or KBAs). As the first group went home, six more teams would rotate in. During the next sixty days, the first group of teams used the analytical tools to sample customers, identify segments, and develop a value proposition. The group would then return to the workshop for a 'peer challenge' – tough give-and-take exchanges with other teams. Then it would go back again for another sixty days to perfect a business plan. At the close of the third workshop, each action lab spent three hours in the 'fishbowl' with Miller and several of his direct reports, reviewing business plans, while the other teams observed the proceedings. At the close of each session, plans were approved, rejected, amended. Financial commitments were made in exchange for promised results. (The latter were incorporated in the country's operating goals for the year.) Then the teams went back to the field for another sixty days to put their ideas into action and returned for a follow-up session.

'Week after week, team after team,' continues Miller, "my six direct reports and I and our internal coaches reached out and worked directly with a diverse cross-section of customers, dealers, shop stewards, and young and mid-level professionals. And it worked. Operating company CEOs, historically leery of any "help" from headquarters, saw their people return energized and armed with solid plans to beat the competition. The grassroots employees who participated in the program got to touch and feel the new Shell – a far more informal, give-and-take culture. The conversation down in the ranks of the organization began to change. Guerrilla leaders, historically resigned to Shell's conventional way of doing things, stepped forward to champion ingenious marketplace innovations (such as the Coca-Cola Challenge in Malaysia – a free Coke to any service-station customer who is not offered the full menu of forecourt services. It sounds trivial, but it increased volume by 15 percent). Many, if not most, of the ideas come from the lower ranks of our company who are in direct contact with the customer. Best of all, we learned together. I can't overstate how infectious the optimism and energy of these committed employees was for the many managers above them. In a curious way, these front-line employees taught us to believe in ourselves again.'

As executives move up in organizations, they become removed from the work that goes on in the fields. Directives from the top become increasingly abstract as executives tend to rely on mechanical cause-and-effect linkages to drive the business: strategic guidelines, head-count controls, operational expense targets, pay-for-performance incentives, and so forth. These are the tie rods and pistons of 'social engineering' – the old model of change. Complexity theory does not discard these useful devices but it starts from a different place. The living-systems approach begins with a focus on the intelligence in the nodes. It seeks to ferret out what this network sees, what stresses it is undergoing, and what is needed to unleash its potential. Other support elements (e.g., controls and rewards) are orchestrated to draw on this potential rather than to drive down solutions from above.

Miller was pioneering a very different model from what had always prevailed at Shell. His 'design for emergence' generated hundreds of informal connections between headquarters and the field, resembling the parallel networks of the nervous system to the brain. It contrasted with the historical model of mechanical linkages analogous to those that transfer the energy from the engine in a car through a drive train to the tires that perform the 'work'.

Edge of Chaos

Nothing novel can emerge from systems with high degrees of order and stability – for example, crystals, incestuous communities, or regulated industries. On the other hand, complete chaotic systems, such as stampedes, riots, rage, or the early years of the French Revolution, are too formless to coalesce. Generative complexity takes place in the boundary between rigidity and randomness.

Historically,[19] science viewed 'change' as moving from one equilibrium state (water) to another (ice). Newtonian understandings could not cope with the random, near-chaotic messiness of the actual transition itself. Ecologists and economists similarly favored equilibrium conditions because neither observation nor modeling techniques could handle transition states. The relatively inexpensive computational power of modern computers has changed all that. Nonequilibrium and nonlinear simulations are now possible. These developments, along with the study of complexity, have enabled us to better understand the dynamics of 'messiness'.

Phase transitions occur in the realm near chaos where a relatively small and isolated variation can produce huge effects. Consider the example of *lasers:* while only a complex system and not an adaptive one, the infusion of energy into plasma excites a jumble of photons. The more the energy, the more jumbled they become. Still more and the seething mass is transformed into the coherent light of a laser beam. What drives this transition, and how can we orchestrate it? Two determinants – (1) a precise tension between amplifying and damping feedback, and (2) (unique to mankind) the application of mindfulness and intention – are akin to rudder and sail when surfing near the edge of chaos.

Two factors determine the level of excitation in a system. In cybernetics, they are known as amplifying (positive) and damping (negative) feedback.[20] Damping feedback operates like a thermostat, which keeps temperatures within boundaries with a thermocouple that continually says 'too hot, too cold'. Amplifying feedback happens when a microphone gets too close to a loudspeaker. The signal is amplified until it oscillates to a piercing shriek. Living systems thrive when these mechanisms are in tension.

Getting the tension right is the hard part. Business obituaries abound with examples of one or the other of these feedback systems gone amok. IT&T under Harold Geneen or Sunbeam under 'Chainsaw' Al Dunlap thrive briefly under stringent damping controls, then fade away owing to the loss of imagination and creative energy. At the opposite end, Value Jet thrives in an amplifying phase, adds more planes, departures, and staff without corresponding attention to the damping loop (operational controls, safety, reliability, and service standards).

Psychologists tell us that pain can cause us to change, and this is most likely to occur when we recontextualize pain as the means by which significant learning occurs. When the great Austro-American economist Joseph Schumpeter described the essence of free-market economies as 'creative destruction', it could be interpreted as a characterization of the hazards near the edge of chaos. Enduring competitive advantage entails disrupting what has been done in the past and creating a new future.

Hewlett-Packard's printer business was one of the most successful in its portfolio. Observing a downward spiral of margins as many 'me too' printers entered the market, HP reinvented its offering. Today, HP's printers are the 'free razor blade' – the loss leader in a very different strategy. To maintain scale, HP abandoned its high-cost distribution system with a dedicated sales force, opting instead for mass channels, partnering, and outsourcing to lower manufacturing costs. To protect margins, it targeted its forty biggest corporate customers and formed a partnership to deliver global business printing solutions – whether through low-cost, on-premise equipment, or networked technology. States Tim Mannon, president of HP's printer division: 'The biggest single threat to our business today is staying with a previously successful business model one year too long.[21]

Shaping the Edge of Chaos at Shell

Shell moved to the edge of chaos with a multipronged design that intensified stress on all members of the Shell system.[22] First, as noted, Miller and his top team performed major surgery on their calendars and reallocated approximately half their time to teaching and coaching wave after wave of country teams. When the lowest levels of an organization were being trained, coached, and evaluated by those at the very top, it both inspired – and stressed – everyone in the system (including mid-level bosses who were not present). Second, the design, as we have seen, sent teams back to collect real data for three periods of sixty days (interspersed with additional workshop sessions). Pressure to succeed and long hours both during the workshops and back in the country (where these individuals continued to carry their regular duties along with project work) achieved the cultural 'unfreezing' effects. Participants were resocialized into a more direct, informal, and less hierarchical way of working.

Miller states: 'One of the most important innovations in changing all of us was the fishbowl. The name describes what it is: I and a number of my management team sit in the middle of a room with one action lab in the center with us. The other team members listen from the outer circle. Everyone is watching as the group in the hot seat talks about what they're going to do and what they need from me and my colleagues to be able to do it. That may not sound revolutionary – but in our culture, it was very unusual for anyone lower in the organization to talk this directly to a managing director and his reports.

'In the fishbowl, the pressure is on to measure up. The truth is, the pressure is on me and my colleagues. The first time we're not consistent, we're dead meat. If a team brings in a plan that's really a bunch of crap, we've got to be able to call it a bunch of crap. If we cover for people or praise everyone, what do we say when someone brings in an excellent plan? That kind of straight talk is another big culture change for Shell.

'The whole process creates complete transparency between the people at the coal face and me and my top management team. At the end, these folks go back home and say, "I just cut a deal with the managing director and his team to do these things". It creates a personal connection, and it changes how we talk with each other and how we work with each other. After that, I can call up those folks anywhere in the world and talk in a very direct way because of this personal connectedness. It has completely changed the dynamics of our operations.'

Disturbing a Living System

An important and distinct property of living systems is the tenuous connection between cause and effect. As most seasoned managers know, the best-laid plans are often perverted through self-interest, misinterpretation, or lack of necessary skills to reach the intended goal.

Consider the war of attrition waged by ranchers and the U.S. Fish and Wildlife Service to 'control' the coyote. A cumulative total of $3 billion (in 1997 dollars) has been spent during the past 100 years to underwrite bounty hunters, field a sophisticated array of traps, introduce novel morsels of poisoned bait, and interject genetic technology (to limit fertility of females) – all with the aim of protecting sheep and cattle ranchers from these wily predators. Result? When white men first appeared in significant numbers west of the Mississippi in the early 1800s, coyotes were found in twelve western states and never seen east of the Mississippi. However, as a direct result of the aggressive programs to eliminate the coyote, the modern day coyote is 20 percent larger and significantly smarter than his predecessor. The coyote is now found in forty-nine of the fifty states – including suburbs of New York City and Los Angeles. How could this occur? Human intervention so threatened the coyote's survival that a significant number fled into Canada where they bred with the larger Canadian wolf. Still later, these visitors migrated south (and further north to Alaska) and, over the decades, bred with (and increased the size of) the U.S. population. The same threats to survival that had driven some coyotes into Canada drove others to adapt to climates as varied as Florida and New Hampshire. Finally, the persistent efforts to trap or hunt or poison the coyote heightened selection pressures. The survivors were extremely streetwise and wary of human contact. Once alerted by a few fatalities among their brethern, coyotes are usually able to sniff out man's latest stratagem to do them harm.

As the tale of the coyote suggests, living systems are difficult to direct because of these weak cause-and-effect linkages. The best laid efforts by man to intervene in a system, to do it harm, or even to replicate it artificially almost always miss the mark. The strategic intentions of governments in Japan, Taiwan, and Germany to replicate Silicon Valley provide one example. The cause-and-effect formula seemed simple: (1) identify a region with major universities with strong departments in such fields as microelectronics, genetics, and nuclear medicine and having a geography with climate and amenities suitable to attract professionals, and (2) invest to stimulate a self-reinforcing community of interests. But these and many similar efforts have never quite reached a critical mass. The cause-and-effect relationships proved unclear.[23] A lot depends on chance. One is wiser to acknowledge the broad possibilities that flow from weak cause-and-effect linkages and the need to consider the second- and third-order effects of any bold intervention one is about to undertake.

Disturbing a Complex System at Shell

In today's fast-changing environment, Shell's Steve Miller dismisses the company's old traditional approach as mechanistic. 'Top-down strategies don't win ballgames', he states. 'Experimentation, rapid learning, and seizing the momentum of success is the better approach'.[24]

Miller observes: 'We need a different definition of strategy and a different approach to generating it. In the past, strategy was the exclusive domain of top management. Today, if you're going to have a successful company, you have to recognize that the top can't possibly have all the answers. The leaders provide the vision and are the context setters. But the actual solutions about how best to meet the challenges of the moment, those thousands of strategic challenges encountered every day, have to be made by the people closest to the action – the people at the coal face.

'Change your approach to strategy, and you change the way a company runs. The leader becomes a context setter, the designer of a learning experience – not an authority figure with solutions. Once the folks at the grassroots realize they own the problem, they also discover that they can help create and own the answers, and they get after it very quickly, very aggressively, and very creatively, with a lot more ideas than the old-style strategic direction could ever have prescribed from headquarters.

'A program like this is a high-risk proposition, because it goes counter to the way most senior executives spend their time. I spend 50 percent to 60 percent of my time at this, and there is no direct guarantee that what I'm doing is going make something happen down the line. It's like becoming the helmsman of a big ship when you've grown up behind the steering wheel of a car. This approach isn't about me. It's about rigorous, well-taught marketing concepts, combined with a strong process design, that enable front-line employees to think like business people. Top executives and front-line employees learn to work together in partnership.

'People want to evaluate this against the old way, which gives you the illusion of "making things happen". I encountered lots of thinly veiled skepticism: "Did your net income change from last quarter because of this change process?" These challenges create anxiety. The temptation, of course, is to reimpose your directives and controls even though we had an abundance of proof that this would not work. Instead, top executives and lower-level employees learn to work together in partnership. The grassroots approach to strategy development and implementation doesn't happen overnight. But it does happen. People always want results yesterday. But the process and behavior that drive authentic strategic change aren't like that.

'There's another kind of risk to the leaders of a strategic inquiry of this kind – the risk of exposure. You're working very closely and intensely with all levels of staff, and they get to assess and evaluate you directly. Before, you were remote from them; now, you're very accessible. If that evaluation comes up negative, you've got a big-time problem.

'Finally, the scariest part is letting go. You don't have the same kind of control that traditional leadership is used to. What you don't realize until you do it is that you may, in fact, have more controls but in a different fashion. You get more feedback than before, you learn more than before, you know more through your own people about what's going on in the marketplace and with customers than before. But you still have to let go of the old sense of control'.

Miller's words testify to his reconciliation with the weak cause-and-effect linkages that exist in a living system. When strategic work is accomplished through a 'design for emergence', it never assumes that a particular input will produce a particular output. It is more akin to the study of subatomic particles in a bubble chamber. The experimenter's design creates probabilistic occurrences that take place within the domain of focus. Period. Greater precision is neither sought nor possible.

Notes

1. E.D. Beinhocker, 'Strategy at the Edge of Chaos,' *McKinsey Quarterly*, 1.
2. For an entertaining treatment of this inquiry, see: M.M. Waldrop, *Complexity* (New York: Simon & Schuster, 1992).
3. A. Trosiglio, 'Managing Complexity' (unpublished working paper, June 1995), p. 3; and D. Deutsch, *The Fabric of Reality* (New York: Penguin, 1997), pp. 3–21.
4. See S. Kauffman, *At Home in the Universe* (New York: Oxford University Press, 1995), p. 21; and G.Hamel and C.K. Prahalad, 'Strategic Intent', *Harvard Business Review*, 67, May–June 1989, pp. 63–76.
5. See Kauffman (1995), p. 205; and J.H. Holland, *Hidden Order* (Reading, Massachusetts: Addison-Wesley, 1995), p. 3.
6. See Kauffman (1995), p. 230; and M. Gell-Mann, *The Quark and the Jaguar* (New York: Freeman, 1994), p. 249.
7. See Gell-Mann (1994), pp. 238–9; and Holland (1995), pp. 38–9 and p. 5.
8. W. Ashby, *An Introduction to Cybernetics* (New York: Wiley, 1956).
9. R. Pascale, interviews with James Cannavino, May 1996.
10. See Gell-Mann (1994), p. 64 and p. 253; and S.J. Gould, *Full House* (New York: Crown Publishing, 1996), p. 138.
11. G. Hamel, 'Strategy as Revolution', *Harvard Business Review'*, 74, July–August 1996, pp. 69–82.
12. 18, 22 and 24, Information and quotations in these sections are drawn from: R. Pascale, interviews with Steve Miller, London, The Hague and Houston, October 1997 through February 1998.
13. Kauffman (1995), pp. 80–6.
14. Waldrop (1992), p. 110.
15. J. Kao, *Jamming The Art and Discipline of Business Creativity* (New York: HarperCollins, 1997).
16. I. Marshall and D. Zohar, *Who's Afraid of Schrodinger's Cat?* (New York: Morrow, 1997), p. 16, p. 19, pp. 153–8.
17. Seldon's work is unpublished. He considers it proprietary and solely for consulting purposes.
19. Gell-Mann (1994), pp. 228–30.
20. Waldrop (1992), pp. 138–9.
21. R. Hof, 'Hewlett Packard', *Business Week'*, 13 February 1995, p. 67.
23. A. Saxenian, 'Lessons from Silicon Valley', *Technology Review*, 97, 5, July 1994, pp. 42–5.

Index